7/85

The 8086/8088 Primer

The 8086/8088 Primer

An Introduction to Their Architecture, System Design, and Programming

SECOND EDITION

STEPHEN P. MORSE

HAYDEN BOOK COMPANY, INC.
Rochelle Park, New Jersey

To Megan

Library of Congress Cataloging in Publication Data

Morse, Stephen P.
  The 8086/8088 primer.

  Previous ed. published as: The 8086 primer. c1980.
  Includes bibliographical references and index.
  1. INTEL 8086 (Computer)   2. INTEL 8088 (Computer)
I. Title.
QA76.8.I292M67   1982   001.64   82-6152
ISBN 0-8104-6255-9   AACR2

		6	7	8	9		PRINTING		
83	84	85	86	87	88	89	90	YEAR	

Preface

This book is an introduction to the 8086 microprocessor. It describes the 8086 architecture, shows how to design a system incorporating an 8086, and discusses how to write programs that run on the 8086. Since the treatment is detailed and relies heavily on examples and illustrations, it can be useful to both the computer novice and the computer professional.

The book is composed of three main topics—8086 architecture, 8086 system design, and 8086 programming. The architecture is broken down into 8086 machine organization (register and memory structure, addressing modes), covered in Chap. 2, and 8086 instruction set, covered in Chap. 3. The 8086 and 8088 system designs in Chaps. 4 and 5 show how to put these microprocessors together with other components to form a complete microcomputer system. Programming is divided into 8086 assembly-language programming (Chap. 6) and 8086 high-level-language programming (Chaps. 7 and 8).

The first chapter is intended to bring a heterogeneous group of readers up to a common level of knowledge about computers and microcomputers. If you already have that knowledge and you're anxious to learn about the 8086, skip ahead to Chap. 2.

The first edition of this primer did not discuss the language Pascal because no 8086 Pascal compilers were available at the time of that writing. The only 8086 high-level language then in existence was PL/M. Today several 8086 Pascal compilers exist, and each language is now covered in its own chapter (Chap. 7 for PL/M and Chap. 8 for Pascal).

Another topic not in the original edition is the 8088. The primary difference between the 8086 and 8088 processors is the amount of data that each can transfer to and from the outside world at one time—the 8086 can transfer 16 bits, whereas the 8088 can transfer only 8 (both processors can manipulate 16 bits of data internally). This difference has its greatest impact on system design, and hence each processor has its own system design chapter (Chap. 4 for the 8086 and Chap. 5 for the 8088). All other chapters are applicable to both processors, although, for convenience, only the 8086 is mentioned (constantly writing 8086/8088 is awkward).

I would like to thank those same people whom I thanked in the original edition (plus a few new ones) who contributed many hours of their own time to reading the drafts and finding my numerous errors. They are Richard Altmaier, John Crawford, Rodney Farrow, Joseph Friedrich, Stephen Hanna, Marek Jeziorek, Jeffrey Katz, Phillip Kaufman, John Palmer,

Samuel Quiring, Andrew Rabinowitz, Joseph Sharp, and Thomas Wilcox. A special thanks goes to Alice Morse, my mother and lifelong proofreader.

Finally, let me thank my wife Anita for graciously relinquishing her place on the dedication page to our daughter, Megan, who should be born at about the same time as this book is published.

STEPHEN P. MORSE

San Francisco, California

Foreword

In 1972, Intel announced the 8008, the first commercially available 8-bit microprocessor, which ultimately led to the 8080, the industry standard microprocessor. When they were introduced, some observers wondered what these new gadgets could be used for. To date, over three million have been used, not counting support and peripheral circuits, for thousands of different uses from telephone switching systems to TV games.

Since 1972, the microprocessor revolution has opened a multitude of component and system applications, from one-device engine control to single-board computers for complex industrial control tasks. In 1978, Intel introduced the first high-performance 16-bit microprocessor, the 8086.

The thrust of the 8086 has always been to help users get their products to market faster using compatible software, peripheral components, and system support. In this "family" concept, the CPU is the heart of a system, extending to interfaces, memories, peripherals, communications, computer systems, and software. This 8086 family consists of several CPUs as well as complete support for bus control. For example, Intel provides the 8088 CPU, which utilizes the same 16-bit internal architecture as the 8086 but has an external 8-bit bus, thus bridging the gap between 8-bit and 16-bit processors. The 8089 is designed as a special high-performance I/O processor for offloading and processing in parallel the host CPU (also available is the 8086-2, an 8-MHz version of the standard 5-MHz 8086). The 8086 family was designed as a multiprocessing family such that a system consisting of multiple processors is easily implemented, supported not only by the 8086 family of CPUs but also by "family" bus support circuitry. The 8289 Bus Arbiter, in conjunction with the 8288 Bus Controller, provides a powerful and efficient means of arbitrating multiple CPUs residing on a shared system bus. Whether designing a single CPU system or a high-performance multiple processor system, the 8086 family supports the "total system" solution.

At first glance, the complexity of 16-bit microprocessor system design seems to govern the choice between diverse component products. The key issue is actually synergism. The ease of use among Intel products offers building-block solutions to entire system design problems. One can use the same components for designing a single microprocessor-based system with one common bus or a very powerful multiple processor system with a host of shared resources.

With the common thread of compatible architecture, user language (like PLM or PASCAL), and a series of development systems that support each and every programmable device, Intel has endeavored to ease the design task for engineers working on microprocessor-based systems, both large and small.

We recommend Stephen Morse's book to those interested in using the 16-bit universe as the solution to their design problems.

DAVE GELLATLY
Microprocessor Marketing Manager
Intel Corporation

Contents

1

Introduction

The aim of this first chapter is to gain a technical and historical perspective on microcomputers in general and the 8086 in particular. Microcomputers are not unlike any other computer except in size. So we'll start by summarizing the fundamentals of computers and then describe the evolutionary process that led to the microcomputer. Finally, we'll show where the 8086 fits into the picture.

Computer Overview

Before we talk about a microcomputer, let's briefly summarize the notion of a computer. Besides serving as a review, this section will introduce some of the terms and concepts used throughout the book.

The basic units that make up a computing system are shown in Fig. 1.1. Figure 1.2 shows the same system except all the recognizable components are replaced by impersonal boxes. Let's examine the behavior of such a system by focusing on the function of each box.

The role of a computer is to obtain data from an *input device,* process the data, and deliver the final results to an *output device.* The particular processing to

Fig. 1.1 Primitive computing system.

1

Fig. 1.2 Modern general-purpose computing system.

be done is specified by a list of instructions called the *program*. The program is stored in the *program area*.

The operations of the computer are controlled by a device called a *control unit*. The control unit does the following three steps repeatedly:

1. *Fetches* an instruction from the program area
2. *Decodes* the instruction to determine what operations are to be performed
3. *Executes* the instruction by sending control signals to devices that perform the operations

The operations that are performed during instruction execution consist of moving data between devices and performing computations on data within a device. Computations are performed by the *arithmetic device*. The *data area* is used to supply inputs for the computations and to hold the intermediate results of the computations.

To see how all this ties together, let's analyze the execution of a particular instruction, namely an "add" instruction. The control unit sends a control signal to the program area requesting the next instruction. The program area responds by sending an instruction to the control unit. The control unit then decodes the instruction and discovers it's an "add" instruction. It then sends out control signals to (1) the data area telling it to move two values to the arithmetic device, (2) the arithmetic device telling it to add the two values it received, and (3) the data area telling it to receive the result of the addition.

The program area and the data area are similar in that both consist of memory in which information is stored. However, there is a big difference in the kind of information each area holds. The data area holds intermediate results, which are frequently changed during the execution of the program. The program area holds the program, which usually doesn't change while it is being executed. (Programs that modify themselves have fallen from favor in recent years.) In some systems the program is actually "engraved" into the memory so it can no longer be changed; it can only be read. Memories having this property are called read-only memories (*ROM* for short). A ROM would obviously be unsuitable for use in the data area. The data area consists of readable-writable memory that came to be called *RAM* by accident; it should have been called *RWM*. (RAM stands for random access memory, which unfortunately is not a very descriptive title.)

A memory is a collection of sequential *locations*, each having a unique *address*. Each location contains a sequence of *bits* (short for *b*inary dig*its*). These bits are the *contents* of the location. Each bit is either 0 or 1. More will be said about binary digits later in this chapter.

The data area consists of *registers* and *flags* in addition to memory. Like memory, the registers are also used to hold intermediate results. It's usually easier and faster to access values in registers than in memory. The computer uses the flags as indicators to keep track of what's going on. There are two kinds of flags—those that record information about the results generated by previously executed instructions (*status flags*) and those that control the operations of the computer (*control flags*). An example of a status flag is a flag that indicates a result is too big for the computer to handle. An example of a control flag is a flag that tells the computer to execute instructions at a slower rate, such as one per hour.

Another device in a computing system is a *port*. A port is the door through which information passes when coming from or going to an input or output device. For the sake of simplicity, ports were not shown in Figs. 1.1 and 1.2.

Data Formats

The contents of a memory location can represent either an instruction in the program or a piece of data. The ways instructions are stored—as a sequence of bits in a location—are called the *instruction formats* and may vary from one computer to another. The instruction formats of the 8086 are presented in Chap. 3. The *data formats* used in the 8086 are described here.

Data processed by a computer can be either numeric (numbers) or non-numeric (characters). A payroll program might make extensive use of numeric data, whereas a text-editing program would be concerned with non-numeric data. The format used for storing non-numeric data is known as ASCII.

Number Systems We are accustomed to representing numbers as a sequence of decimal digits, such as 365. This is interpreted as 3 hundreds, 6 tens, and 5 ones. It is sometimes called a base-10 representation. It's no accident that we have ten fingers, and we use a base-10 representation for our numbers. Computers don't have fingers; they count with voltages. For reliability, they use

Table 1.1 Hexadecimal Representation

Group of Four Bits	Hexadecimal Digit	Value
0000	0	zero
0001	1	one
0010	2	two
0011	3	three
0100	4	four
0101	5	five
0110	6	six
0111	7	seven
1000	8	eight
1001	9	nine
1010	A	ten
1011	B	eleven
1100	C	twelve
1101	D	thirteen
1110	E	fourteen
1111	F	fifteen

only two voltage levels. They either have a voltage or they don't, and it's pretty difficult (though not impossible) to confuse the two situations. So it follows that computers want to represent numbers as a sequence of binary digits (bits), such as 11010. This is the base-2 representation of 1 sixteen, 1 eight, 0 fours, 1 two, and 0 ones. Binary numbers can be added, subtracted, multiplied, and divided directly (no need to convert them to decimal numbers first) as long as we remember that 1 plus 1 is 10 (1 two and 0 ones) and not 2. For example:

```
  1001      binary representation of nine
+ 0101      binary representation of five
  1110      binary representation of fourteen
```

We tend to get confused with long sequences of binary digits, although computers aren't perturbed the least bit. For example, 10110101 is the binary representation for one hundred eighty-one. To make things simpler, we have devised a scheme of compressing long sequences of binary digits by grouping the bits four at a time. Each group of four is represented by a single character, as shown in Table 1.1. Thus 10110101 is abbreviated to B5. This is called a *hexadecimal* number and is exactly the number system we would have used if we had been born with 16 fingers.

Signed Numbers   The binary notation is perfect for describing positive numbers and zero. But when we want to allow for negative numbers, we need to have an additional mechanism to indicate the sign of the number. The simplest way to do this is to use the most significant (leftmost) bit of the number to indicate the sign. For example:

0000 0100	would be +4
1000 0100	would be −4
0111 1111	would be +127
1111 1111	would be −127

Such a representation is called *sign-magnitude* representation and has one serious drawback: it requires a new set of arithmetic rules. This becomes obvious when we try to use binary arithmetic to subtract +1 from 0 and expect to get −1.

0000 0000	0	in sign-magnitude
− 0000 0001	+1	in sign-magnitude
1111 1111	−127	in sign-magnitude

If we want to use the same binary arithmetic on signed numbers that we used on unsigned numbers, we need a signed-number representation in which 1111 1111 represents −1, not −127. Furthermore, subtracting +1 from −1 should give −2. Let's perform this subtraction to see what −2 should look like.

1111 1111	here's −1
− 0000 0001	subtract +1
1111 1110	and call this −2

So it seems that we should represent positive and negative numbers as follows:

.
.
.

0000 0011	plus three
0000 0010	plus two
0000 0001	plus one
0000 0000	zero
1111 1111	minus one
1111 1110	minus two
1111 1101	minus three

.
.
.

This is called a *two's complement* representation, and it has the property that binary additions and subtractions will give the correct two's complement result. For example:

0000 0011	+3 in two's complement
+ 1111 1110	−2 in two's complement
0000 0001	+1 in two's complement

It also has the property that the most significant bit of every non-negative (positive or zero) number is 0 and of every negative number is 1. Thus, just like in sign-magnitude representation, this bit serves as a sign bit. Properties of signed numbers are explored in more detail in Chap. 3.

The sign of a two's complement number can be changed by changing the value of each bit and adding +1. For example, we can obtain the two's complement representation of −3 from the two's complement representation of +3 as follows:

0000 0011	+3 in two's complement

1111 1100	+3 with each bit changed
+ 0000 0001	+1 in two's complement
1111 1101	−3 in two's complement

There is one precaution to note about two's complement numbers. If an 8-bit two's complement number is to be extended to 16 bits (so that it can be added to a 16-bit two's complement number, for example), some thought must be given as to what goes into the additional eight bits.

Suppose we wanted to add 0000 0001 (+1 in two's complement) to 0000 0000 0000 0011 (+3 in two's complement). In this case there's no doubt that we would simply append eight 0's on the left side of the +1 and then add:

0000 0000 0000 0011	(+3 in two's complement)
+ 0000 0000 0000 0001	(+1 in two's complement)
0000 0000 0000 0100	(+4 in two's complement)

However, if we wanted to add 1111 1111 (−1 in two's complement) to 0000 0000 0000 0011 (+3 in two's complement), we must append eight 1's to the left side of −1 (appending 0's would make it a positive number). The addition is then:

0000 0000 0000 0011	(+3 in two's complement)
+ 1111 1111 1111 1111	(−1 in two's complement)
0000 0000 0000 0010	(+2 in two's complement)

Thus the extension of an 8-bit number to a 16-bit number looks like this:

Value	*8-bit Representation*	*16-bit Representation*
+1	0000 0001	0000 0000 0000 0001
−1	1111 1111	1111 1111 1111 1111

The rule for extending a two's complement number is to append additional bits on the left side of the number with each such appended bit having the same value as the original sign bit. This process is called *sign extending*.

Characters Characters can be represented as a sequence of bits. As a minimum we need to be able to represent 26 letters and 10 digits for a total of 36 characters. But it also would be nice to be able to distinguish between upper case and lower case letters (another 26 characters) and to be able to represent some special characters (+ and * for example). So now we have over 64 characters and thus need at least seven bits to represent a single character (the largest value that a 6-bit number can have is only 64). A commonly used 7-bit encoding is called *ASCII* (*A*merican *S*tandard *C*ode for *I*nformation *I*nterchange) and is shown in Appendix C. An 8-bit memory location is called a *byte* of memory and is conveniently used for the storage of an ASCII-encoded character (the eighth bit is sometimes used as a check on the validity of the other seven).

Stacks

A stack is a concept that is frequently found in microprocessors as well as in larger machines. Other names for stacks are "pushdown lists" or "last-in-first-out queues." These names are intended to convey the image of a device for stacking cafeteria trays. When a new tray is placed on top of the stack of trays, it pushes all trays beneath it down one level. When the top tray is removed from the stack, all trays pop up one level. The last tray placed on the stack will be the first tray to be removed.

To understand what all this has to do with computers, we have to look at subroutines. *Subroutines* (sometimes called *procedures*) are parts of a program that are called upon to perform specific tasks. This provides a means of subdividing the total problem to be solved into smaller and simpler parts. A subroutine itself might call upon other subroutines to further subdivide the work. After a subroutine finishes its task, it returns control back to the routine that called upon it. The result is a sequence of subroutines, each calling upon other subroutines, until the last subroutine called upon decides to return. In other words, the last subroutine called will be the first subroutine to return.

When a subroutine is called upon, there is a certain amount of information that must be saved. This might include the current contents of some of the registers and the current settings of the flags. It certainly includes the address in the calling routine to which the subroutine will eventually return control. When the subroutine completes its task, it will retrieve this saved information so that it can restore the contents of the affected registers, set the flags to their original settings, and use the "return address" to return control to the appropriate instruction. But since the last subroutine called is the first subroutine to return, the last piece of information saved must be the first to be retrieved. Thus the information must be stacked like cafeteria trays.

So far we have described how a stack behaves and why a stack would be a useful thing in a computer. Now let's see how a computer stack can be implemented. Since the stack has to hold information, it must be some kind of memory. Actually any portion of the available memory (other than the read-only memory) can be used as a stack. All that is needed is a pointer to the last piece of information that was placed in the stack portion of memory. This pointer is often called the *stack pointer,* and the information it points at is usually called the *top of the stack.* When a new piece of information is placed on the stack (a process referred to as *pushing*), the stack pointer is updated so that it points to the next memory location, and the information is placed in that location. When a piece of memory is retrieved from the stack (a process referred to as *popping*), the

information is retrieved from the memory location that the stack pointer is pointing at, and the stack pointer is again updated—but this time in the opposite
direction.

8086 Memory Utilization (A Sneak Preview)

The preceding sections have illustrated that memory may be used to hold
the program (code), to store data (numeric and character), and as a stack. Thus it
is not surprising that the 8086 actually separates its memory into code segments,
data segments, and stack segments. These segments of memory are discussed in
Chap. 2.

The Microcomputer Story

Now that we've summarized the basic concepts of a computer, let's take a
look at the history of computers and see how they evolved into microcomputers.

From Big Computers to Microcomputers

In the 1950s all electronic
devices (radios and televisions, as well as computers) were built of bulky
vacuum-tube devices. Computers of that vintage are sometimes referred to as
first-generation computers. Examples are IBM's 650 and 704. These computers
were housed in large rooms containing several racks of electronic equipment. By
the end of the decade, transistors and other solid-state devices began to replace
vacuum tubes. Computers using this technology are called second-generation
computers (the IBM 7090 and the Burroughs B5500, for example).

In the 1960s many discrete electronic components (resistors, capacitors,
transistors, etc.) were combined into one single complex electronic component
called an *integrated-circuit* (*IC* for short). The IC is fabricated on a wafer of
silicon smaller than a postage stamp. It is mounted on a centipede-like structure
that can be plugged into a system. This pluggable integrated-circuit became
known as a *chip*. Computers built out of IC chips are the third-generation computers (the IBM 360, the GE 635, and the Burroughs B6700). But the
integrated-circuit technology continued to advance, and by the early 1970s many
of the components in Fig. 1.2 could be put together onto a single chip (Intel's
4004 and 8008). This led to the coining of the term *computer-on-a-chip*.

By this time, not only had the size of computers been drastically reduced,
but so had the price. The vacuum-tube computers were priced in the millions of
dollars. Computers-on-a-chip were initially priced around $300, and within a few
years competition drove that price down to less than $10.

Computers-on-a-chip are called microcomputers or microprocessors. Although the terms are sometimes used interchangeably, there is a difference. A
microprocessor is a single chip. It usually consists of a control unit, an arithmetic
and logical unit, registers, flags, and interfaces to both memory and input/output
devices. Program and data memory, as well as input/output devices, are usually
not on the chip. A *microcomputer* is an entire computer system consisting of a
microprocessor chip, memory chips, and input/output devices. Sometimes the

Fig. 1.3 Special-purpose computer system.

entire computer system is contained on one chip (Intel's 8048). This is called a *single-chip microcomputer*.

As computers became small and inexpensive, it became economical to build them into special-purpose systems such as cash registers, calculators, and typewriters. An example of a computer built into a traffic light is shown in Fig. 1.3. It is not surprising that microprocessors are frequently found in such special-purpose control applications.

From 8008 to 8086 The microprocessor era started with the introduction of Intel's 4004 and 8008 processors in 1971. This was the first generation of microprocessors. Both of these chips were designed for specialized applications—the 4004 in a calculator and the 8008 in a computer terminal. These microprocessors were somewhat of a novelty and not taken seriously. But by 1974 when the 8008 matured into the 8080 (the second-generation microprocessor), the computer industry began to take notice. The 8080 was the first microprocessor deliberately designed to be useful in a great variety of applications. It quickly became the "standard" microprocessor.

The microprocessor was now able to perform the computational tasks of the older and bulkier equipment and was inexpensive enough to find its way into the hands of the hobbyist. Many companies other than Intel began building 8080 chips, and some companies (notably Zilog) built enhanced versions of the 8080. Intel, itself, introduced an enhanced version in 1976 called the 8085. But the basic 8080 character wasn't significantly changed until 1978 when Intel produced the 8086. The 8088, a modified version of the 8086, appeared the following year. These processors are compatible enough with the 8080 so that software written for the 8080 can be preserved. But they are sufficiently advanced to be considered the third generation of microprocessors.

Secret of 8086's Success   What did the 8086 offer that made it an instant success? To appreciate the answers, we must look at the limitations and restrictions of the 8080.

The early success of the 8080 encouraged its use in larger and larger systems. Eventually these systems became so large that they could no longer tolerate the upper limit of 65,000 locations of 8-bit memory addressed by the 8080. The 8086 addresses over one million locations of memory. The 8080 was also being used more and more in areas requiring rapid processing of data longer than eight bits. The 8080's 8-bit data size meant that longer data had to be broken down into small pieces, and each piece had to be operated on separately, thereby increasing the processing time. The 8086 operates on data that is 16 bits long, while at the same time retaining the ability to process 8-bit data items so that shorter pieces of data can still be processed efficiently. As the 8080 was starting to be used as a general-purpose computer, the lack of multiply and divide instructions and the lack of operations on signed numbers were making it cumbersome to use. The 8086 provides these previously missing arithmetic facilities. More and more 8080 programs were being written in a high-level language and then translated into a language understood by the 8080. The means by which the 8080 could address its data did little to provide for the creation of efficient 8080 code from programs written in a high-level language. The addressing modes of the 8086 were designed to accommodate high-level-language processing. A fair number of applications found the 8080 pitifully trying to juggle strings of data, a task for which it was ill-prepared. The 8086 was designed to process data strings efficiently. And, finally, as systems became more and more complex, no single processor could be expected to perform all the functions of the system. But the 8080 never learned how to cooperate with other processors. The 8086, on the other hand, was designed to be used in a multiprocessor environment.

Secret of 8088's Success   What did the 8088 offer that also made it a success? For one thing, it contained all the advanced features found in the 8086. But the amount of data transferred between the 8086 processor and memory at one time is twice as much as the 8080 is able to transfer. Although being able to transfer more data at a time is usually a desirable feature (that's why the 8086 was given this ability), it makes it difficult to use the 8086 in systems designed for the 8080. The amount of data transferred by the 8088 at one time is exactly the same as the amount transferred by the 8080.

2

8086
Machine Organization

Overview

One way to describe a computer is to describe the functional components that make up that computer. A description of these components and the interaction between them is sometimes referred to as the *architecture* of the computer. It is concerned with such things as how many registers are in the computer, what functions the registers serve, how much memory can be connected, how the memory is addressed, and what sort of input/output facilities are available.

The 8086 is a single integrated-circuit chip containing most of the components that make up a computer. The circuitry that controls all the functions of the computer is contained on that chip. Also contained on the chip are all of the registers and flags. The memory and input/output ports are not contained on the chip but can be easily connected to the chip to form a computer. The collection of all those things on the chip is sometimes referred to as the *processor*.

If we had to summarize the architecture of the 8086 in one paragraph, it would be as follows: "The 8086 has four sets of registers. One set contains general registers that are used to hold intermediate results. The second set contains pointer and index registers that are used to locate information within a specified portion of memory. The third set contains segment registers that are used to specify these portions of memory. And the fourth set contains the instruction pointer. There are also nine flags in the 8086. These flags are used to record the state of the processor and to control its operation. The 8086 can access up to 1,000,000 bytes of memory and up to 65,000 input or output ports." The first half of this chapter will elaborate on these features.

Typical computer instructions involve locating designated *operands* (data to be processed), performing an operation on the values of these operands, and storing the result back into a designated *result* location. The locations of the operands and of the result can be either in memory or in a register as designated by the instruction. The facilities available for designating these locations are referred to as the *operand-addressing modes* of the computer. The operand-

12

Fig. 2.1 Memory addresses.

Fig. 2.2 Examples of words in memory.

addressing modes of the 8086 will be described in the second half of this chapter. The actual instructions that operate on the designated operands are described in Chap. 3.

Memory Structure

The memory in an 8086 system is a sequence of up to 2^{20} (approximately 1,000,000) 8-bit quantities called *bytes*. Each byte is assigned a unique address (unsigned number) ranging from 0 to $2^{20}-1$ (0000 0000 0000 0000 0000 to 1111 1111 1111 1111 1111 in binary, 00000 to FFFFF in hexadecimal). This is illustrated in Fig. 2.1

Any two consecutive bytes in memory are defined as a *word*. Each byte in a word has a byte address, and the smaller of these two addresses is used as the address of the word. Examples of words are shown in Fig. 2.2

Fig. 2.3 Example of "backwords" storage in memory.

A word contains 16 bits. The byte with the higher memory address contains the eight most significant bits of the word, and the byte with the lower memory address contains the eight least significant bits. On first reading, this seems very natural. Of course the most significant byte should have the higher memory address. But then when you consider that memory is a sequence of bytes starting at the lowest address and going toward the highest address, it becomes apparent that the 8086 stores its words backwards (perhaps they should be called *backwords*). This is illustrated in Fig. 2.3.

The 8086, as well as the 8088, has some instructions that access (read or write) bytes and other instructions that access words. Now here comes the difference between the two processors. Let's consider the 8088 first. The amount of information that the 8088 transfers to or from memory at one time is always 8 bits. A byte instruction in the 8088 can perform its function with one memory access, whereas an 8088 word instruction must do two memory accesses to two consecutive bytes. Examples of 8088 byte and word reads are shown in Fig. 2.4.

Now for the 8086. The amount of information it transfers to or from memory at one time is always 16 bits. In the case of byte instructions, only eight of those bits are used and the other eight are ignored. The 16 bits are always the contents of two consecutive bytes in memory starting with a byte at an even address. That means that a word instruction that reads or writes a word starting at an even address can perform its function with one memory access. However, word instructions for words starting at odd addresses must do more work; they must do two memory accesses to two consecutive even-address words, ignore the unwanted half of each, and do some byte juggling with the remaining halves. Examples of the various byte and word reads are shown in Fig. 2.5.

The program in the 8086 (or 8088) is oblivious to all of these memory-accessing contortions; an instruction merely requests the accessing (reading or writing) of a particular byte or word, and the processor does whatever is necessary to perform such an access.

Memory Segmentation

Since the 8086 can address up to 2^{20} bytes of memory, it would seem that, within the 8086 processor, byte and word addresses must be represented as 20-bit

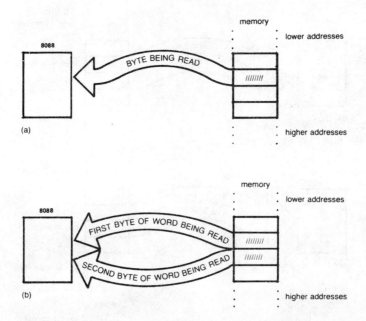

Fig. 2.4 Reading bytes and words from 8088 memory. (a) Reading in a byte.
(b) Reading in a word.

quantities. But the 8086 was designed to perform 16-bit arithmetic, and thus the address objects it manipulates can only be 16 bits in length. An additional mechanism is therefore required to build addresses.

We can conceive of the one megabyte memory as an arbitrary number of *segments,* each containing at most 2^{16} (approximately 65,000) bytes. Each segment begins at a byte address that is evenly divisible by 16 (i.e., the four least significant bits of the byte address are '0'). At any given moment, the program can immediately access the contents of four such segments. These four segments are called the *current code segment,* the *current data segment,* the *current stack segment,* and the *current extra segment.* (The extra segment is a general-pupose area often treated as an additional data segment.) We identify each current segment by placing the 16 most significant bits of the address of its first byte into one of four dedicated registers. These registers are called *segment registers.* Segments need not be unique and they may overlap. Examples of segments are shown in Fig. 2.6.

As an example, assume that the 16-bit code segment register contains the hexadecimal value C018. This makes the code segment start at byte address C0180 and extend for a total of 2^{16} (10000 hexadecimal) bytes. The last byte in the code segment is therefore at byte address D017F.

We refer to bytes or words within a segment by using a 16-bit *offset address* within the 2^{16} byte segment. The processor constructs the 20-bit byte or

The 8086/8088 Primer

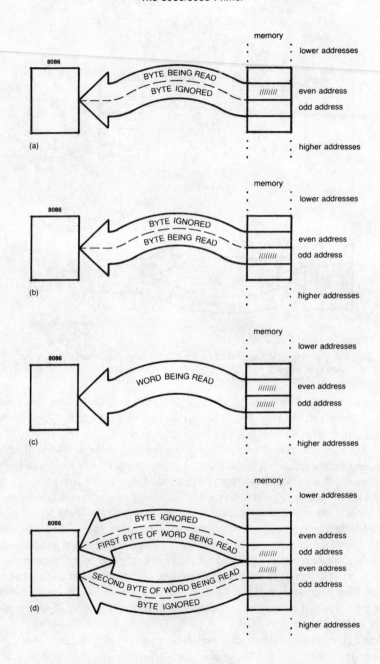

Fig. 2.5 Reading bytes and words from 8086 memory at even and odd addresses. (a) Reading in even-addressed byte. (b) Reading in odd-addressed byte. (c) Reading in even-addressed word. (d) Reading in odd-addressed word requires two memory accesses.

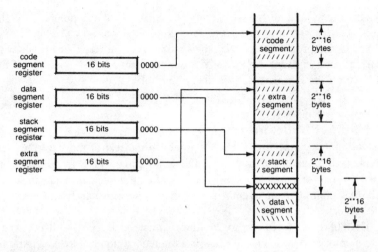

Fig. 2.6 Example of segments. Note that the stack segment and the data segment overlap in this example.

Fig. 2.7 Constructing byte or word addresses.

Fig. 2.8 Example of constructing byte address (see text).

word address by adding the 16-bit offset address to the contents of a 16-bit segment register with four low-order zeros appended, as shown in Fig. 2.7.

So, in the previous example, the byte at byte-address CFFFF lies within the current code segment. Specifically, it has an offset address of FE7F (CFFFF-C0180) within the segment. This is illustrated in Fig. 2.8.

Input/Output Structure

The things connecting an 8086 system to the rest of the world are called *ports*. It is through these ports that the 8086 can receive information about external events (for example, passenger's seat belt not buckled) and can send out signals that control other events (for example, prevent car from starting and heckle driver).

The 8086 can access up to 2^{16} (approximately 65,000) 8-bit ports analogous to memory bytes. Each 8-bit port is assigned a unique address ranging from 0 to $2^{16}-1$. Any two consecutive 8-bit ports can be treated as a 16-bit port analogous to memory words; and, like memory words, 16-bit ports at odd addresses (all 16-bit ports in the case of the 8088) will require two accesses instead of one each time they are used. In fact, ports are addressed in the same manner that memory bytes or words are addressed except there are no port segment registers. In other words, all ports are considered to be in one segment.

Register Structure

The 8086 processor contains a total of thirteen 16-bit registers and nine 1-bit flags. For descriptive purposes, the registers are subdivided into four sets. Three of the sets each contain four registers. A thirteenth register, namely the instruction pointer, is not directly accessible to the programmer and is therefore in a set by itself. The 8086 registers and flags are shown in Fig. 2.9.

The three sets of accessible registers are the general registers, the pointer and index registers, and the segment registers. The general registers are used primarily for holding operands for arithmetic and logical operations. The pointer and index registers are used for holding offset addresses within segments. The segment registers are used for specifying starting addresses of segments.

General Registers   In a processor without general registers, each instruction would fetch its operands from memory and return its result to memory. But memory accesses take time. This time could be reduced by temporarily keeping frequently used operands and results in a quickly accessible place. The set of general registers in the 8086 processor is such a place.

The general registers of the 8086 are the 16-bit registers AX, BX, CX, and DX. The upper and lower halves of each general register can be used separately as two 8-bit registers or together as one 16-bit register. Thus each half of a general register is given its own name. The least significant *low* halves are named AL, BL, CL, and DL, and the most significant *high* halves are named AH, BH,

Fig. 2.9 The 8086 registers and flags.

CH, and DH. The dual nature of these registers permits them to handle both byte and word quantities with equal ease.

For the most part, the contents of the general registers can participate interchangeably in the arithmetic and logical operations of the 8086. For example, the ADD instruction can add the contents of any 8- or 16-bit general register to any other general register of the same size and store the result into either of the registers. However, there are a few instructions that dedicate certain general registers to specific uses. For example, the string instructions require the CX register to contain the count of the number of elements in the string. Neither the AX, BX, nor DX register may be used for this purpose. This specialized use of the CX register suggests the descriptive name COUNT for the CX register. Specialized uses for the AX, BX, and DX registers (to be described later) suggest the descriptive names ACCUMULATOR, BASE, and DATA.

These specialized uses of the general registers have the disadvantage of making the processor harder to learn because there are more special rules to memorize. And it appears that programs will be longer because of the need to move data from one general register to another prior to executing certain instructions. However, let's consider how we would write a program for a processor that treated all the general registers as equals all the time. In order to keep track of where things are, we would probably organize the program so that particular kinds of data always reside in particular registers. We might choose to always use the CX register to keep track of the number of elements in a string. We would never have to move the string size into CX; it would always be there. But since the string instruction in our hypothetical processor can obtain the string size from any general register, each string instruction would have to specify where its string size is to be found. This could be done either by making each string instruction longer (two bytes instead of one) or by having more 1-byte string instructions. The first solution has a direct impact on making programs longer. The second also makes programs longer because there are only a small number of 1-byte instructions (256 of them) and having more 1-byte string instructions means that some other 1-byte instructions must be increased to two bytes. So, by having dedicated registers for certain instructions, the 8086 architecture has actually resulted in a decrease in program size.

Pointer and Index Registers An instruction that accesses a location in memory could specify the address of that location directly. This address takes up space in the instruction, thereby increasing the size of the code. If addresses of frequently used locations were stored in special registers, instructions that access these locations would no longer need to contain the address but could instead specify the register that contained the address. Such registers are sometimes called pointer or index registers.

This use of registers is not unlike abbreviated telephone dialing. You can call anyone in your town by dialing his (or her) 7-digit phone number. Or, if your telephone company provides this service, you can enter some frequently called phone numbers into a set of "registers." Then you can call these selected people by dialing only the one or two digits that specify the register.

The pointer and index registers of the 8086 consist of the 16-bit registers SP, BP, SI, and DI. These registers generally contain offset addresses for addressing within a segment. For example, an ADD instruction could specify that one of its operands is located in the current data segment of memory at an offset contained in a particular pointer or index register (say SI).

Pointer and index registers serve another (and perhaps more important) function besides reducing the size of instructions; they permit instructions to access locations whose offset addresses are the result of previous computations performed while the program is running. It is often necessary to perform such computations in order to establish the offset address of variables, especially in high-level language programs. These computations could be performed in a general register and the result moved to a pointer or index register to be used as an offset. Elimination of such moves would result in shorter programs. For this reason, the values contained in pointer and index registers are permitted to participate in arithmetic and logical operations along with the 16-bit general registers. Thus the ADD instruction mentioned above could specify that its other operand is the contents of the DI register.

There are some differences among the registers that result in dividing this set of registers into the pointer registers SP and BP, and the index registers SI and DI. The pointer registers are intended to provide convenient access to data in the current stack segment as opposed to the data segment. This use of the stack segment as a "data area" has certain advantages (which will be discussed at the end of this chapter) for the implementation of high-level languages. Thus, unless a segment is specifically designated, offsets contained in the pointer registers are assumed to refer to the current stack segment, whereas offsets contained in the index registers are generally assumed to refer to the current data segment. (If the word "generally" is used, you can bet there'll be an exception mentioned soon.) For example, if an ADD instruction specifies that SI contains the offset of one of its operands, that operand will be assumed to be in the current data segment unless the ADD instruction explicitly designates some other segment.

There are some instructions that distinguish between the two pointer registers SP and BP. The PUSH and POP instructions obtain the offset for the top-of-stack location from the SP register, thereby suggesting the descriptive name STACK POINTER for this register. The BP register may not be used for this purpose. This leaves the BP register free to contain the offset of the "base" of a data area in the stack segment, thereby suggesting the descriptive name BASE POINTER.

Furthermore, the string instructions make a distinction between the two index registers SI and DI. Those string instructions requiring a source operand obtain the offset for the source operand from SI; similarly, DI contains the offset of the destination operand. This suggests the descriptive names SOURCE INDEX and DESTINATION INDEX. For those string instructions, the roles of SI and DI may not be interchanged. As an example, the string-move instruction will move the string located in the current data segment starting at the offset contained in SI and relocate it to the current extra segment (there's the exception you were promised) at the offset contained in DI; the SI and DI registers are not explicitly mentioned by the string-move instruction. (Incidentally, the destination string is in the extra segment instead of in the data segment so that each string would have a segment of its own and could be up to 2^{16} bytes long.)

Segment Registers   You will recall that the 8086 has a one megabyte memory, but addresses contained in instructions and in pointer and index registers are only 16 bits long. These addresses cannot be addresses in the one megabyte memory but must be address offsets into some particular 65,000 byte segment. But which one?

The segment registers of the 8086 are the 16-bit registers CS, DS, SS, and ES. These registers are used to identify the four segments that are currently addressable. Each register identifies a particular current segment, and they cannot be used interchangeably: CS identifies the current code segment, DS the current data segment, SS the current stack segment, and ES the current extra segment.

OK. An instruction specifies an offset into a segment, and the segment registers specify the four segments we could use. Which one do we select? The answer depends on how the offset is to be used. An offset might be specifying the next instruction to be executed, or it might be specifying an operand for an instruction.

All instruction fetches are taken from the current code segment. So we need a register that contains the offset in the current code segment of the next instruction to be executed. This is the purpose of IP, the INSTRUCTION POINTER. For example, if CS contains hexadecimal 1FF7 and IP contains hexadecimal 003A, then the next instruction fetched would come from memory location 1FFAA because:

1FF70	code segment start address
+ 003A	offset contained in IP
1FFAA	memory address of next instruction

(You will recall from Fig. 2.6 that the hexadecimal digit ''0'' is appended to the value in the segment register when constructing memory addresses.)

The segment for operand fetches can generally be designated by preceding the instruction with a special 1-byte prefix. This prefix specifies from which of the four current segments the operand is to be fetched. In the absence of such a prefix (the usual case), the operand is taken from the current data segment unless (1) the offset address was calculated from the contents of a pointer register, in which case the current stack segment is used; or (2) the operand is the destination operand of a string instruction, in which case the current extra segment is used. (The reasons for these two exceptions were mentioned in the previous section.)

As an example, consider an ADD instruction that has one of its operands in the data segment and at the offset contained in SI. The instruction would specify SI in its operand field but would make no mention of DS. When executing the instruction, the processor would know to use the contents of DS along with the contents of SI in order to locate the operand. Next, consider an ADD instruction for which the operand is in the code segment (as might be the case with constants in ROM) and at the offset contained in SI. This ADD instruction would, as before, specify SI in its operand field; but, in addition, the instruction would be preceded by a prefix byte specifying CS.

Flags   The 8086 contains nine flags that are used to record processor status information (*status flags*) or to control processor operations (*control flags*). The status flags are generally set after the execution of arithmetic or logical instructions to reflect certain properties of the results of such operations. These flags are the carry flag (CF), indicating if the instruction generated a carry out of the most significant bit; the auxiliary carry flag (AF), indicating if the instruction generated a carry out of the four least significant bits; the overflow flag (OF), indicating if the instruction execution generated a signed result that is out of range; the zero flag (ZF), indicating if the instruction generated a zero result; the sign flag (SF), indicating if the instruction generated a negative result; and the parity flag (PF), indicating if the instruction generated a result having an even number of "1" bits.

The control flags are the direction flag (DF), which controls the direction of the string manipulation instructions; the interrupt-enable flag (IF), which enables or disables external interrupts; and the trap flag (TF), which puts the processor into a single-step mode for program debugging.

More details will be given on each of these flags throughout Chap. 3, and the final section of that chapter summarizes the behavior of the flags.

Instruction Operands and Operand-Addressing Modes

Instructions in the 8086 usually perform operations on one or two operands. For example, the ADD instruction adds the value contained in one operand to the value contained in a second operand and stores the result back into one of these operands. The INCrement instruction adds 1 to the value contained in the operand and stores this result back into the operand. The time has come to show how an instruction specifies its operands (more formally referred to as its *operand-addressing modes*).

Single Operand Let's examine an instruction that specifies a single operand, such as the INCrement instruction. The most common uses of the INCrement instruction are to increment the contents of a pointer or index register (when computing offset addresses) or of a 16-bit general register (when performing arithmetic computations). For such operands, the instruction takes a very simple 1-byte form as shown in Fig. 2.10. It contains a 3-bit **reg** field that

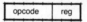

Fig. 2.10 Single-operand instruction where operand is in a 16-bit register.

specifies one of the eight 16-bit registers (general, pointer, or index). The register encodings used in the **reg** field are shown in the first two columns of Table 2.1. The remaining five bits of the instruction identify the operation and are collectively referred to as the *opcode*. In the case of INCrement, the opcode is 01000. As an example, the instruction that increments the contents of the BP register is shown in Fig. 2.11. This operand-addressing mode is sometimes referred to as the *register-mode*. Table 2.2 summarizes all the operand-addressing modes. addressing modes.

```
        opcode     reg
       0 1 0 0 0  1 0 1
         INC        BP
```

Fig. 2.11 Instruction that increments contents of BP.

In its most general form, the INCrement instruction can increment any general, pointer, or index register (eight or 16 bits) or any byte or word of memory. This form is two bytes long as shown in Fig. 2.12. The opcode field is now split; seven bits of opcode are contained in the first byte and three in the second. The opcode for INCrement in this form is 1111111,000. The **w** field is a 1-bit field specifying the width of the operand. If **w** = 0, the operand is eight bits; otherwise it is 16 bits. The **mod** field specifies whether the operand is in a register or in memory. If **mod** = 11, the operand is in a register; otherwise it is in

Fig. 2.12 Single-operand instruction where operand is in a register or memory.

memory. If the operand is in a register, the **r/m** field specifies which register; if the operand is in memory, the **r/m** field tells where in memory it is (**r/m** stands for register or memory).

First consider the case where the operand is in a register (**mod** = 11). The register encodings used in the **r/m** field are shown in Table 2.1. This is another instance of the register operand-addressing mode. As an example, the instruction that increments the contents of the CL register is shown in Fig. 2.13.

Fig. 2.13 Instruction that increments contents of CL.

Now consider the case where the operand is in memory (**mod** = 00, 01, or 10). This operand-addressing mode is sometimes referred to as *indirect memory addressing* because the operand is in memory but the offset is not specified directly. Instead, it is obtained by adding together a seemingly strange assortment of values. (The usefulness of such a mode will be justified in the next section.) The offset is the sum of up to three numbers: a 16-bit value (called a *displacement*) specified in the instruction, the contents of an index register (SI, DI, or none) specified in the instruction, and the contents of a base register (BX, BP, or none) specified in the instruction. The **r/m** field specifies the base and index register as shown in Table 2.3. The **mod** field specifies the displacement as shown in Table 2.4. The offset thus formed locates the operand within its segment. The operand is in the current data segment (unless the contents of pointer register BP were used in computing the offset address, in which case the operand

Fig. 2.14 An example of memory operand (see text).

Table 2.1 Register Encoding

	16-bit Register	8-bit Register
000	AX	AL
001	CX	CL
010	DX	DL
011	BX	BL
100	SP	AH
101	BP	CH
110	SI	DH
111	DI	BH

Table 2.2 Operand Addressing Modes

IMMEDIATE
REGISTER
DIRECT MEMORY ADDRESSING
INDIRECT MEMORY ADDRESSING
    base register
    index register
    base register + index register
    base register + displacement
    index register + displacement
    base register + index register + displacement

Table 2.3 Base and Index Register Specified by r/m for Operands in Memory (mod ≠ 11)

r/m Field	Base Register	Index Register
000	BX	SI
001	BX	DI
010	BP	SI
011	BP	DI
100	none	SI
101	none	DI
110	BP	none
111	BX	none

*If **mod** = 00 and r/m = 110, see note below Table 2.4.*

is in the current stack segment). Still another addition, involving the contents of a segment register, is necessary to form the 20-bit memory address of the operand.

As an example, consider the instruction shown in Fig. 2.14. The opcode field is 1111111 000, which is the INCrement instruction. The **w** field is a 1, which indicates the operand is 16 bits. The **mod** field is 01, which indicates the operand is in memory; and, furthermore, the displacement is the contents of the next byte of the instruction sign extended to 16 bits. Thus the displacement is 0000 0000 0101 1100. The **r/m** field is 100, which indicates that the contents of the index register SI are to be added to the displacement to form the offset address. Assume SI contains 1010 0000 1000 0110. Then the offset address is as follows:

**Table 2.4 Displacement as Specified by mod for
Operands in Memory (mod ≠11)**

Mod	Displacement	Comment
00	zero (16 bits worth)	
01	8-bit contents of next byte of instruction sign extended to 16 bits	Instruction contains an additional byte
10	16-bit contents of next two bytes of instruction (next byte contains least significant eight bits and byte after that contains most significant eight bits).	Instruction contains two additional bytes

*If **mod** = 00 and **r/m** = 110, then:*
1. Tables 2.3 and 2.4 do not apply
2. Instruction contains two additional bytes
3. Offset address is contained in those bytes (least significant eight bits precede most significant eight bits)

$$\begin{array}{ll} 1010\ 0000\ 1000\ 0110 & \text{contents of SI} \\ +\ 0000\ 0000\ 0101\ 1100 & \text{displacement} \\ \hline 1010\ 0000\ 1110\ 0010 & \text{offset address} \end{array}$$

Since BP was not used in computing the offset address, the offset refers to the current data segment. Assume DS contains 1111 0000 1111 0000. Then the memory address of the operand is as follows:

$$\begin{array}{ll} 1111\ 0000\ 1111\ 0000 & \text{data segment} \\ +\ 1010\ 0000\ 1110\ 0010 & \text{offset address} \\ \hline 1111\ 1010\ 1111\ 1110\ 0010 & \text{memory address} \end{array}$$

The operand is 16 bits wide (specified by the **w** field) so the operand is the contents of the bytes located at address 1111 1010 1111 1110 0010 and at address 1111 1010 1111 1110 0011 with the higher-addressed byte being the most significant.

Fig. 2.15 Segment-overriding prefix.

The operand need not be restricted to the current data segment or stack segment. It can be fetched from any one of the four current segments by preceding the instruction with a 1-byte prefix denoting a segment register. This 1-byte prefix is shown in Fig. 2.15. As an example, Fig. 2.16 shows the same instruction as Fig. 2.14 except that now the operand is in the current extra segment.

Fig. 2.16 Example of using segment-overriding prefix (see text).

So far we have shown how to specify the offset of an operand in memory by going through a base and/or index register. But often we know exactly where the operand is, and we want to specify the offset directly in the instruction. This mode of operand addressing is called *direct memory addressing*. In this mode, the offset is contained in two bytes of the instruction ("backwords," of course). The remainder of the instruction must specify the opcode and the fact that the mode is direct memory addressing. It would be convenient to use a combination of the bits in the **mod** and **r/m** fields to indicate this mode. Unfortunately, all the combinations have already been accounted for by the indirect memory-addressing mode and the register mode. But one of these combinations corresponded to an infrequently used indirect memory-addressing mode and so was chosen to correspond to direct memory addressing instead. This combination is **mod** = 00 and **r/m** = 110. For example, the instruction which increments the byte at offset 0101 1010 1111 0000 in the current data segment is shown in Fig. 2.17.

The infrequently used mode that was lost to the direct memory-addressing mode is indirect through BP (no index register and no displacement). So now an instruction that forms its offset from just the BP register and a zero displacement will need to have **mod** = 01 and use one byte in the instruction to specify the zero displacement.

Fig. 2.17 Instruction that increments byte at offset 0101 1010 1111 0000 in current data segment.

Two Operands Now that we've mastered the one-operand instruction, let's consider an instruction that has two operands such as ADD. As mentioned previously, ADD takes the value of one operand, adds it to the value of the other operand, and stores the result back in the location of either operand. If both operands could be in memory, the instruction would need a **mod** field and an **r/m** field for each. To keep the instruction short, it was decided that at least one of the operands must be in a register. Now the instruction needs a **mod** and **r/m** field for one of the operands but only a **reg** field for the other. This is shown in Fig. 2.18.

Fig. 2.18 Typical two-operand instruction.

The two-operand instruction uses the **w** field to indicate if the operands are eight bits (**w** = 0) or 16 bits (**w** = 1). Also present is a new field not encountered before, namely the **d** field (**d** stands for destination). The **d** field specifies whether the result should be stored back into the operand specified by the **mod** field and **r/m** field (**d** = 0) or into the operand specified by the **reg** field (**d** = 1). The operand into which the result is to be stored is called the *destination operand,* and the remaining operand is called the *source operand.*

As an example, consider the ADD instruction shown in Fig. 2.19. The opcode for ADD is 000000. The **w** field is 0, specifying that both operands are eight bits. The operand specified by the **reg** field is CH. The **mod** field is 11, specifying that the **mod r/m** operand is in a register, and the **r/m** field identifies the register as being BL. The **d** field specifies that the result is to be placed back into the operand specified by the **reg** field, namely CH. Thus the instruction will add the contents of register BL, the source operand, to the contents of register CH, the destination operand, and store the result back into CH.

Fig. 2.19 Example of two-operand instruction (see text).

Fig. 2.20 Simplest immediate-operand instruction.

Fig. 2.21 Example of immediate-operand instruction (see text).

Fig. 2.22 Immediate-operand instruction using **mod** and **r/m** fields.

Fig. 2.23 Example of immediate-operand instruction using **mod** and **r/m** fields (see text).

One of the operands of a two-operand instruction can be a constant contained in the instruction itself (referred to as an *immediate operand*). Since instructions are frequently located in read-only memories (ROMs), this would be an ideal place to keep constant operands. But forget about trying to store a result back into such an operand. The memory won't allow it.

An instruction that can specify an immediate operand is the MOVe instruction. The most common use of such an instruction is to move a constant into a register (general, pointer, or index). In such cases, the non-immediate operand can be specified by a **reg** field, and the instruction takes the simple form shown in Fig. 2.20. The **w** field indicates if the operands (immediate as well as non-immediate) are eight bits (**w** = 0) or 16 bits (**w** = 1); if eight bits, the immediate operand occupies one byte in the instruction; otherwise it occupies two bytes and is stored "backwards." As an example, Fig. 2.21 shows an instruction that moves the value 1111 0000 0000 1111 to the 16-bit DI register.

A slightly more complicated immediate-operand instruction uses the **mod** and **r/m** fields instead of the **reg** field to specify the non-immediate operand. This is more general (non-immediate operand can be in memory) but requires an additional byte as illustrated in Fig. 2.22. Figure 2.23 shows an instruction that moves the value 1111 0000 0000 1111 into a word in memory in the data segment at the offset contained in DI.

Since two-operand instructions have only one **w** field, either both operands must be eight bits or both must be 16 bits. However, immediate operands are frequently small numbers that don't require 16 bits. This is particularly true of immediate operands used with addition, subtraction, and comparison instructions; it is less true of immediate operands used with logical instructions. It follows that we could reduce the size of immediate-operand instructions if we didn't have to use 16 bits to house small numbers. To accomplish this, some of the immediate-operand instructions (additions, subtractions, and comparisons) contain an **s** field (**s** means sign-extend). This field only has significance for 16-bit operands (**w** = 1) and signifies whether all 16 bits of the immediate operand are contained in the instruction (**s** = 0) or whether only the eight least significant bits are contained in the instruction and must be sign-extended to form the 16-bit operand (**s** = 1). This form is illustrated in Fig. 2.24.

Figure 2.25 shows an example of such an instruction. In this example, the value 0000 0000 0000 1111 is added to the contents of a word in memory and the

Fig. 2.24 Immediate-operand instruction containing **s** field.

Fig. 2.25 Example of immediate-operand instruction containing an **s** field.

result placed back into the memory word. The memory word is in the data segment at the offset contained in DI. Note that one byte is eliminated by having the **s** field.

Comments about Operand-Addressing Modes

After having read and understood the operand-addressing modes just described, you might be asking the following questions:

1. Do I really have to fill in the **mod, r/m, reg, w, s, d,** etc., fields every time I want to use an instruction that has operands?
2. Why are there so many memory-addressing modes?

The answer to the first question is NO, unless you are of the conviction that the only proper way to write a program is in terms of 1's and 0's. But if you believe in automatic programming aids such as assemblers or compilers, you'll never have to look at a **mod, r/m, reg,** etc., field again; any decent assembler and every compiler will make these details invisible to you.

To understand the answer to the second question, you will recall that the 8086 was designed so that a program written in a high-level language could be translated into efficient code. Typical high-level language features were examined to determine what kinds of operand-addressing modes would best support them. Some of these features will now be discussed.

Most programming languages have the concept of simple variables and arrays. A *simple variable* is a variable that represents a single value; an *array* is a variable that represents a sequence of values. Consider an assignment statement typical of the kind found in many high-level languages.

$$A(I) = X$$

This statement is read "Ith element of A becomes X." It could be translated into code that moves the contents of the memory location corresponding to the simple variable X into a register, say BL, and then moves the contents of BL into the memory location corresponding to the Ith element in the array A. Assume that X is the contents of the memory location at offset 0FF0 (hexadecimal) in the current data segment. Furthermore, assume A(0), the first element of the array A, is at offset 0FF1 in that segment. The machine instruction that moves (the contents of) X into BL is shown in Fig. 2.26 (a). This utilizes the special case of **mod** and **r/m** chosen for direct memory addressing. Since accessing of simple variables such as

X is a frequent occurrence, it is not surprising that a special addressing mode was provided. The machine instruction that moves the contents of BL into A(I) is shown in Fig. 2.26 (b). Here it is assumed that the value of the index I already exists in an index register. Such array accesses point out the need for the indirect memory-addressing mode "index register + displacement." Assignments of the form A(I) = B(J) point out the need for at least two index registers, each with the addressing mode just mentioned, specifically "SI + displacement" and "DI + displacement." Accesses to array elements such as A(I + 2) present no additional complication; the displacement field of Fig. 2.26 (b) would merely contain 0FF3, the offset of A(2), instead of the offset of A(0).

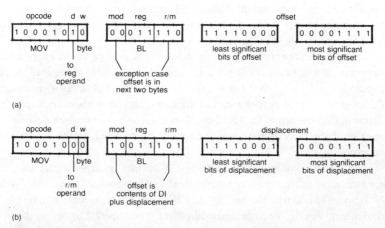

Fig. 2.26 Machine instruction for A(I) = X. (a) Moving X to BL. (b) Moving BL to A(I).

Certain high-level languages have the concept of a based variable. A *based variable* corresponds to the memory location whose address is contained in some other variable called a *pointer*. If the value of the pointer (i.e., the value contained in the memory location corresponding to the pointer) changes, the based variable will correspond to a different memory location. A convenient way to access a based variable is to place the value of the pointer in BX and then use the operand-addressing modes involving BX. Specifically, the mode "BX" would be used to access a simple based variable and "BX + SI" or "BX + DI" would be used to access an element in a based array.

Some high-level languages employ the concept of a record. A *record* (also called a *structure* in some languages, notably PL/M) is a collection of named data items possibly of differing types. This is in contrast to an array, which is a sequence of (unnamed) data items all of the same type. A payroll program, for example, might have a record corresponding to each employee. Each record might contain the employee's name, social security number, year-of-hire, and salary. A particular record item such as year-of-hire is in the same position in every employee record. For example, if year-of-hire is contained in the fourth byte from the start of each employee record and the employee record for John Doe starts at offset 03B4 (hexadecimal), then John Doe's year of hire is contained in the memory location at offset 03B7. Thus the location of any given item in a record is at a fixed location and can be accessed with direct addressing; it is in essence no different from a simple variable.

Consider now a based record and assume that the value of the pointer on which the record is based is contained in the BX register. The operand-addressing mode to access an item from such a record would be "BX + displacement" where displacement would be the position in the record corresponding to the item. For example, displacement would be 3 if the item were year-of-hire in a based employee record. Unless the record is quite large (more than 256 bytes), the displacement can be contained in eight bits and a single-byte displacement (**mod** = 01) can be used.

Although the operand-addressing mode for accessing items in based records appears similar to the mode for accessing array elements (both are "register + displacement"), there is a big difference. In the case of array elements, the displacement corresponds to the start of the array, and the register corresponds to the distance into the array. In the case of based records, the register corresponds to the start of the record, and the displacement corresponds to the distance into the record.

Arrays and records can be combined. Consider an array where each element of the array is an employee record. And, furthermore, consider that this is a based array. Assume that the pointer is in BX and an index corresponding to an array element is in SI. The operand-addressing mode needed to access the year-of-hire item of the particular record being indexed is "BX +SI +displacement" where displacement would be a 3. This justifies the need for the 8086's most complicated operand-addressing mode, namely "base register + index register + displacement." So it appears as though the operand-addressing modes aren't overkill after all.

What still remain to be justified are the operand-addressing modes involving BP as the base register and the corresponding use of the stack segment instead of the data segment. These modes have been provided to allow for an efficient implementation of block-structured languages and reentrant subroutines. A reentrant subroutine is a subroutine that may be invoked (called upon) while it is already in execution from a previous invocation. This could occur if (1) the subroutine invoked itself, (2) the subroutine invoked some other subroutine that in turn invoked the original subroutine, or (3) the execution of the subroutine was suspended because an interrupt occurred, and during the processing of the interrupt, the subroutine was invoked again.

All the data (local variables and parameters) utilized by a reentrant subroutine must have a unique memory location for each concurrent invocation of the subroutine, otherwise the data being used by one invocation of the subroutine might be corrupted by a subsequent invocation. This means that memory must be allocated for the subroutine's data every time the subroutine is invoked. Such memory is called an *activation record*. Although it's not essential, it would be highly desirable for the subroutine to release this memory when the subroutine finishes. Since the last subroutine invoked is the first to finish, the stack serves as a convenient place from which to allocate such memory. Each time a subroutine is invoked, a block of memory on the top of the stack is reserved for the activation record by simply changing the contents of register SP, the stack pointer. During the execution of the subroutine, it is necessary to maintain a pointer to the beginning of the activation record; this is the reason for having BP, the base pointer. Accesses to items within the activation record can be performed with the operand-addressing modes involving BP. Specifically, a simple variable within the activation record can be accessed by the mode "BP + displacement," and an array element within the activation record can be accessed with "BP + SI + displacement." Since BP was involved in the address calculation, the access will be to the current stack segment (as opposed to the current data segment), which is exactly where the activation record is.

The uses of the memory-addressing modes in high-level languages are summarized in Table 2.5.

Table 2.5 Use of Direct and Indirect Memory-Addressing Modes in High-Level Languages

	Not Based	Based	Activation Record
SIMPLE VAR	direct	BX	BP+placement
ARRAYS	SI+displacement	BX+SI	BP+SI+displacement
	DI+displacement	BX+DI	BP+DI+displacement
RECORDS	direct	BX+displacement	BP+displacement
ARRAYS OF REC	SI+displacement	BX+SI+displacement	BP+SI+displacement
	DI+displacement	BX+DI+displacement	BP+DI+displacement

3

8086
Instruction Set

The previous chapter described the source and destination operands of an instruction; this chapter describes the operation an instruction performs on these operands. The instructions are described in an informal manner. A more formal description can be found in the *Intel MCS-86 User's Manual*.

Several of the instructions have a general (long) form as well as a restricted (short) form. The short form uses fewer bytes but is more limited in the operands it allows. The purpose of the short form is to allow the most frequent cases to be programmed in the fewest number of bytes. For example, the general form of the PUSH instruction pushes an operand that is either in a register or in memory. It requires two bytes to specify the operand. The short form of PUSH operates only on registers and is only one byte long. Unless you're planning to write your programs directly in 1's and 0's, you won't have to be concerned about instructions having multiple forms; a good assembler will let *you* specify the instructions, and *it* will select the most efficient forms. Appendix A summarizes the possible forms of each instruction and Appendix B summarizes the opcodes.

For convenience, the instructions are grouped into the following categories: data-transfer instructions, arithmetic instructions, logical instructions, string instructions, transfer-of-control instructions, interrupt instructions, flag instructions, and synchronization instructions. Each of these categories will now be described in detail.

Data Transfer Instructions
The 8086 has four classes of data transfer instructions: general-purpose transfers, accumulator-specific transfers, address-object transfers, and flag transfers. These are summarized in Table 3.1.

General-Purpose Transfers   The general-purpose transfers are MOV (move), PUSH, POP, and XCHG (exchange). A segment register may be used as one of the operands of these instructions so that new values may be placed into segment registers and the old values saved. Once a value is placed in segment register, it makes little sense to perform any calculations using that value. Therefore, none of the other instructions permit segment registers as operands. (The segment register is specified with a 2-bit **seg** field where 00 denotes ES, 01 denotes CS, 10 denotes SS, and 11 denotes DS; if the instruction has a **d** field, then **d** = 1 denotes that the segment register is the destination operand.)

Table 3.1 Data Transfer Instructions

General Purpose

MOV (move):	SOURCE	= > DEST
PUSH (push):	SOURCE	= > stack
POP (pop):	stack	= > DEST
XCHG (exchange):	SOURCE	< = > DEST

Accumulator Specific

IN (input):	port	= > AL or AX
OUT (output):	AL or AX	= > port
XLAT (translate):	f(AL)	= > AL

Address Object Transfers

LEA (load effective address into register):   offset of SOURCE = > REGISTER

LDS (load pointer into register and DS):   SOURCE, SOURCE +1 = > REGISTER
SOURCE +2, SOURCE+3 = > DS

LES (load pointer into register and ES):   SOURCE, SOURCE +1 = > REGISTER
SOURCE+2, SOURCE+3 = > ES

Flag Transfers

LAHF (load AH with flags):	SF,ZF,AF,PF,CF = > AH
SAHF (store AH into flags):	AH = > SF,ZF,AF,PF,CF
PUSHF(push flags):	flags = > stack
POPF (pop flags):	stack = > flags

The MOV instruction performs a byte or word transfer from the source operand to the destination operand. One of the operands is specified with a **mod** field and an **r/m** field. The other operand can be specified either by a **reg** field, a **seg** field (segment register operand), or a **data** field (immediate operand). In order to optimize frequently occurring cases, several short forms of the MOV instruction also are provided, as shown in Fig. 3.1.

The 8086/8088 Primer

Fig. 3.1 Formats of MOV instruction.

The PUSH instruction transfers a word from the source operand to the stack. The POP instruction does just the opposite; it transfers a word from the stack to the destination operand. The stack is a portion of memory contained in the current stack segment. The SP register contains the offset of the last word entered onto the stack. This word is called the *top of the stack*. As successive words are pushed onto the stack, they are placed in consecutively lower memory addresses (the stack grows toward lower memory and shrinks toward higher memory). The PUSH instruction *starts* by *decrementing* the contents of SP by 2, thereby locating the next free stack word. The POP instruction *finishes* by *incrementing* the contents of SP by 2, thereby removing the word just accessed from the stack. Figure 3.2 illustrates the effect of a PUSH instruction and a POP instruction.

The operand of a PUSH or POP instruction is specified either by a **mod** field and an **r/m** field, a **reg** field, or a **seg** field, as shown in Fig. 3.3.

A word of caution is in order at this time. Consider what would happen if an instruction changed the contents of the CS register. The effect of such an instruction would be to cause a new segment to become the current code segment. But the usual incrementing of the IP register will cause IP to contain the offset of the next sequential instruction in the *previous* code segment. Thus the combination of CS and IP will specify a meaningless memory address, and the processor will attempt to fetch the next instruction for execution from this meaningless address. So, unless the instruction that alters the contents of CS also puts a related value in IP, the processor will wind up making a wild transfer. For this reason, certain instructions that permit a segment register to be used as an operand may not use one particular segment register—namely CS. This occurs in (1) a MOV instruction when the seg field denotes CS as the destination operand

Fig. 3.2 Example of pushing and popping entries on stack. (a) Initial stack configuration. (b) Stack configuration after executing a PUSH instruction that pushes the value of A01F onto the stack. (c) Stack configuration after executing a POP instruction.

Fig. 3.3 Formats of PUSH and POP instructions.

and (2) the POP instruction. The actions of the processor when encountering such instructions are undefined. The undefined instructions are shown in Fig. 3.4.

The final general-purpose data-transfer instruction is the XCHG instruction. This instruction performs a byte or a word interchange between the two operands. There is no need to distinguish the operands as source and destination, and hence the instruction contains no **d** field (thereby making room for another opcode). The XCHG instruction has a general form and a short form as shown in Fig. 3.5.

Accumulator-Specific Transfers The accumulator-specific transfers include IN (input), OUT (output), and XLAT (translate). Unlike the previous

Fig. 3.4 Undefined instructions. (a) Moving a new value into CS. (b) Popping a new value into CS.

XCHG—exchange register/memory with register

XCHG—exchange with accumulator

Fig. 3.5 Formats of XCHG instruction.

transfers, which treated all registers other than the segment registers as equals, these transfers discriminate by permitting only the accumulator to serve as the operand. The reason they were made accumulator-specific was to avoid the need for any **mod, r/m,** or **reg** fields.

The IN instruction transfers data (byte or word) from an input port to the accumulator (AL or AX). Similarly, the OUT instruction transfers data from the accumulator to an output port. The port number can be specified either directly by a byte in the instruction or indirectly by the contents of the DX register. Note that this is a specialized use of the DX register: none of the other general-purpose registers can be used for this function. Only the first 256 ports can be specified directly in the instruction, whereas any of the 2^{16} (approximately 65,000) ports can be specified indirectly. The direct specification, although requiring the instruction to contain an additional byte, has the advantage of not requiring the execution of an additional instruction to preload the port number into a register. The indirect access has the advantage that program loops can be used to access consecutive ports. The formats of the IN and OUT instruction are shown in Fig. 3.6. The difference between the direct and the indirect port specification is shown in Fig. 3.7.

The XLAT instruction (shown in Fig. 3.8) transfers a byte from a table into the accumulator AL. The beginning of the table is specified by register BX (another specialized use of a general-purpose register). The index into the table is the original contents of AL.

IN—input to AL/AX from fixed port

IN—input to AL/AX from variable port

OUT—output from AL/AX to fixed port

OUT—output from AL/AX to variable port

Fig. 3.6 Formats of IN/OUT instructions.

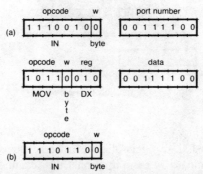

Fig. 3.7 Contrasting direct and indirect port specification for inputting the byte from port 3C (hexadecimal). (a) Direct specification: port number in instruction. (b) Indirect specification: port number first loaded into DX register.

XLAT—translate byte to AL

Fig. 3.8 Format of XLAT instruction.

The XLAT instruction is useful for translating an encoded value into the same value under a different encoding. For example, consider the following encoding of the decimal digits 0 through 9:

Digit	Encoding
0	1 1 0 0 0
1	0 0 0 1 1
2	0 0 1 0 1
3	0 0 1 1 0
4	0 1 0 0 1
5	0 1 0 1 0
6	0 1 1 0 0
7	1 0 0 0 1
8	1 0 0 1 0
9	1 0 1 0 0

This encoding is of practical interest because each encoded value contains exactly two "1" bits (sometimes referred to as a 2-out-of-5 code) and is actually used in telephone signaling applications. Suppose we want to translate the binary digit 7 into a 2-out-of-5 code. The steps to perform this translation are as follows:

1. Place the offset of a table containing the encodings into BX.
2. Place binary 7 (0000 0111) into AL.
3. XLAT—this will fetch the seventh entry from the table (0001 0001) and place it in AL.

This translation is illustrated in Fig. 3.9.

Address-Object Transfers   The address-object transfers are LEA (load effective address), LDS (load pointer into DS), and LES (load pointer into ES). These instructions provide the programmer with some control over the addressing mechanism. The formats for these instructions are shown in Fig. 3.10. Note that although these instructions use a **mod** and an **r/m** field to specify one operand and a **reg** field to specify the other operand, there is no **d** field to specify which operand is the source and which is the destination. The **d** field is unneces-

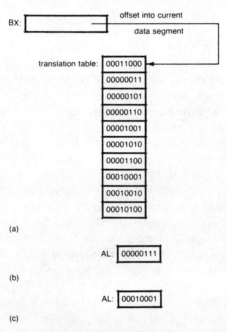

(a)

(b)

(c)

Fig. 3.9 Example of using XLAT instruction to translate the digit 7 from binary encoding to a 2-out-of-5 encoding. (a) Translation table for converting binary to 2-out-of-5 code. (b) Contents of register AL before executing XLAT instruction. (c) Contents of register AL after executing XLAT instruction.

Fig. 3.10 Formats of address-object transfer instructions.

sary because the source operand of these instructions always comes from or refers to memory and hence has to be specified by the **mod** and **r/m** fields. The reason the source operand must come from or refer to memory will become apparent as each of the address-object transfers is described.

The LEA instruction provides access to the offset address of the source operand as opposed to the value of the operand. Hence this instruction would be meaningless if the source operand did not refer to memory. The effect of the instruction is to transfer the 16-bit offset address of the source operand to the 16-bit register designated as the destination operand. This facility is useful for passing the offset address of a variable from one part of the program to another so that the other part of the program can modify the value of the variable if it so desired. Objects that are passed between different parts of the program are called *parameters,* and the different parts of the program are called *subroutines*. For example, suppose one subroutine had the responsibility for incrementing variables. Other parts of the program could call on this incrementing subroutine and have it increment a specific variable. The offset address of the variable to be incremented could be passed as a parameter to the incrementing subroutine by placing the offset address in a mutually agreed upon register, such as BX, prior to calling the incrementing subroutine. The LEA instruction is tailor-made to do just that. The **reg** field of the LEA instruction would designate the BX register (011), and the **mod** and **r/m** fields would designate the offset address of the variable. The instruction would be executed prior to calling the subroutine. The subroutine could then access the variable by using the appropriate operand-address mode involving BX (**mod**=00, **r/m**=111). Note that if the value of the variable instead of its offset were passed to the incrementing subroutine, the subroutine would know the value but would be unable to alter the variable.

The LDS instruction transfers four consecutive bytes (32 bits) from a source operand to a pair of 16-bit destination registers. The source operand must be in memory. One destination register is the 16-bit destination operand specified by the **reg** field in the instruction; the other destination register is DS. The LES instruction is similar to LDS except that the other destination register is ES instead of DS. The actual data transferred is illustrated in Fig. 3.11. The LDS and LES instructions provide an efficient means for setting up the segment start address and offset address of a variable so that the variable can be accessed by succeeding instructions. This combination of segment start address and offset address is called a *pointer;* the LDS (or LES) instruction transfers a pointer from memory into registers appropriate for the operand-addressing modes. For example, assume offset addresses 0F1C to 0F1F (four bytes) in the current data segment contain a pointer to a 1-byte variable as shown in Fig. 3.12 (a). The two-instruction sequence for loading the value of the variable in the AL register is shown in Fig. 3.12 (b).

Flag Transfers   The flag transfer instructions (Fig. 3.13) provide access to the set of processor flags. The instructions are LAHF (load AH with flags), SAHF (store AH into flags), PUSHF (push flags), and POPF (pop flags).

Fig. 3.11 Data movement for LDS and LES instruction.

Fig. 3.12 Example of using LDS instruction. (a) Memory containing a pointer to a variable. (b) Instructions that (i) load pointer into registers DS and BX; (ii) use operand-addressing mode involving DS and BX to access variable being pointed at.

Fig. 3.13 Formats of flag-transfer instructions.

Fig. 3.14 Correspondence between flags and bits of AH.

Fig. 3.15 Correspondence between flags and bits on the stack.

The LAHF instruction transfers the flag registers SF (sign flag), ZF (zero flag), AF (auxiliary carry flag), PF (parity flag), and CF (carry flag) into specific bits of the AH register. The SAHF instruction transfers specific bits of the AH register into these flags. These five flags were singled out for no other reason than that they were the five flags present in the 8080 processor. (The LAHF and SAHF instructions exist mainly to permit programs written for the 8080 to be translated into efficient 8086 programs.) The correspondence between bits in AH and the five flags is shown in Fig. 3.14.

The PUSHF instruction enters a word on the stack and transfers all nine of the flags into specific bits of this word. The POPF instruction removes a word from the stack and transfers specific bits of this word into the nine flag registers. The correspondence between bits of the stack word and the nine flags is shown in Fig. 3.15.

Arithmetic Instructions

The 8086 provides the four basic mathematical operations in a number of different varieties. The arithmetic instructions of the 8086 are shown in Table 3.2. Both 8- and 16-bit operations and both signed and unsigned arithmetic are provided. Furthermore, correction operations are provided to allow arithmetic to be performed directly on decimal rather than on binary digits.

Table 3.2 Arithmetic Instructions

Addition

ADD (add):	DEST+SOURCE => DEST
ADC (add with carry):	DEST+SOURCE+CF => DEST
INC (increment):	DEST+1 => DEST

Subtraction

SUB (subtract):	DEST−SOURCE => DEST
SBB (subtract with borrow):	DEST−SOURCE−CF => DEST
DEC (decrement):	DEST−1 => DEST
NEG (Negate	0−DEST => DEST
CMP (compare):	DEST−SOURCE => ?

Multiplication

MUL (multiply): $AL*SOURCE_8 => AX$
or $AX*SOURCE_{16} => DX,AX$

IMUL (integer multiply): Same as above but signed multiply

Division

DIV (divide): $AX/SOURCE_8 => AL$;remainder $=> AH$
or $DX,AX/SOURCE_{16} => AX$;remainder $=> DX$

IDIV (integer divide): Same as above but signed divide

| | unsigned | | | | signed | | | |

	number	representation		number	representation
8-bit	0	0000 0000		-128	1000 0000
	1	0000 0001		-127	1000 0001
	2	0000 0010		-126	1000 0010
	.			.	
	126	0111 1110		-1	1111 1111
	127	0111 1111		0	0000 0000
	128	1000 0000		+1	0000 0001
	.			.	
	253	1111 1101		+125	0111 1101
	254	1111 1110		+126	0111 1110
	255	1111 1111		+127	0111 1111

(a) unsigned 8-bit numbers   (b) signed 8-bit numbers

	number	representation		number	representation
16-bit	0	0000 0000 0000 0000		-32,768	1000 0000 0000 0000
	1	0000 0000 0000 0001		-32,767	1000 0000 0000 0001
	2	0000 0000 0000 0010		-32,766	1000 0000 0000 0010
	.			.	
	32,766	0111 1111 1111 1110		-1	1111 1111 1111 1111
	32,767	0111 1111 1111 1111		0	0000 0000 0000 0000
	32,768	1000 0000 0000 0000		+1	0000 0000 0000 0001
	.			.	
	65,533	1111 1111 1111 1101		32,765	0111 1111 1111 1101
	65,534	1111 1111 1111 1110		32,766	0111 1111 1111 1110
	65,535	1111 1111 1111 1111		32,767	0111 1111 1111 1111

(c) unsigned 16-bit numbers   (d) signed 16-bit numbers

Fig. 3.16 Range of 8- and 16-bit signed and unsigned numbers.

The difference between signed and unsigned numbers is in your interpretation of the bit patterns. Unsigned numbers are interpreted in binary notation. Signed numbers are interpreted in the two's complement notation described in Chap. 1. Figure 3.16 shows the range and representation of signed and unsigned numbers. Addition and subtraction operations are the same on both types of numbers. Thus the ordinary binary addition and subtraction instructions designed for unsigned numbers will also give the correct results when applied to signed numbers. The only difference between signed and unsigned addition and subtraction is the mechanism for detecting out-of-range results. The add and subtract instructions set the CF flag if the result, when interpreted as an unsigned number, is out of range; and set the OF flag if the result, when interpreted as a signed number, is out of range. It is possible for either the signed or unsigned result to be out of range with the other result being in range. Figure 3.17 illustrates this.

The six status flags are set or cleared by most arithmetic operations to reflect certain properties of the result of the operations. We have just discussed two of these flags, CF and OF. In general, the six flags are set to recognize the following conditions:

1. CF is set if the operation resulted in an unsigned result being out of range.
2. OF is set if the operation resulted in a signed result being out of range (called *signed overflow*).
3. ZF is set if the result of the operation is zero (signed or unsigned).
4. SF is set if the most significant bit of the result of the operation is a '1', thereby indicating a negative result.
5. PF is set if the result of the operation contains an even number of '1' bits (called *even parity*).
6. AF is set if a correction is needed for decimal operations (discussed in detail later).

A summary of the behavior of these flags appears at the end of this chapter.

Multiple-precision arithmetic is a means of dealing with unsigned numbers larger than 16 bits by breaking the numbers into 8- or 16-bit fields and performing repeated operations on successive fields starting with the least significant. If any of these operations yields an out-of-range result, the result is still valid, but a '1' is carried into (addition) or borrowed from (subtraction) the operation on the next field. As an example, consider adding the 24-bit number 0011 1010 0000

	representation	interpretation as unsigned numbers		interpretation as signed numbers	
(a) both signed and unsigned results in range	0000 0100 + 0000 1011 ――― 0000 1111	4 11 ― 15	CF = 0	+ 4 + 11 ― + 15	OF = 0
(b) unsigned result out of range	0000 0111 + 1111 1011 ――― 0000 0010	7 251 ― 2 •••out of range•••	CF = 1	+ 7 − 5 ― + 2	OF = 0
(c) signed result out of range	0000 1001 + 0111 1100 ――― 1000 0101	9 124 ― 133	CF = 0	+ 9 + 124 ― − 123 •••out of range•••	OF = 1
(d) both signed and unsigned result out of range	1000 0111 + 1111 0101 ――― 0111 1100	135 245 ― 124 •••out of range•••	CF = 1	− 121 − 11 ― + 124 •••out of range•••	OF = 1

Fig. 3.17 Examples of out-of-range results in unsigned and signed additions.

0111 1011 0010 to the 24-bit number 0100 0000 1100 0010 0101 0011. This can be done in three successive additions on 8-bit numbers, as shown below:

1. The least significant eight bits are added together:

$$
\begin{array}{l}
1011\ 0010 \\
0101\ 0011 \\
\hline
0000\ 0101 \qquad \text{with CF} = 1
\end{array}
$$

2. The middle eight bits are added together along with any carry generated by the previous addition:

$$
\begin{array}{ll}
1 & \text{(last CF)} \\
0000\ 0111 & \\
1100\ 0010 & \\
\hline
1100\ 1010 & \text{with CF} = 0
\end{array}
$$

3. The most significant eight bits are added together along with any carry generated by the previous addition:

$$
\begin{array}{ll}
0 & \text{(last CF)} \\
0011\ 1010 & \\
0010\ 0000 & \\
\hline
0101\ 1010 &
\end{array}
$$

Thus the result is 0101 1010 1100 1010 0000 0101. This example points out the need to have an instruction (add-with-carry) that adds the values of the two operands and the value in CF all together. A similar instruction, subtract-with-borrow, is useful for multiple-precision subtraction.

An unsigned addition or subtraction result going out of range can be planned for when performing tasks such as multiple-precision arithmetic. It is a normal event and does not indicate an error condition. A signed result going out of range, on the other hand, is usually unanticipated. It indicates that a fault has occurred and that the results must be corrected before computations can proceed.

Addition Instructions   The addition instructions are ADD (add), ADC (add-with-carry), and INC (increment). These instructions may, in general, be applied to any operands.

The ADD instruction (Fig. 3.18) performs a byte or word addition of the contents of the source and destination operands and stores the result back in the destination operand. One of the operands can be in a register or in memory (**mod** and **r/m** field); the other operand can be in a register (**reg** field) or in the instruction (immediate field). Both a general form and short form of the immediate-operand ADD instruction are provided.

The ADC instruction is similar to the ADD instruction except it includes the initial value of CF in the addition. This facilitates the multiprecision arithmetic discussed above. The forms of the ADC instruction are the same as the forms for the ADD instruction and are summarized in Fig. 3.19.

Fig. 3.18 Formats of ADD instruction.

Fig. 3.19 Formats of ADC instruction.

Fig. 3.20 Formats of INC instruction.

The INC instruction has only one operand. The instruction adds '1' to the contents of the operand and stores the result back in that operand. The INC instruction has a general form and a short form as shown in Fig. 3.20.

The INC instruction is identical to the ADD instructions with an immediate operand of 1 but requires fewer bytes. INC was included in the instruction set because adding (and subtracting) 1 is a very frequent operation and should therefore be done in as few bytes as possible.

Subtraction Instructions The subtraction instructions are SUB (subtract), SBB (subtract with borrow), DEC (decrement), NEG (negate), and CMP (compare). The first three are analogous to the three addition instructions, and their formats are shown in Fig. 3.21.

The NEG instruction (Fig. 3.22) changes the sign of its operand. For example, if the operand contained the representation of −1 (1111 1111), the NEG instruction would change it to +1 (0000 0001).

The CMP instruction is similar to the subtract instruction except the result is not stored back into the destination operand. In fact, the result is not stored anywhere; it is just lost inside the processor. No doubt you're probably wondering, "Of what use is an instruction that loses its result?" It turns out that the flag

Fig. 3.21 Formats of SUB, SBB, and DEC instructions.

NEG—change sign (negate)

Fig. 3.22 Formats of NEG instruction.

**Table 3.3 Flag Setting after a CMP
Instruction Is Executed**

Relationship of Destination Operand to Source Operand		CF	ZF	SF	OF
	EQUAL	0	1	0	0
Signed Operands	LESS THAN	—	0	1	0
	LESS THAN	—	0	0	1
	GREATER THAN	—	0	0	0
	GREATER THAN	—	0	1	1
Unsigned Operands	BELOW	1	0	—	—
	ABOVE	0	0	—	—

*Unspecified entries in above table can be either '0' or '1' depending on the actual values
of the operands.*

settings that reflect certain properties of the result are more important than the result itself. From these flag settings, we can deduce the relationship between the value of the two operands that entered into the subtraction. For example, if the ZF flag is set to '1', then the result is zero and the value of the two operands must have been identical. The flag settings for each of the various possible relationships are shown in Table 3.3. A CMP instruction is typically followed by a conditional jump instruction (discussed later) that tests the flag settings to see if a particular relationship was satisfied. The forms of the CMP instruction are the same as the forms of the SUB instruction and are shown in Fig. 3.23.

Multiplication and Division Instructions Multiplication of two 8-bit numbers has the potential for yielding a product up to 16 bits long. Consider, for example, the multiplication of the unsigned numbers shown in Fig. 3.24.

Similarly, the multiplication of two 16-bit numbers can give a 32-bit product. The 8086 multiplication instructions permit multiplying either an 8- or 16-bit quantity contained in AL or AX by an operand of the same size specified in the instruction itself. The 16- or 32-bit product is placed back into AX and, if necessary, into DX. This is illustrated in Fig. 3.25.

The division instructions of the 8086 are designed to undo what the multiplication instructions did. Specifically, the division instructions divide the 16-bit number in AX (or the 32-bit number in AX and DX) by an operand of half that size specified in the instruction. The remainder is placed in AH (AX in the bigger case), and the quotient is placed in AL (DX in the bigger case). This is illustrated in Fig. 3.26.

Fig. 3.23 Formats of CMP instruction.

Fig. 3.24 Example illustrating that product can be up to twice as long as operands.

Fig. 3.25 Source and destination operands for multiplication.

Fig. 3.26 Source and destination operands for division. (a) 8-bit divisor. (b) 16-bit divisor.

Unlike addition and subtraction, the ordinary binary multiplication and division instructions that work for unsigned numbers do not give the correct results when applied to signed numbers. This is illustrated in Fig. 3.27. Thus special multiplication and division instructions must be provided for signed numbers. The 8086 multiplication and division instructions are MUL (unsigned multiply), IMUL (signed multiply, sometimes called integer multiply), DIV (unsigned divide), and IDIV (signed divide, sometimes called integer divide). The formats of the multiply and divide instructions are shown in Fig. 3.28.

A word about signed division is in order. If we divide -26 by $+7$, we could get a quotient of -4 and a remainder of $+2$. Or we could get a quotient of -3 and a remainder of -5. Either pair of results would be correct. In one case the remainder is positive, and in the other case it is negative. The 8086 signed division instruction was designed so that the remainder will have the same sign as the dividend. For the above division, the 8086 will produce a quotient of -3 and a remainder of -5. Division, defined in this manner, will give quotients (and remainders) with the same absolute value for -27 divided by $+7$, -27 divided by -7, $+27$ divided by $+7$, and $+27$ divided by -7.

Table 3.4 summarizes the number of bits in the operands and the results of various arithmetic instructions. The instructions were designed so that the double-length result of a multiplication could be used in a future division. What if you want to use the result of a multiplication for something other than division? For instance, how would you multiply 17 (0001 0001) by 10 (0000 1010) and add 20 (0001 0100) to the product? That's simple. Just ignore the eight most significant bits of the product. But now comes the problem of performing a division on a number that was not generated by a previous multiplication. For example, try to divide a plain old 8-bit version of 35 (0010 0011) by 7 (0000 0111). The division instruction expects a 16-bit dividend to be in AX. Simply putting an 8-bit dividend into AL won't work because the division instruction will use whatever

representation	interpretation as an unsigned number	interpretation as a signed number
1111 1111 1111 1111	255 255	−1 −1
1111 1111 1 1111 111 11 1111 11 111 1111 1 1111 1111 1 1111 111 11 1111 11 111 1111 1		
1111 1110 0000 0001	65,025 (correct result)	−511 (incorrect result)

Fig. 3.27 Example demonstrating that ordinary binary multiplication does not give correct result for signed numbers.

Fig. 3.28 Formats of multiply and divide instructions.

Table 3.4 Size of Operands and Results

	First Operand	Second Operand	Result
ADD	8 (addend) 16 (addend)	8 (augend) 16 (augend)	8 (sum) 16 (sum)
SUBTRACT	8 (minuend) 16 (minuend)	8 (subtrahend) 16 (subtrahend)	8 (difference) 16 (difference)
MULTIPLY	8 (multiplicand) 16 (multiplicand)	8 (multiplier) 16 (multiplier)	16 (product) 32 (product)
DIVIDE	16 (dividend) 32 (dividend)	8 (divisor) 16 (divisor)	8 (quotient), 8 (remainder) 16 (quotient), 16 (remainder)

garbage it finds in AH as the eight most significant bits of the dividend. Well, that's no problem. Just make sure to zero out AH before doing an 8-bit by 8-bit division or zero out DX before doing a 16-bit by 16-bit division.

Zeroing out the most significant half of the double-length dividend works fine for unsigned division, but how about signed division? Converting the 8-bit version of -2 (1111 1110) to the 16-bit version (1111 1111 1111 1110) involves setting the eight most significant bits to all 1's, whereas converting the 8-bit version of $+3$ (0000 0011) to the 16-bit version (0000 0000 0000 0011) involves setting the eight most significant bits to all 0's. The rule is simple: just extend the leftmost bit (sometimes called the sign bit) of the 8-bit version into every bit position in the most significant half of the 16-bit version. The process of stretching numbers by extending the sign bit is called *sign extension*. The 8086 provides instructions (Fig. 3.29) to facilitate the task of sign extension. These instructions were initially named SEX (*s*ign *ex*tend) but were later renamed to the more conservative CBW (*c*onvert *b*yte to *w*ord) and CWD (*c*onvert *w*ord to *d*ouble word). The CBW instruction extends the sign bit of AL into all bits of AH; the CWD instruction extends the sign bit of AX into all bits of DX. Figure 3.30 summarizes the steps for performing 8-bit by 8-bit or 16-bit by 16-bit divisions.

Decimal Arithmetic   All the arithmetic operations discussed so far have been on binary numbers. That's because computers think in binary. But people don't. Our world is decimal. If God had intended for us to think in binary, we would have been born with only two fingers. So the first obstacle we face when doing arithmetic operations with computers is converting input numbers from our

1	0	0	1	1	0	0	0

CBW—convert byte to word

1	0	0	1	1	0	0	1

CWD—convert word to double word

Fig. 3.29 Formats of sign-extension instructions.

	SIGNED	UNSIGNED
8-bit by 8-bit	move divisor into AL sign extend AL into AH (CBW) divide AH by dividend	move divisor into AL put zero into AH divide AH by dividend
16-bit by 16-bit	move divisor into AX sign extend AX into DX (CWD) divide BX,AX by dividend	move divisor into AX put zero into DX divide DX,AX by dividend

Fig. 3.30 Performing equal length divisions.

Table 3.5 BCD Encoding of Decimal Digit

Digit:	0	1	2	3	4
Encoding:	0000	0001	0010	0011	0100
Digit:	5	6	7	8	9
Encoding:	0101	0110	0111	1000	1001

language to theirs and then converting results back the other way. The fact that the conversions waste time is unfortunate. But what's worse is that the computer is thinking about a different problem than we are thinking about, and this could result in some surprising results. For example, we would be justifiably upset if our computer-controlled car odometer wrapped around after 131,071 (instead of 99,999) miles just because 131,072 is a power of 2.

Why then must computers be so stubborn and insist on "thinking" in binary? Just because they work with only two voltage levels, 0 and 1, they need not represent their numbers in binary notation. Certainly these 0's and 1's could be used to encode each decimal digit in a number separately. For example, instead of representing the decimal number 37 by its binary equivalent 0010 0101, it could be represented by a binary encoding for 3 (0011), followed by a binary encoding for 7 (0111), resulting in the representation 0011 0111. Note that this is a binary encoding of the demical digits and is appropriately referred to as *binary-coded decimal* or BCD. Table 3.5 lists the encoding of each demical digit. The reason computers typically "think" in binary notation instead of in BCD is that the binary notation is more compact. For example, the number 125 can be represented in eight bits in binary notation (0111 1101) but requires 12 bits in BCD (0001 0010 0101).

How about arithmetic on numbers represented in BCD notation? Can BCD numbers be added, subtracted, multiplied, and divided? One way to do this is to have BCD addition, BCD subtraction, BCD multiplication, and BCD division included in the instruction set of the computer in place of (or in addition to) the conventional binary addition, binary subtraction, binary multiplication, and binary division instructions. Another solution is to use the binary arithmetic instructions on the BCD numbers, knowing full well that the wrong BCD answer will be obtained and then executing a special *adjustment* instruction that will convert the answer to the correct answer in BCD notation. The latter is used by the 8086.

Consider, for example, adding the BCD representation of 23 to the BCD representation of 14 by using the (8-bit) binary addition instruction. The addition is shown below:

$$\begin{array}{r} 0010\ 0011 = 2\ 3 \\ +\ \underline{0001\ 0100} = 1\ 4 \\ 0011\ 0111 = 3\ 7 \end{array}$$

Lo and behold, the binary addition gives the correct BCD result! So in this example, no adjustment is necessary. Let's push our luck further and try to add 29 in BCD to 14 in BCD. This addition is as follows:

$$
\begin{array}{r}
0010\ 1001 = 2\ 9 \\
+\ 0001\ 0100 = 1\ 4 \\
\hline
0011\ 1101 = 3\ ?
\end{array}
$$

This answer is not correct because the encoding 1101 does not represent a decimal digit. What's happened is that a 4-bit encoding can represent up to 16 distinct digits, but there are only 10 distinct decimal digits. Thus any addition of two digits whose sum is greater than 9 will enter into the forbidden 6-digit range and give the incorrect answer. The way to adjust for this is to add 6 to the sum in any digit position that treads in the forbidden range, thereby compensating for the six forbidden digits that must be passed over. Thus the sum of the previous example is adjusted as follows:

$$
\begin{array}{r}
0011\ 1101 = 3\ ? \\
+\ \ \ \ \ \ 0110 = 0\ 6 \\
\hline
0100\ 0011 = 4\ 3
\end{array}
$$

And 43 is the correct answer. In this example, the journey through the forbidden range was easy to detect because the result was "caught in the act." A more subtle case occurs when the sum passes completely through the forbidden range and winds up on a valid digit of the other side. The addition of BCD 29 and BCD 18 illustrates this.

$$
\begin{array}{r}
0010\ 1001 = 2\ 9 \\
+\ 0001\ 1000 = 1\ 8 \\
\hline
0100\ 0001 = 4\ 1
\end{array}
$$

In this case, the result is incorrect because the rightmost digit of the sum passed completely through the forbidden range, and thus that digit should be adjusted by adding 6. However, there is no way to determine that such an adjustment is necessary by inspecting the result. One property of a digit passing completely through the forbidden range is that, during the addition, a carry is generated out of the corresponding digit position. In the above example, a carry is generated out of the low-order digit position into the high-order digit position. Thus results could be adjusted if we had some way of knowing when carries are generated out of either digit position. The carry flag (CF), already discussed, indicates when an addition generates a carry out of the most significant bit (and hence out of the most significant digit). The auxiliary-carry flag (AF) exists solely to indicate when an addition generates a carry out of the least significant digit, so the BCD adjustment can be applied. In the above example, CF is set to 0, and the AF is set to 1 after the addition.

Multiple precision arithmetic can be performed on BCD numbers. This is illustrated by adding the number 2889 to the number 3714. It involves two successive additions and adjustments as shown below:

1. The least significant pairs of digits are added together:

$$
\begin{array}{rll}
1000\ 1001 &= 8\ 9 \\
+\ 0001\ 0100 &= 1\ 4 \\
\hline
1001\ 1101 &= 9\ ? & \quad CF = 0 \qquad AF = 0
\end{array}
$$

2. Adjustment is applied:

$$
\begin{array}{rll}
1001\ 1101 &= 9\ ? \\
+\ \qquad 0110 &= \text{adjustment} \\
\hline
1010\ 0011 &= ?\ 3 \\
+\ 0110 \qquad &= \text{adjustment} \\
\hline
0000\ 0011 &= 0\ 3 & \quad CF = 1 \qquad AF = 1
\end{array}
$$

3. The most significant pairs of digits are added together along with the last value of CF:

$$
\begin{array}{rll}
1 & \text{(last CF)} \\
0010\ 1000 &= 2\ 8 \\
+\ 0011\ 0111 &= 3\ 7 \\
\hline
0110\ 0000 &= 6\ 0 & \quad CF = 0 \qquad AF = 1
\end{array}
$$

4. Adjustment is applied:

$$
\begin{array}{rll}
0110\ 0000 &= 6\ 0 \\
+\ \qquad 0110 &= \text{adjustment} \\
\hline
0110\ 0110 &= 6\ 6
\end{array}
$$

5. The final result:

$$0110\ 0110\ 0000\ 0011 = 6\ 6\ 0\ 3$$

The 8086 instruction that performs the decimal adjustment is DAA (decimal adjust for addition). The DAA instruction assumes the sum is in AL. Based on the value in AL and the settings of CF and AF, the DAA instruction determines the necessary adjustment and applies it to AL. A similar instruction, DAS (decimal adjust for subtraction), will adjust the result after a subtraction operation. It is not possible to apply an adjustment for multiplication because the BCD result is buried under and indistinguishable from the cross-terms generated. Similarly, a divide adjustment is not possible. So, if you need to perform multiplication or division on decimal numbers, you'll have to use a different decimal representation as described below.

The BCD representation discussed so far is more accurately referred to as *packed BCD* because two digits are packed into a byte. Another representation, called *unpacked BCD*, contains only one digit per byte. The digit is contained in the four least significant bits; the most significant bits have no bearing on the

Table 3.6 ASCII Representations of Digits

Digit	ASCII
0	0011 0000
1	0011 0001
2	0011 0010
3	0011 0011
4	0011 0100
5	0011 0101
6	0011 0110
7	0011 0111
8	0011 1000
9	0011 1001

value of the represented number. One example of unpacked BCD is the ASCII representations of digits. ASCII is a 7-bit representation of a set of characters (see Appendix C). The ASCII representations of digits are shown in Table 3.6. The four most significant bits contain 0011, which is not relevant to the digit value.

Addition and subtraction of unpacked BCD representations can be adjusted in a manner similar to the packed BCD adjustments, except only the least significant digit is affected. Unlike packed BCD, multiplication and division adjustments are possible for unpacked BCD. The instructions that perform these four adjustments are called ASCII adjustment instructions (because ASCII is the most common example of unpacked BCD) and are AAA (ASCII adjust for addition), AAS (ASCII adjust for subtraction), AAM (ASCII adjust for multiplication), and AAD (ASCII adjust for division). The forms of the decimal and ASCII adjust instructions are shown in Fig. 3.31.

Fig. 3.31 Format of decimal and ASCII adjust instructions.

As an example of unpacked BCD multiplication, consider multiplying 9 by 4. Assume unpacked 9 (0000 1001) is in the BL register and unpacked 4 (0000 0100) is in the AL register. Applying the (unsigned) binary multiplication instruction specifying BL as the source (multiplier) will put the 16-bit binary product, namely 36 (0000 0000 0010 0100), in AX. The multiplication adjustment (AAM) must decompose the binary 36 in AX into 3 (0000 0011) in AH and into 6 (0000 0110) in AL. This is nothing more than dividing the contents of AL by ten and placing the quotient in AH and the remainder in AL. In fact, it's no coincidence that the AAM instruction is two bytes long (it appears as though one byte would have sufficed) with the second byte being nothing more than the binary representation of ten (0000 1010). In reality, the AAM instruction is a kind of division instruction (although it doesn't put the remainder and quotient in the same places that DIV and IDIV do) with the divisor operand contained in the second byte of the instruction. Don't be surprised if changing the second byte from ten (0000 1010) to seven (0000 0111) results in a divide-by-seven instruction (although Intel makes no such promise). And it follows that putting sixteen (0001 0000) in the second byte should result in converting a packed BCD number in AL into an unpacked BCD number in AH and AL.

Observe that in the example just presented, the operands 0000 1001 and 0000 0100 were unpacked BCD numbers having all zeros in the most significant four bits. If this were not the case, the multiplication would generate cross-terms that would hide the desired result 0010 0100 (it was just such cross-terms that made adjustments for packed BCD multiplication impossible). Thus before multiplying unpacked BCD numbers, you must zero the most significant four bits of each operand unless you know that they are already zero. A convenient instruction for zeroing selected bits of a byte is the AND instruction (to be discussed later).

So far we have seen how to multiply a 1-digit unpacked BCD number by another 1-digit unpacked BCD number. Let's now try to multiply a multidigit number by a 1-digit number. For example, 539 times 6. When we first learned arithmetic, we were taught to perform such multiplication as follows:

> "Nine times six is 54. Write down the four and carry the five. Three times six is 18, plus five to carry makes 23. Write down the three and carry the two. Five times six is 30, plus two to carry makes 32. Write it down."

In summary form it looked something like this:

$$
\begin{array}{r}
25 \qquad \text{(carries)} \\
539 \\
\times \quad 6 \\
\hline
3234
\end{array}
$$

Now let's see how an 8086 would tackle this problem. Assume the number 539 is stored as unpacked BCD in variables a3, a2, and a1 respectively. Also assume that the number 6 is stored as unpacked BCD in variable b. Furthermore, assume that the most significant four bits of a_3, a_2, a_1, and b are all zero. We want to multiply a_3, a_2, a_1 by b and put the result in variables c_4, c_3, c_2, c_1. This is represented diagrammatically as follows:

$$
\begin{array}{ccccc}
 & a_3 & a_2 & a_1 \\
\times & & & b \\
\hline
c_4 & c_3 & c_2 & c_1 \\
\end{array}
$$

The steps in an 8086 program to perform this multiplication would be something like this:

1.	al * b −>AX	;nine times six is . . .
2.	AAM	; 54 (five in AH, four in AL)
3.	AL −>c1	;write down the four
4.	AH −>c2	; and carry the five
5.	a2 * b −>AX	;three times six is . . .
6.	AAM	; 18 (one in AH, eight in AL)
7.	AL + c2 −>AL	;plus five to carry makes . . .
8.	AAA	; 23 (two in AH, three in AL)
9.	AL −>c2	;write down the three
10.	AH −>c3	; and carry the two
11.	a3 * b −>AX	;five times six is . . .
12.	AAM	; 30 (three in AH, zero in AL)
13.	AL + c2 −>AL	;plus two to carry makes . . .
14.	AAA	; 32
15.	AL −>c3	;so write
16.	AH −>c4	; it down

Observe the use of additions and the corresponding AAA adjustments in the above example. Let's examine one of those AAA's in detail. When the AAA on line 8 adjusted AL from invalid (0000 1101) to three (0000 0011), it generated a carry out of the least significant digit of AL. That carry did not go into the most significant digit of AL but rather went into the least significant digit of AH, thereby adjusting AH from one (0000 0001) to two (0000 0010). Thus the AAA instruction involves an adjustment not just to AL but to both AH and AL. This side effect of AAA would not have been necessary if AAA were used solely for additions and not for multiplications.

A more elegant algorithm (involving a loop) for doing multidigit unpacked BCD mutiplication is outlined in Fig. 3.32. Although only single-digit mutipliers are discussed here, the extension to multidigit multipliers is straightforward.

Next consider an unpacked BCD division, such as 42 divided by 6. Assume unpacked 42 is in AX (0000 0100 in AH, 0000 0010 in AL) and unpacked 6 (0000 0110) is in BL. The unpacked representation of a single-digit number, such as 6, is nothing more than its binary representation. So let's put the dividend, 42, into binary. This can be done by multiplying the contents of AH by ten and adding it to the contents of AL. A binary division of AL (binary 42) by BL

addition

addend: $a(n)\ a(n-1)\ a(n-2)\ \ldots\ a(3)\ a(2)\ a(1)$
augend: $b(n)\ b(n-1)\ b(n-2)\ \ldots\ b(3)\ b(2)\ b(1)$

sum: $c(n+1)$ $c(n)\ c(n-1)\ c(n-2)\ \ldots\ c(3)\ c(2)\ c(1)$

clear the carry flag CF
do the following once for each integer value of i from 1 to n
  move $a(i)$ into AL
  add-with-carry $b(i)$ to AL
  add-adjust AL into AH,AL
  move AL into $C(i)$
move AH into $C(n+1)$

subtraction

minuend: $a(n)\ a(n-1)\ a(n-2)\ \ldots\ a(3)\ a(2)\ a(1)$
subtrahend: $b(n)\ b(n-1)\ b(n-2)\ \ldots\ b(3)\ b(2)\ b(1)$

difference: $c(n+1)$ $c(n)\ c(n-1)\ c(n-2)\ \ldots\ c(3)\ c(2)\ c(1)$

clear the carry flag CF
do the following once for each integer value of i from 1 to n
  move $a(i)$ into AL
  subtract-with-borrow $b(i)$ from AL
  subtract-adjust AL into AH,AL
  move AL into $C(i)$
move AH into $C(n+1)$

multiplication

multiplicand: $a(n)\ a(n-1)\ a(n-2)\ \ldots\ a(3)\ a(2)\ a(1)$
multiplier: b

product: $c(n+1)$ $c(n)\ c(n-1)\ c(n-2)\ \ldots\ c(3)\ c(2)\ c(1)$

clear most significant four bits of b
clear $c(1)$
do the following once for each integer value of i from 1 to n
  clear most significant four bits of $a(i)$; put result into AL
  multiply AL by b
  multiply-adjust AL into AH,AL
  add $c(i)$ to AL
  add-adjust AL into AH,AL
  move AL into $c(i)$
  move AH into $c(i+1)$

division

dividend: $a(n)\ a(n-1)\ a(n-2)\ \ldots\ a(3)\ a(2)\ a(1)$
divisor: b

quotient: $c(n)\ c(n-1)\ c(n-2)\ \ldots\ c(3)\ c(2)\ c(1)$

clear most significant four bits of b
clear AH
do the following once for each integer value of i from n to 1
  clear most significant four bits of $a(i)$; put result into AL
  divide-adjust AH,AL into AL
  divide AL by b with remainder going into AH
  move AL into $c(i)$

Fig. 3.32 Multi-digit unpacked BCD arithmetic.

(6) would then give the binary representation of 7 in AL. But binary 7 is nothing more than unpacked 7, so the unpacked division is complete.

There are three points to note from the preceding example. First, division adjustment (AAD) consists of multiplying AH by ten and adding in AL (again, it's no coincidence that the second byte of the AAD instruction is a ten). Second, division adjustment *precedes* the division operations, whereas addition, subtraction, and multiplication adjustments *follow* the corresponding arithmetic operation. In other words, the addition, subtraction, and multiplication adjustments correct a bad (i.e., non-BCD) result, whereas the division adjustment prevents a bad result from occurring. Third, the unpacked BCD dividend and divisor must have all zeros in the most significant four bits. This requirement applies to multiplication as well but is not necessary for addition and subtraction.

A multidigit dividend can be divided by a single-digit divisor in much the same manner as was already illustrated for mutiplication. An algorithm for doing such multidigit unpacked BCD division is shown in Fig. 3.32. Unfortunately, this method does not generalize to divisions with multidigit divisors. Such divisions can be done by "guessing" at the quotient, using unpacked BCD multiplication and subtraction to see how close the guess was, and then successively refining the guess. This is exactly what we do in the ordinary pencil-and-paper method of long division. More refined algorithms for performing long divisions are discussed in the book entitled *The Art of Computer Programming–Volume 2* by Donald E. Knuth.

Logical Instructions

The 8086 logical instructions consist of Boolean instructions and shift/rotate instructions as summarized in Table 3.7.

Table 3.7 Logical Instructions

AND:	DEST and SOURCE = > DEST
TEST:	DEST and SOURCE = > ?
OR:	DEST or SOURCE = > DEST
XOR:	DEST xor SOURCE = > DEST
NOT:	not DEST = > DEST
SHL (shift logical left):	CF<——DEST<——0
SHR (shift logical right):	0——>DEST——>CF
SAL (shift arithmetic left):	same as SHL
SAR (shift arithmetic right):	sign——>DEST——>CF
ROL (rotate left):	
ROR (rotate right):	
RCL (rotate left through carry):	
RCR (rotate right through carry):	

Fig. 3.33 Formats of Boolean instructions.

Boolean Instructions The Boolean instructions are NOT, AND, OR (inclusive-or), XOR (exclusive-or), and TEST. The forms of these instructions are shown in Fig. 3.33

The AND, OR, and XOR instructions perform a logical function between each bit of a source operand and the corresponding bit of a destination operand and place the result back in the bit of the destination operand. The NOT instruction has only one operand; it performs its function on each bit of that operand and places the result back in that same bit. The logical functions performed by these instructions are defined in Table 3.8.

Table 3.8 Definition of Logical Functions

One Operand	
Source Bit	Not
0	1
1	0

Two Operands				
Source Bit	Destination Bit	And	Or	Exclusive-Or
0	0	0	0	0
0	1	0	1	1
1	0	0	1	1
1	1	1	1	0

The "and" function is useful for clearing (sometimes called *masking*) specified bit positions in a number; one operand specifies the bit positions and the other specifies the number. For example, we can clear the most significant four bits in an 8-bit number by "anding" that number with 0000 1111. (You will recall that it was necessary to clear the most significant four bits of an unpacked decimal number prior to performing a decimal multiplication or division.)

In a similar manner, the "or" function and "exclusive-or" function are useful for setting and complementing specified bit positions in a number. For example, we can set the most significant bit in an 8-bit number by "oring" the number with 1000 0000, and we can complement the middle four bits in an 8-bit number by "exclusive-oring" that number with 0011 1100. The "not" function is useful for complementing every bit in a number; it is equivalent to "exclusive-oring" that number with all 1's.

The TEST instruction is similar to the AND instruction in that both perform an "and" function between corresponding bits of two operands. However, the TEST instruction retains only the flag settings and not the result. Such an instruction is useful for examining specified bit positions in a number to determine if any of them are 1. Again, one operand specifies the bit positions and the other specifies the number. If the (discarded) result is non-zero, as indicated by the ZF flag (ZF = 0 means result is not zero), then at least one of the specified bits is a 1. For example, to determine if any of the least significant four bits of BL are 1, place 0000 1111 into BH, execute a TEST instruction that designates BL and BH as its operands, then execute a conditional jump instruction that jumps if ZF is 0. Note that the AND instruction could have been used in place of the TEST instruction, but this would have destroyed the initial value of one of the operands because the AND instruction doesn't discard its result.

Shift/Rotate Instructions   The shift instructions provide a very efficient mechanism for doubling or halving a number (fewer bytes and fewer cycles than doing a multiplication or division). To double an unsigned number, just shift all bits one position to the left and fill in the vacated rightmost bit with a 0. And if the bit that was shifted off the left end is placed into CF, an out-of-range result can be detected by testing CF for a 1. For example, doubling the number 65 (0100 0001) by shifting left results in 130 (1000 0010) with CF becoming 0 (in-range), whereas shifting left the number 130 (1000 0010) results in 4 (0000 0100) with CF becoming 1 (out-of-range). Similarly, halving an unsigned number is accomplished by shifting all bits one position to the right, filling in the vacated bit position with a 0, and placing into CF the bit that was shifted off the right end. In this case, CF = 1 indicates that the number was not even. For example, halving the number 9 (0000 1001) results in 4 (0000 0100) with CF becoming 1.

The instructions that perform the doubling and halving of unsigned numbers are SHL (shift left) and SHR (shift right). Two other shifts, SAL (shift arithmetic left) and SAR (shift arithmetic right), are useful for doubling and halving signed numbers. The forms of these instructions, along with the rotate instructions, are shown in Fig. 3.34.

The difference between halving a signed number, SAR, and halving an unsigned number, SHR, is that in the former the leftmost bit (sign bit) must remain unchanged. For example, halving +6 (0000 0110) should result in +3 (0000 0011), and halving −120 (1000 1000) should result in −60 (1100 0100). Thus SAR will shift all bits one position to the right but at the same time leave the sign bit unchanged.

Observe that using the SAR instruction to halve +5 (0000 0101) gives +2 (0000 0010), and using it to halve −5 (1111 1011) gives −3 (1111 1101). Right-shifting an odd number always gives a result that is smaller than half the number (−3 is smaller than −2½).

Fig. 3.34 Formats of shift/rotate instructions.

There is no distinction between doubling a signed number and doubling an unsigned number. So, in fact, SHL and SAL are simply two different names for the same instructions.

The rotate instructions provide the ability to rearrange the bits in a number. ROL (rotate left) and ROR (rotate right) permit left or right rotation of the bits: the bit that falls off one end is rotated around to fill in the vacated position on the other end. Two other rotate instructions, RCL (rotate with carry left) and RCR (rotate with carry right), permit the carry flag CF to participate in the rotation: the bit that falls off one end winds up in CF, and the bit that was in CF is rotated around into the vacated bit—sort of a computerized version of musical chairs.

The operand to be shifted or rotated can be in memory or in a register (specified by a **mod** field and an **r/m** field in the instruction). Furthermore, the operand can be 8 or 16 bits (specified by a **w** field). Another field, **v**, specifies whether the shift or rotation is to be for a distance of one bit ($v = 0$) or any number of bits ($v = 1$). In the latter case, the distance is specified in CL, the COUNT register (another example of a specialized use of one of the general-purpose registers).

Admittedly, one purpose of the **v** field is to provide for more efficient multiple-bit shifts and rotations. (But be aware that it is more efficient to do a 2-bit shift by executing two 1-bit shifts with $v = 0$ than by loading a 2 into CL and doing a shift with $v = 1$.) The primary purpose of the **v** field, however, is to permit shifts and rotations over a variable number of bits (hence the reason the field is called **v**). The variable shift instruction is used when the number of bits to be shifted over is the result of a previous computation. Figure 3.35 shows an example of a variable shift.

String Instructions

A *string* is simply a sequence of bytes or words in memory. A string operation is an operation that is performed on each item in a string. An example is a string move, which moves an entire string from one area of memory to

Fig. 3.35 Example of a variable shift.

Table 3.9 String Primitives

MOVS	move	SOURCE = > DEST UPDATE SI, DI
CMPS	compare	SOURCE−DEST = > ? UPDATE SI, DI
SCAS	scan	AL−DEST = > ? UPDATE DI
LODS	load	SOURCE = > AL UPDATE SI
STOS	store	AL = > DEST UPDATE DI

AX is used in place of AL for word operations.

another. Since string operations usually involve repetitions, they could take a long time to execute. The 8086 has a set of instructions that decreases the time required to perform string operations. This speed up is accomplished by (1) having a powerful set of primitive instructions so that the time taken to process each item in the string is reduced, and (2) eliminating bookkeeping and overhead that are usually performed between the processing of successive items. The string primitives are summarized in Table 3.9.

Elementary String Instructions To illustrate how string instructions speed up the processing of strings, consider how a sequence of bytes would be moved. We'll need some way of denoting where the bytes are now and where we'd like them to be. Let's use SI (SOURCE INDEX) and DI (DESTINATION INDEX) for that purpose. Into SI we'll place the offset in the current data segment of the first byte in the sequence. Into DI we'll place the offset to which that byte should be moved. A likely place to store the count of the number of bytes to be moved would be CX, the count register. If CX is initially zero, no bytes should be moved. The steps for performing the string move are as follows:

1. If CX contains zero, we're done.
2. Fetch the byte whose offset is contained in SI.
3. Store that byte into the location whose offset is contained in DI.
4. Increment SI by 1.
5. Increment DI by 1.
6. Decrement CX by 1.
7. Go back to step 1 and repeat.

Steps 2 and 3 perform the actual move of each byte. Steps 4 through 6 are bookkeeping. Steps 1 and 7 are overhead. The actual move of each byte can be speeded up by having a 1-byte primitive instruction that transfers the byte whose offset is contained in SI to the byte whose offset is contained in DI. Furthermore, if that primitive instruction also incremented SI and DI, part of the explicit bookkeeping would be eliminated. With such a primitive, the string move is simplified to the following:

1. If CX contains zero, we're done.
2. Perform "move-primitive."
3. Decrement CX by 1.
4. Go back to step 1 and repeat.

Steps 1, 3, and 4 could be eliminated if the move-primitive were "souped up" to incorporate a test-decrement-and-repeat based on CX. The result is a single step that incorporates the move-primitive within it. The string move now becomes as follows:

1. Soup up the accompanying primitive
   1a. Move-primitive

The 8086 has an instruction, MOVS (move string element), which is the move-primitive described above. Furthermore, any string primitive can be "souped up" by preceding it with a special 1-byte prefix called a *repeat prefix*. The combination of the repeat prefix and the MOVS primitive forms a 2-byte instruction.

There can be a problem if the place that the sequence of bytes goes to overlaps the place that it came from. For example, consider moving the five bytes starting at offset 100 into the five bytes starting at offset 102 as shown in Fig. 3.36. The bytes at 100 and 101 are copied successfully into 102 and 103. But when it comes time to copy the byte from 102 into 104, a problem occurs; the byte in 102 is not the byte that was there originally but rather the byte that came from 100. So the byte from 100 gets copied again, this time into 104. Eventually it will also get into 106. Similarly, the byte from 101 will wind up in 103 and 105.

This problem would have been avoided completely if the bytes were moved in reverse order, specifically the byte from 104 moved first, then the byte from 103, and so forth. However, if the overlap were in the opposite direction (100 through 104 into 98 through 102), the reverse move would have the problem, and the forward move would work properly.

Fig. 3.36 An overlapping move.

Let me point out that one man's problem might be another man's blessing. The "problem" with overlapped string moves becomes a useful feature when we need to repeat a pattern of bytes over a portion of memory.

The 8086 has a flag called DF (direction flag), which governs the direction in which strings are processed. If DF = 0, strings are considered as progressing in the forward direction (toward higher addresses) starting from the offsets in SI and DI. If DF = 1,they progress in the reverse direction. This will tell the string primitives to decrement rather than increment SI and DI. Thus, if an overlapped move moves bytes to higher offsets (thereby necessitating a reverse move), DF should be initialized to 1. Depending on the setting of DF, SI and DI will contain either the lowest offsets (DF = 0) or the highest offsets (DF = 1) in the strings. Instructions for setting and clearing DF (STD, CLD) will be discussed later under Flag Instructions.

To facilitate moving strings from one segment to another, it would be convenient if SI and DI were offsets into different segments. We stated that SI contains the offset into the current data segment. However, we didn't reveal to which segment the offset in DI refers. It would be most fortunate if the primitive string instructions were designed so that they use DI as an offset into the current extra segment. They were! Now to move a string from one segment to another, start by loading DS and ES with the appropriate segment start addresses, and SI and DI with the appropriate offsets within those respective segments. A string move within a segment is accomplished by loading DS and ES with the same value.

Certain string operations are more efficiently performed on words instead of bytes. A move, for example, would go much faster if the elements being moved were words. To allow for word strings, each string primitive instruction contains a 1-bit **w** (width) field that distinguishes between byte operations (**w** = 0) and word operations (**w** = 1). The move-primitive for words is similar to the move-primitive for bytes except that SI and DI are incremented (decremented if DF = 1) by 2 instead of by 1. CX, however, is always decremented by 1, and we must therefore initialize it to contain the number of words (not bytes) if we are using word primitives.

Now let's consider another string operation, namely scanning through a sequence of bytes to find a particular value. For example, if the bytes contain ASCII character codes, this operation finds the first occurrence of a specific character in a message. Let us use DI to contain the offset of the sequence and CX to contain the number of bytes in the sequence. Place the specific byte being searched for into AL. The steps for performing the scan are shown below:

1. If CX contains zero, we're done.
2. Fetch the byte whose offset is contained in DI.
3. Compare it to the byte in AL (comparing means subtracting and setting flags, ZF in particular).
4. Increment (decrement if DF = 1) DI by 1.

Fig. 3.37 Format of REP prefix and string primitives.

5. Decrement CX by 1.
6. If ZF = 0, then the two bytes were not identical; so go back to step 1 and repeat.

Steps 2, 3, and 4 are done by the 8086 scan-primitive SCAS (scan string element). Steps 1, 5, and 6 are done if the scan-primitive is "souped up" with the repeat prefix. Word scanning (**w** field = 1) is similar to byte scanning except that AX is used in place of AL, and DI is incremented (decremented) by 2 instead of by 1.

Note that the repeat prefix behaves slightly differently with the scan-primitive than it does with the move-primitive: with the scan it tests the ZF flag before deciding to repeat. In general, the repeat prefix will test the ZF flag whenever the accompanying primitive string instruction is one which may modify the ZF flag. (MOVS never affects the ZF flag; SCAS sets or clears ZF depending on whether the bytes match or not.)

Another string operation is scanning through a sequence of bytes looking for any byte other than a particular byte. An example would be finding the first non-zero entry in a table. This is done by using the repeat prefix on the scan-primitive instruction as was done in the previous scanning operation, except that now the condition for repetition is ZF = 1. Since the testing of ZF is dictated by the repeat prefix, that prefix must indicate which value of ZF is to cause repetitions. This is specified by a 1-bit **z** field in the repeat prefix. The **z** field is ignored when the repeat prefix is used with string primitives, such as MOVS, which never modify the ZF flag. The form of the repeat prefix and of the string primitives (including a sneak preview of those primitives about to be discussed) is shown in Fig. 3.37.

The next string operation is comparing two sequences of bytes to see which one should come first. In particular, if the bytes contain ASCII character codes, this operation puts the sequence in lexicographical order (lexicographical is simply a fancy term for alphabetical but takes non-alphabetic characters into account as well). Again assume that the offsets of the two sequences are in SI and DI, and the number of bytes to be compared (size of the shorter sequence) is contained in CX. The steps for performing the string comparisons are as follows:

1. If CX contains zero, we're done.
2. Fetch the byte whose offset is contained in SI.
3. Compare it to the byte whose offset is contained in DI.
4. Increment (decrement if DF = 1) SI by 1.
5. Increment (decrement if DF = 1) DI by 1.
6. Decrement CX by 1.
7. If ZF = 1, the two bytes are identical, so go back to step 1 and repeat.

Steps 2, 3, 4, and 5 are done by the 8086 compare primitive CMPS (compare string elements), and the remaining steps are done if a repeat prefix (with a 1 in the z field) is appended to the CMPS instruction. Word comparing is similar to byte comparing, except SI and DI are incremented or decremented by 2 instead of by 1.

A word of explanation is in order here. As long as the bytes being compared in step 3 are identical, the zero flag (ZF) will be set to 1 and step 7 will keep looping back. The looping ends when either the two bytes are not identical (step 7 will no longer loop back) or the end of the shorter string is reached (step 1 will skip us out of the loop). After the looping ends, we can test ZF to see if we reached the end of the shorter string. (ZF will still be 1 in that case.) If we did not, we can test the carry flag (CF) to determine which string is greater (CF = 1 means the string pointed at by DI is greater).

The final two string primitives are LODS (load string element) and STOS (store string element). The load-primitive loads the byte or word whose offset is contained in SI into AL or AX and increments (decrements if DF = 1) SI by 1 or 2. The store-primitive stores the byte or word contained in AL or AX into the byte or word whose offset is contained in DI and increments (decrements if DF = 1) DI by 1 or 2. Unlike the previous primitives, these two primitives were not intended to be used with the repeat prefix. They were included for use in building up more complicated string operations. However, the store primitive does perform a useful function when used in conjunction with the repeat prefix: it fills every byte or word of a sequence with the same value. (This could also be done with an overlapped string move but slightly less efficiently, requiring two strings instead of one.) A repeat prefix on the load-primitive does nothing useful: it repeatedly loads AL or AX with successive bytes or words in a sequence, each time destroying the previous value loaded.

Complex String Instructions The five primitive string instructions provide the most common string operations. It would be a hopeless task to provide a primitive instruction for all conceivable operations. A strategy that makes more sense is to provide a means of building up efficient complicated string instructions, possibly using some of the primitives as building blocks. As an example, consider the operation of negating a sequence of bytes where each byte represents an 8-bit signed number. Let SI contain the offset of the first byte of the sequence, and let DI contain the offset of where the first byte of the negated sequence is to be placed. Let CX contain the count of the number of bytes in the sequence. The steps for performing this operation are as follows:

1. If CX contains zero, we're done, so skip over the following steps.
2. Fetch the byte whose offset is contained in SI.
3. Increment SI by 1.
4. Negate the byte fetched.
5. Store the result into the byte whose offset is contained in DI.
6. Increment DI by 1.
7. Decrement CX by 1.
8. Go back to step 1 and repeat.

Analogous to the previous examples, we would like to have a primitive instruction that performs steps 2, 3, 4, 5, and 6. There is none! So the next best thing would be to build up these steps from 8086 instructions. If some of the building blocks are string primitives, the incrementing of SI and DI can be done at no additional expense. Specifically, steps 2 and 3 can be done by the load-primitive, 4 by a negate instruction, and 5 and 6 by a store-primitive. This simplifies the task to:

1. If CX contains zero, we're done; so skip over the following steps.
2. Perform "load-primitive."
3. Negate byte in AL.
4. Perform "store-primitive."
5. Decrement CX by 1.
6. Go back to step 1 and repeat.

Steps 1, 5, and 6 were previously accomplished by "souping up" a string primitive with the repeat prefix. In this case, the body of the loop consists of more than just a string primitive, and thus the repeat prefix cannot be used. What is needed are a few efficient instructions that simulate the complex actions of the repeat prefix. Step 1 requires a conditional jump instruction that jumps if CX contains zero. The destination of the jump should be specified in as few bits as possible. So naturally the 8086 has an instruction, JCXZ, that will jump if CX contains zero. The destination of the jump is specified in a single byte of the instruction; that byte contains the difference (as a signed number) between the offset of the destination and the offset of the JCXZ instruction. Our next wish would be for an instruction that decrements CX and then jumps unconditionally. That instruction also exists and is called LOOP; the destination of the jump in a

LOOP instruction is specified in a single byte exactly as was done in JCXZ. The example now becomes the following:

1. JCXZ over the following steps.
2. Perform "load-primitive."
3. Negate the byte in AL.
4. Perform "store-primitive."
5. LOOP back to step 1.

Each step represents a single 8086 instruction.

The LOOP instruction introduced above does an unconditional jump. But we have already seen that for some string operations, it is desirable to loop based on the setting of the ZF flag. The corresponding 8086 instructions are LOOPZ (loop if ZF set) and LOOPNZ (loop if not ZF set). Of course, both LOOPZ and LOOPNZ decrement CX before looping. Alternate names for these instructions are LOOPE (loop if equal) and LOOPNE (loop if not equal); these names more clearly indicate the underlying condition on which we are looping.

As an example of using the LOOPNZ instruction, consider the previous example of negating a sequence of bytes. However, this time the number of bytes is unspecified. It is known that none of the bytes in the sequence is zero. However, the sequence is followed by a zero byte. The steps now become as follows:

1. Perform "load-primitive."
2. Negate byte in AL.
3. Perform "store-primitive."
4. LOOPNZ back to step 1.

Note that the initial JCXZ instruction is not necessary here (why?).

The forms of the instructions that simulate the repeat prefix are shown in Fig. 3.38.

Let us wrap up the discussion on strings by considering an example that translates numbers between 0 and 15 into a *Gray code*. A Gray code has the

Fig. 3.38 Format of instructions simulating REP prefix.

property that only one bit changes between adjacent values. An example of a Gray code for the numbers 0 through 15 is the following:

Binary	Gray
0000	0000
0001	0001
0010	0011
0011	0010
0100	0110
0101	0100
0110	0101
0111	0111
1000	1111
1001	1110
1010	1100
1011	1101
1100	1001
1101	1011
1110	1010
1111	1000

Assume that there is a sequence of bytes starting at offset 100 in the current data segment and containing binary numbers between 0 and 15. Also assume that CX contains the number of bytes in the sequence. Furthermore, assume that BX contains the offset of the first byte of a 16-byte Gray code translation table, which is simply the 16 values given above. Notice that conditions are ideal for using the XLAT instruction. Let us place the translated sequence into the extra segment starting at offset 50. The steps for pulling this off are as shown:

1. Move 100 into SI.
2. Move 50 into DI.
3. JCXZ over the following steps.
4. Perform "load-primitive."
5. XLAT.
6. Perform "store-primitive."
7. LOOP back to step 3.

The XLAT instruction fits in perfectly with string loops as if it were designed for this purpose. It was!

Unconditional Transfer Instructions

The main types of unconditional transfer instructions in the 8086 are jumps, calls, and returns. Jumps load a value into the instruction pointer, thereby breaking the sequential execution of instructions. Calls do the same thing, but first they save the current value of the instruction pointer on the stack so that at some time in the future execution can continue from where it left off. Returns occur at that time in the future: they remove an entry from the stack and place it back into the instruction pointer, thereby resuming the previous execution. Calls and returns are the mechanism used to invoke subroutines. But all this is nothing new.

What is new is that the calls, jumps, and returns come in two flavors— intrasegment and intersegment. The intrasegment ones transfer control within the current code segment. The intersegment ones transfer control to an arbitrary code segment (by changing the contents of CS), which then becomes the current code segment.

Obviously, intersegment transfers can do everything that intrasegment transfers can do and then some. Why then do we need both? Simply because intersegment transfers take longer to execute (they have more to do); and, with the exception of returns, they require more bytes of code (they have more to say).

As an example of an intersegment jump, suppose the current code segment starts at B0000 (hexadecimal) and that the instruction pointer contains 00A0 (hexadecimal). That means the next instruction to be executed is at B00A0. Suppose at location B00A0 we have placed a jump instruction that will transfer control to location A0100 (hexadecimal). But the current code segment ranges from B0000 to BFFFF, and hence a jump to location A0100 would have to be an intersegment jump. Such an intersegment jump would have to specify a new value for CS (possibly A000) as well as a new value for IP (0100). This example is shown in Fig. 3.39.

An intersegment call saves the current value of the code segment register, as well as the instruction pointer, on the stack. An intersegment return removes two 16-bit values from the stack and places them into the instruction pointer and code segment register. This is in contrast to the intrasegment call and return, which save and restore the instruction pointer only.

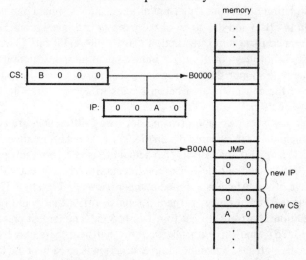

Fig. 3.39 Example of an intersegment jump instruction.

The preceding example, besides illustrating an intersegment jump, illustrates another concept—namely a direct jump. A direct jump (or call) tells us immediately where to go. An indirect one gives us the runaround: it tells us where to go to find out where to go. Indirect transfers are useful when we don't know where we want to go but must first compute it. For example, an indirect intersegment jump or call uses a **mod** field and an **r/m** field to specify the first of four consecutive bytes in memory (there are no 4-byte registers). These four bytes would contain the new value of IP (two bytes) followed by the new value of CS (two bytes). These values could have been computed by the preceding instructions.

Returns never tell us where to go; instead, they tell us to return from where we came. Thus the concept of an indirect return makes no sense. The forms of the unconditional jumps, calls, and returns are shown in Fig. 3.40.

An intrasegment jump specifies a new value for the instruction pointer but not for the code segment register. Consider, for example, a jump instruction at offset 01A8 in the current code segment. This jump instruction is to cause the program to jump back by eight bytes to offset 01A0. The value 01A0 could have been contained in two bytes of the jump instruction; and, indeed, in many other processors it is. But this has two disadvantages. First, many jumps are to nearby places, and yet the instruction must dedicate two bytes to specifying the jump destination. Second, if for some reason the entire section of code from offset 01A0 to 01B0 must be moved and placed at offset 0500 to 0510, the jump instruction specifying offset 01A0 would no longer jump back by eight bytes. (Sections of code that can be moved and still execute properly are sometimes called *position-independent code*.) If the jump instruction did not specify 01A0 but merely specified -8, then (1) the jump destination fits in one byte and (2) the code is position-independent. Thus direct intrasegment jumps and calls specify not the destination offset, but rather the difference (as a signed number) between the destination offset and the offset of the jump or call instruction. Furthermore, if that difference for a jump instruction can fit into eight bits (a very frequent occurrence), a short form of the direct intrasegment jump instruction can be used which is one byte shorter than the regular direct intrasegment jump. There is no short form of the call instruction because calls to nearby locations are not that frequent an occurrence.

We've just seen two good reasons for using differences (relative offsets) rather than actual offsets as jump destinations. Let's make sure there isn't a good reason for *not* using relative offsets. An actual offset is a 16-bit unsigned number (from 0 to 65535) and can designate any location in the current code segment. Can a relative offset, which is a signed number (from -32768 to $+32767$), cover the same range? For instance, is there a relative offset that could be used by a jump instruction at offset 0 to get to offset 65535? The largest positive relative offset is $+32767$, and this will take us only halfway there. So let's consider negative relative offsets. Since the jump instruction is already at the lowest offset in the segment, where will a negative relative offset of -1 take us? Answer: to the highest offset in the segment, namely 65535 (by processor design). In fact, the jump instruction at offset 0 can get to any offset from 32768 to 65535 by using a negative relative offset. It is clear from this discussion that relative offsets can take us from a jump instruction located anywhere in the segment to any other location in the segment.

Fig. 3.40 Formats of unconditional jumps, calls, and returns.

The preceding discussion about using relative offsets rather than actual offsets does not apply to indirect jumps or calls, nor does it apply to intersegment jumps or calls. There are several reasons for this:

1. Indirect jumps and calls do not specify the destination; they specify where to find the destination. More than one indirect jump or call could specify the same place at which the destination is to be found. Thus the concept of relative offset has little meaning since we don't know which instruction it is to be relative to.
2. Intersegment jumps and calls specify destinations in some other code segment. If a section of code containing intersegment jumps or calls is moved, the destination, being in some other segment, would not necessarily also be moved. Hence using relative offsets would not lead to position-independent code.
3. The destination of an intersegment jump or call is not necessarily to a nearby place, and thus there is no reason to expect to save any bytes by using relative offsets.

Before leaving the topic of unconditional transfers, one more thing needs to be said about the return instruction. There is a variation of the return instruction that, after restoring the instruction pointer and possibly the code segment register (with values popped off the stack), adds a constant (contained in the instruction as an immediate operand) to the stack pointer. This has the effect of popping and discarding additional entries off the stack. Such entries could have been placed on the stack prior to issuing the call instruction so that a sequence of values could be passed to the subroutine being called. When the subroutine completes its work and does a return, these values would no longer be needed. Such values are called *parameters*. The form of the return instruction just described provides a convenient way for a subroutine to discard its parameters. If such a return-and-discard instruction were not provided, the parameters would have to be discarded in the following manner:

1. Before using a return, the subroutine removes the saved value of IP (and possibly CS) from the stack and puts it somewhere else in memory for safekeeping. This uncovers the parameters that were sitting on the stack just below the saved values of IP and CS.
2. The subroutine then adds a constant to SP. This has the effect of popping and discarding the parameters.
3. The subroutine then replaces the saved values of IP and CS (that were put somewhere for safekeeping) back onto the stack.
4. The subroutine then executes a return instruction.

Certainly the return-and-discard instructions make this task much simpler.

Another way to discard parameters is by decrementing the stack pointer after the subroutine executes the return instruction. On first reading, this seems almost as efficient as the return-and-discard instruction. But the decrementing of the stack pointer cannot be done by the subroutine (it already returned), so it would have to be done at every place the subroutine returns to. And when you realize that the subroutine could be called from a large number of different places, this solution starts looking less attractive.

The return-and-discard instructions use 16 bits to contain the number of parameters (value that must be added to SP). Eight bits would have been sufficient in all but exceptional cases, and the resulting instructions would have been one byte shorter. However, in those rare cases where eight bits would be insufficient, the alternative method of parameter discarding as described above is too unpleasant to think about. So the extra byte was put onto the instruction.

Conditional Transfer Instructions

The 8086 provides conditional jumps that, along with the compare instruction (CMP), determine the relationship between two numbers. This is done in two steps. First the 8086 executes the compare instruction that performs a subtraction of the two numbers, sets the flags based on the result, and discards the difference. It then executes a conditional jump instruction that tests the flags and performs a jump if the flags indicate the two numbers satisfy a particular relation. For example, suppose we wanted to execute certain instructions if the number in BH is equal to the number in BL. This is done as follows:

1. Compare BH to BL (flags become set).
2. Jump to step 5 if zero flag, ZF, is 0.
3. Special instructions to be
4.   executed if BH = BL.
5. . . .

In this example, the compare instruction subtracted BL from BH and set the flags based on the result. If BH = BL, the result is zero, and ZF would be set to 1. Thus a test for equality is a test of ZF, and this is what was done by the conditional jump in step 2. Specifically, if BH   BL, ZF is 0 and steps 3 and 4 are skipped over.

The forms of the conditional jump instructions are shown in Fig. 3.41. Note that each of them consists of an 8-bit opcode followed by eight bits specifying the jump destination. The destination is specified as the difference between the destination offset and the offset of the conditional jump instruction. As already mentioned, this provides for position-independent code (jumps are relative) and code compaction (destination specified in only eight bits). But this also limits conditional jumps to have a jump destination that is relatively close to (within approximately 127 bytes of) the conditional jump instruction. It would have used up too many opcodes if two forms ("close" and "not-so-close") of each conditional jump were provided. The "close" case occurs more frequently and was therefore optimized at the expense of the "not-so-close" case ("not-so-close" conditional jumps can always be done in two instructions with a "close" conditional jump jumping around a "not-so-close" unconditional jump).

Fig. 3.41 Formats of conditional jump instructions.

Besides testing for equality, it is often useful to know which number is bigger. But this poses an interesting question. Is the 8-bit number 1111 1111 bigger than 0000 0000? The answer is both yes and no. If these numbers were considered as unsigned binary numbers, the first number would have a value of 255, and this is indeed bigger than 0. But if the numbers were considered as signed binary numbers, the value of the first number is -1, and this is smaller than 0. So we see that there are two ways of looking at "bigger" and "smaller" depending on whether the numbers are signed or unsigned. We therefore introduce some new terms to distinguish between the two cases. If we are comparing the numbers as signed numbers, we use the terms *less than* and *greater than;* if we are comparing them as unsigned numbers, we use *below* and *above*. So 1111 1111 is above 0000 0000 while, at the same time, it is less than 0000 0000. As another example, 0000 0000 is both below and less than 0000 0001.

To summarize, the various relationships that could exist between two numbers are equal, above, below, less than, and greater than. Each of these conditions can be determined by the flag settings after a compare instruction has been executed; these flag settings were shown in Table 3.3. The 8086 provides conditional jump instructions that test the flags to determine if any particular relationship is or is not satisfied. The specific conditional jumps are as follows:

Name	*Meaning*
JE	jump on equal
JNE	jump on not equal
JL	jump on less than
JNL	jump on not less than
JG	jump on greater than
JNG	jump on not greater than
JB	jump on below
JNB	jump on not below
JA	jump on above
JNA	jump on not above

Some other relationships might come to mind such as "less than or equal," but this is the same as "not greater than." The following is a list of alternate names for the jump instructions listed above:

Name	*Alternate Name*	*Meaning for Alternate Name*
JE	JZ	jump on zero
JNE	JNZ	jump on not zero
JL	JNGE	jump on not greater than or equal
JNL	JGE	jump on greater than or equal
JG	JNLE	jump on not less than or equal
JNG	JLE	jump on less than or equal
JB	JNAE	jump on not above or equal

Name	Alternate Name	Meaning for Alternate Name
JNB	JAE	jump on above or equal
JA	JNBE	jump on not below or equal
JNA	JBE	jump on below or equal

For reference, the actual flag settings for the various conditional jumps are shown below:

Name	Flag Settings
JE/JZ	ZF = 1
JNE/JNZ	ZF = 0
JL/JNGE	(SF xor OF) = 1
JNL/JGE	(SF xor OF) = 0
JG/JNLE	((SF xor OF) or ZF) = 0
JNG/JLE	((SF xor OF) or ZF) = 1
JB/JNAE	CF = 1
JNB/JAE	CF = 0
JA	(CF or ZF) = 0
JNA	(CF or ZF) = 1

There are conditional jump instructions that are not concerned with the relationship between two numbers but rather with the setting of a particular flag. The JZ and JNZ instructions mentioned above are actually tests on the zero flag. Also, it turns out that the JB and JNB instructions mentioned above are nothing more than tests on the carry flag. Other conditional jump instructions that test the setting of a particular flag are shown:

Name	Meaning	Flag Settings
JS	jump on sign	SF = 1
JNS	jump on not sign	SF = 0
JO	jump on overflow	OF = 1
JNO	jump on not overflow	OF = 0
JP	jump on parity	PF = 1
JNP	jump on not parity	PF = 0

Alternate names for the last two are given:

Name	Alternate Name	Meaning for Alternate name
JP	JPE	jump on parity even
JNP	JPO	jump on parity odd

Interrupts

Most modern processors provide facilities for being interrupted by external devices. This frees the processor from having to check periodically on such devices to see if they are in need of any attention. For instance, instead of having a processor frequently ask a keyboard if a key has been pressed and get back negative responses most of the time, it would be more efficient for the processor to ignore the keyboard but allow the keyboard to get the processor's attention when a key is pressed. The former method is referred to as *polling,* the latter as *interrupting.*

Interrupt Mechanism The 8086 has two "apron strings" that external devices can "tug on" to get attention. These "apron strings" are, in reality, two pins on the processor chip called the NMI (non-maskable interrupt) pin and INTR (plain old interrupt) pin. Let's consider the NMI pin first. When an external device places a signal on the NMI pin, the processor will stop whatever it's doing (but not in the middle of an instruction) and take care of this interruption. However, the processor might have been in the middle of a very important task, so external devices should refrain from causing such interruptions except in real emergencies. An example of a real emergency is if an external device notices that the line voltage has just passed through 100 volts and is dropping. The technical term for this condition is "power failure." In this case, the external device is justified in interrupting the processor to inform the processor that it hasn't long to live. In its few remaining milliseconds, the processor could then attempt to put its affairs in order (like transferring important results to a safe place) before its little oscillator stops ticking. Barring such emergencies, if an external device wishes to interrupt the processor, it should use the INTR pin. The processor can choose to ignore this pin if it is not in the mood. The "mood" is set by the interrupt-enable flag (IF): when IF is 0, the processor will not respond to signals on the INTR pin. Interrupts are said to be *enabled* when IF = 1 and *disabled* when IF = 0. Instructions for setting and clearing IF (STI, CLI) will be discussed later under Flag Instructions.

Besides placing a signal on the INTR pin, the external device must convey the reason for the interrupt to the processor. There may be any number of reasons (let's say 256) for an interrupt on the INTR pin, while there is only one reason (impending doom) for an NMI interrupt. The external device will, upon request of the processor, supply a number between 0 and 255 representing the reason for the INTR interrupt. This number is often referred to as the *interrupt type.* For each different interrupt type, the processor has a program that it must execute before resuming its normal tasks. The addresses of these programs are contained in a 256-entry table. Each entry is four bytes long and contains the value of CS and IP corresponding to the beginning of the programs for a particular interrupt type. The table starts at memory address 0 as shown in Fig. 3.42. The programs that are executed when interrupts occur are often referred to as *interrupt routines.*

Now let's see what the processor does when it receives an interrupt on its INTR pin and interrupts are enabled (IF = 1). After completing the execution of the current instruction, the processor stops doing whatever it was doing and prepares to execute the piece of code corresponding to the type of the interrupt. First, the processor saves all relevant information about what it was doing, so when it finishes executing the interrupt routine, it can resume what it was doing. A convenient place to save this information is on the stack. The values to be saved are the current values of all flags, the current value of CS, and the current

Fig. 3.42 Table of interrupt-code addresses.

value of IP. Next, the processor gets the interrupt type from the external device and places the table entries corresponding to that type into IP and CS. For example, suppose the external device supplied type 0001 (hexadecimal). In this case, the 16-bit value starting at address 00004 is placed into IP, and the 16-bit value starting at address 00006 is placed into CS. Thus the next instruction to be executed is the first instruction in the interrupt routine coresponding to interrupt type 1.

When the processor receives an interrupt on its NMI pin (regardless of the setting of the interrupt-enable flag IF), it will do everything that it did for INTR interrupts with one exception. It will not need to get the interrupt type from the external device since there is only one possible reason for an NMI interrupt. The type 2 entry in the interrupt table is reserved for locating the NMI interrupt routine; hence the table entries for type 2 are placed into IP and CS. Other reserved entries in the interrupt table (including those that might be used by future versions of the 8086) are shown in Fig. 3.43.

Two more reserved interrupt types are division by zero (type 0) and signed overflow (type 4). Like the NMI interrupt, processing of these two interrupts does not depend on the value of the interrupt-enable flag (IF). (In fact, this statement is true for all the reserved interrupt types.) The processor itself automatically generates a type 0 interrupt whenever it attempts to divide by zero. Thus the type 0 entry in the table should contain the IP and CS values for a routine that recovers from such a division. Although signed overflow is also a serious matter, the processor does not automatically generate an interrupt when signed overflow occurs. This is because the same ADD instruction is used for both signed and unsigned arithmetic, and the processor has no way of knowing if signed addition was actually intended (the same is true for subtraction). However, the processor does provide an efficient (1-byte) instruction that generates a type 4 interrupt if the overflow flag (OF) is set. This instruction, INTO (interrupt on overflow), should follow every arithmetic instruction applied to signed numbers whenever the potential for overflow exists.

Now let's consider the interrupt routine itself. The interrupt routine does not have to feel guilty about altering values in flags because the initial values of the flags were already saved. However, if the interrupt routine alters any other important item (items that the interrupted program could have been using—AX, for instance), the interrupt routine must first save the initial value of that important item. Before the interrupt routine terminates, it must restore any of these

Fig. 3.43 Reserved interrupt types.

Fig. 3.44 Formats of interrupt instructions.

important items that it saved. Finally, the interrupt routine terminates by executing an instruction called IRET (interrupt return) that restores the values of IP, CS, and the flags saved on the stack. Note that the interrupt return differs from the intersegment return discussed previously only so far as restoring the flags is concerned. They both restore IP and CS.

Another instruction usually associated with interrupts is the HLT (halt) instruction. HLT stops the processor and leaves CS and IP pointing to the instruction following the HLT. When an interrupt comes along, these values of CS and IP are saved on the stack and the processor starts executing instructions—specifically, the instructions in the interrupt routine. When the IRET instruction is encountered, the saved values of IP and CS are restored. At this time the processor doesn't remember that it was resting prior to receiving the interrupt. So it will proceed to execute the instruction that CS and IP are now pointing to—namely the instruction following the HLT. So, in effect, HLT provides the processor with a way to relax while waiting for an interrupt.

Now consider all those interrupt routines, 256 of them, sitting at various places in memory waiting for interrupts to occur so they can get called into execution. Some of them might be useful to invoke even when no interrupt occurs. Since the values of IP and CS needed to execute the routines are contained in four consecutive bytes in memory, it appears as though we could invoke an interrupt routine by simply executing an indirect intersegment call instruction that specifies those four bytes. But beware! The interrupt routine does not end with a normal return instruction; it ends with an IRET, which will attempt to pop the saved flags off the stack. So the flags had better be on the stack if this return is to work properly. This could be accomplished by preceding the indirect intersegment call instruction with a push flag (PUSHF) instruction. But this is getting cumbersome. What would be nice is a single instruction that does everything the processor does when it recognizes an interrupt with one exception—the interrupt type is specified in the instruction rather than supplied by the external device.

This instruction is INT (interrupt), and its format, along with the formats of other instrucfions related to interrupts (IRET, INTO, and HLT), is shown in Fig. 3.44. The value of the interrupt-enable flag (IF) has no effect on the execution of the INT instruction.

Debugger Requirements   Notice that there are two forms for the INT instruction. In the first form, the instruction is two bytes long, and the second byte specifies the interrupt type. In the second form, the instruction is one byte long, and the type is implicitly type 3 (see reserved types in Fig. 3.43). The fact that it is type 3 is irrelevant (it could have been any type), but the fact that it is one byte long is significant. A 1-byte INT instruction is essential for the operation of a software debugging program. To understand why, we have to learn something about how software debuggers work.

A software debugger is an interactive program you can use to find out why the program you wrote doesn't work properly. A common thing you might want to do is tell the debugger to run your bad program until the instruction at a certain address, say 100, is about to be executed. In debugging jargon, this is referred to as "setting a breakpoint" at address 100. The debugger sets a breakpoint by planting an instruction at address 100 that will transfer control back to the debugger. The debugger can now let your program run, and when your program reaches address 100, it will transfer back to the debugger. Naturally the debugger would save the original contents of address 100 prior to setting the breakpoint and will restore the original contents after control returns to the debugger.

Now the question remains as to which 8086 transfer instruction to plant at address 100. A jump instruction would work fine if there were only one breakpoint set at any given time. However, if more than one breakpoint is set, the debugger would need to know which breakpoint was actually reached. The INT instruction is ideal since it saves information (CS and IP) that locates the breakpoint. Using the 2-byte INT instruction to set a breakpoint at address 100 would mean that the contents of both 100 and 101 would have to be overwritten. The debugger would save and eventually restore the original contents of both bytes. In most cases this would present no problems. However, sooner or later you'll write a program, such as the one in Fig. 3.45, that jumps around and executes the instruction at 101 prior to executing the instruction at 100. But the instruction at 101 has been temporarily overwritten by the second byte of the INT instruction planted at 100. This is the reason the debugger must use a *1-byte* INT instruction. The debugger will be using the 1-byte INT instruction to generate type 3 interrupts when programs are being debugged; therefore, you should not use the 1-byte INT instruction or any type 3 interrupts in your program if you ever intend to use a software debugger to debug your program.

Another facility intended for the use of debugger programs is the trap flag (TF). Whenever this flag is set, the processor will execute a single instruction and then generate an interrupt of type 1 (see Fig. 3.46). This permits the debugger to execute your program, one instruction at a time, and examine what was done after each instruction. Such a mode of execution is referred to as *single*

address	instruction
90,91	read value from port 1 into AX (IN — 2 bytes)
92,93	go to 101 (JMP — 2 bytes)
94,...,99	do things involving value in AX
100	increment AX (INC — 1 byte)
101,102	compare AX to 5 (CMP — 2 bytes)
103,104	go to 94 if less than (JL — 2 bytes)

Fig. 3.45 Program that executes address 101 prior to executing address 100.

** indicates occurrence of interrupt of type 50

Fig. 3.46 Executing a program in single-step mode.

stepping. (Don't worry about repeated string instructions; single stepping through them will cause an interrupt after each repetition instead of waiting for the end of the entire instruction.)

The debugger can cause your program to execute in single-step mode by modifying the set of flags saved on the stack by a previous interrupt so that the saved value of TF is 1, and then executing an interrupt return (IRET) instruction. Since it is the debugger and not your program that decides when your program is to switch into single-step mode, there is no need for an instruction to set or clear TF. For example, suppose your program is executing at full speed. You would like to stop it and have it then resume one instruction at a time. After each instruction you want to examine the contents of all the registers so you can determine if the program is behaving the way you expected. You can stop your program by placing a signal on the INTR pin and providing the processor with an interrupt type, say 50. The processor will stop executing your program (providing IF = 1) and save the values of the flags, CS, and IP on the stack. Then it will start to execute the interrupt routine for type 50. In that routine, you have code that goes to the stack and sets the saved value of TF to a 1. The interrupt routine then executes an IRET to restore the saved values of IP, CS, and flags. These are the values that existed when you interrupted your program, except that TF now contains a 1. As a result, your program will execute a single instruction, and then a type 1 interrupt will be generated. In response to this interrupt, the processor will save the values of the flags (with TF = 1), CS, and IP on the stack and will start to execute the interrupt routine for type 1. To prevent the processor from single-stepping through the interrupt routine, TF is automatically cleared after the flags are saved on the stack. The interrupt routine for type 1 should have code that displays the contents of all registers. The final instruction of this interrupt routine is again IRET, which restores the saved values of IP, CS, and flags. So once again TF is 1, and the above process will be repeated. This is illustrated in Fig. 3.46. The type 1 and type 50 interrupt routines just described are part of what we have been calling the debugger.

An 8086 Mistake Let's consider the instruction that moves a new value into the stack segment register (SS). This instruction is one of two MOV instructions that must be executed if we want to change to another stack (a useful operation when the processor is alternately executing more than one program, each with its own stack). The second MOV instruction moves a new value into the stack pointer register (SP). After both MOV's are executed, the SS and SP registers together specify the location of the top of the new stack. However, after the first MOV is executed but before the second, the combination of SS and SP does not have any significance; it certainly does not specify the top of any area reserved for a stack (except possibly by accident). This isn't a problem unless someone tries to push a value on the stack during the stack change. But that is exactly what an external interrupt or a single-step interrupt might try to do if it arrives at the wrong time.

This mistake was not discovered until after the 8086 was designed and built. After the mistake was discovered, the 8086 was modified so that it will not accept any interrupts immediately after executing an instruction that moves a new value into SS.

Flag Instructions

The 8086 has instructions for setting and clearing the carry flag (STC, CLC), the direction flag (STD, CLD), and the interrupt flag (STI, CLI). Furthermore, it has an instruction for complementing the carry flag (CMC). These instructions are summarized in Table 3.10. The uses of these flags have already been discussed—the carry flag (CF) for multiprecision arithmetic, the direction flag (DF) for string processing, and the interrupt flag (IF) for enabling and disabling interrupts. The forms of the flag instructions are shown in Fig. 3.47.

Table 3.10 Flag Operations

CLC	(clear carry)	$0 => CF$
CMC	(complement carry)	$1-CF => CF$
STC	(set carry)	$1 => CF$
CLD	(clear direction)	$0 => DF$
STD	(set direction)	$1 => DF$
CLI	(clear interrupt-enable)	$0 => IF$
STI	(set interrupt-enable)	$1 => IF$

```
1 1 1 1 1 0 0 0
```
CLC—clear carry

```
1 1 1 1 0 1 0 1
```
CMC—complement carry

```
1 1 1 1 1 0 0 1
```
STC—set carry

```
1 1 1 1 1 1 0 0
```
CLD—clear direction

```
1 1 1 1 1 1 0 1
```
STD—set direction

```
1 1 1 1 1 0 1 0
```
CLI—clear interrupt

```
1 1 1 1 1 0 1 1
```
STI—set interrupt

Fig. 3.47 Formats of flag instructions.

Synchronization Instructions

Interrupts provide one means of synchronizing an 8086 with external devices. There are two other forms of synchronization that the 8086 architecture provides. The first involves using a subordinate processor to do things for the 8086 that the 8086 cannot do for itself. The second involves sharing resources (such as memory) with other processors in a multiple-processor system. Both of these cases will now be examined in detail.

Subordinate Processors   Although the 8086 has a powerful instruction set, there are still many instructions that it is lacking. For example, there is no instruction to perform operations on floating-point numbers. Certainly you could write a routine that performs an addition of two floating-point numbers, but this is much less efficient than having a floating-point add instruction. A better solution would be to have a separate processor capable of performing floating-point operations and willing to offer its services to the 8086. If you had such a floating-point processor, you could write floating-point instructions in your program; the 8086 would invoke the floating-point processor whenever it encountered such instructions.

The subordinate processor operates by watching the 8086 and being constantly aware of the instruction being executed. In particular, it is watching for the special instruction ESCape, which is the embodiment of all instructions the 8086 needs help executing. The ESC instruction has a 3-bit field (**x**) indicating which subordinate processor is needed, and a 3-bit field (**y**) indicating the instruction that processor should execute. Both of these fields are ignored by the 8086 processor. (This description is slightly simplified; in reality, the six ignored bits may arbitrarily be used to distinguish 64 combinations of processor and/or instructions.) Furthermore, the ESC instruction has a **mod** field and an **r/m** field that designate a memory operand for the subordinate processor. These two fields are indeed used by the 8086; the 8086 computes the memory address of the operand and then actually reads the value of the operand from memory, although it ignores the value when it gets it. The subordinate processor is watching all this and now knows the address of the operand as well as the value of the operand. The subordinate processor now has everything it needs (instruction and operand) in order to execute the required operation.

The form of the ESC instruction is shown in Fig. 3.48 along with another instruction, WAIT. The WAIT instruction is a synchronizing instruction; it is

Fig. 3.48 Formats of subordinate processor synchronization instructions.

executed by the 8086 to determine when the subordinate processor finishes its execution. When the subordinate processor is done, it puts a signal on a pin named TEST on the 8086 chip. The WAIT instruction will hold up the 8086 until it detects this signal on the TEST pin. Like the string instructions, the WAIT instruction can be interrupted before the instruction is finished.

One way we could use WAIT and ESC is by preceding every ESC instruction with a WAIT instruction. We would then be assured that an instruction will never be sent to the subordinate processor before that processor finishes executing any previous instructions sent to it. By placing the WAIT before the ESC instead of after it, the 8086 can be doing other things while the subordinate processor is executing an instruction.

As an example, suppose we have two floating-point numbers that we wish to add together. Each number is four bytes long. The first number is contained in the current data segment starting at the offset contained in SI, and the second number is contained in the current data segment starting at offset contained in DI. We want the floating-point sum to be placed in the current data segment starting at offset contained in DI. Assume that we have a floating-point processor that responds to ESC instructions having an **x** field value of 101 (binary). Furthermore, assume that the instructions the floating-point processor is capable of executing are as follows:

001:	Load operand into floating-point accumulator.
010:	Add operand to floating-point accumulator.
011:	Subtract operand from floating-point accumulator.
100:	Multiply floating-point accumulator by operand.
101:	Divide floating-point accumulator by operand.
110:	Store floating-point accumulator into operand.

The floating-point accumulator is a register on the floating-point processor.

The 8086 sequence of instructions to accomplish the required addition is shown in Fig. 3.49. The WAIT instructions keep the 8086 and the floating-point processor synchronized while the ESC instruction passes information from one to the other.

Resource Sharing   Another form of synchronization is between two processors sharing a common resource. For example, consider an airline reservation system in which computer processors from all over the country are making entries into a common data base in some shared memory. Suppose one of the processors wants to make a reservation for Harry Jones on a flight from San Francisco to New York. First, the processor will read the data base and discover that there are indeed 15 seats available on that flight. It will then reserve a seat for Harry by writing a 14 into that word of the data base that indicates the number of available seats. But suppose after Harry's processor reads the 15 and before it writes back the 14, some other processor in another corner of the country tries to make a reservation for William Smith on that same flight. William's processor

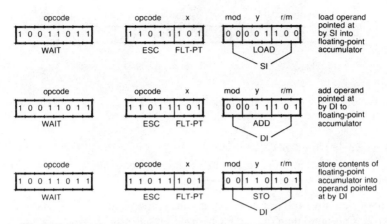

Fig. 3.49 Example of instruction sequence that invokes subordinate processor (see text).

also reads the vacancy count of 15 and reserves a seat by writing back a 14. It doesn't matter which processor writes the 14 first; after both processors complete their transactions, the seat count has gone from 15 to 14 and two people both think they have reservations (is that why airlines get overbooked?).

Perhaps we could have avoided the problem if Harry's processor made Harry's reservation by reading the 15 and writing back the 14 all in one instruction. The DEC (decrement) instruction will do just that. If there are no seats available (count is zero), the DEC instruction will cause the count to go negative (SF becomes 1); in that case, no reservation can be made, and an INC (increment) instruction should be executed to restore the count back to zero.

Now there is no way for both processors to decrement the same initial count . . . *unless* William's processor comes along right in the middle of Harry's DEC instruction, and you can just bet that one day that's going to happen. In that case, Harry's DEC instruction will fetch a value of 15, then do the subtraction (while William's DEC instruction fetches the same 15), and then store back a 14 (while William's DEC instruction does the subtraction). Finally, William's DEC instruction will store back a 14.

So it appears as though updating the count all in one instruction did not completely solve the problem; it only reduced the likelihood of its occurrence. What is still needed is a way for Harry's processor to prevent all other processors from accessing the data base while it is executing the DEC instruction. The 8086 accomplishes this by allowing any instruction to be preceded by a 1-byte lock prefix. Execution of such an instruction will cause the processor to place a signal on an 8086 output pin (called the LOCK pin) for the duration of the instruction. The hardware of the airline reservation system can now be designed to give exclusive memory access to any processor asserting the lock signal (if no other processor can use the memory, then no other processor can access the data base).

Fig. 3.50 Example of an instruction with a lock prefix.

An example of the decrement instruction preceded by the lock prefix is shown in Fig. 3.50.

A Postscript on Prefixes

We've now encountered all three 8086 instruction prefix bytes—segment-override, repeat, and lock. Two questions come to mind:

1. Can any prefix be used on any instruction?
2. Can more than one prefix be used on an instruction?

With one exception, any prefix can be used with any instruction. The exception is the repeat prefix, which may be used only with the string primitives. Applying it to any other instruction could give unexpected results because of the way the facility was implemented. The lock prefix can be applied to any instruction and will cause the processor to place a signal on its LOCK pin for the duration of the instruction. This signal is typically used to provide exclusive memory access to a processor (in a multiprocessor system) while executing an instruction that both reads and writes memory (for example INC, DEC, XCHG). However, the processor doesn't care if you use the lock prefix with any other instruction, even one that doesn't access memory. And, finally, the segment-overriding prefix can be used with any instruction. If the instruction accesses an operand in memory, this prefix specifies the segment; otherwise it has no effect.

Now, let's consider combinations of prefixes. The lock prefix and the segment-overriding prefix can be used together and each will perform its designated function. The behavior of the instruction is not affected by the ordering of the prefixes. The repeat prefix, however, has some problems when used with other prefixes. For one thing, it must always be the last prefix because it can be applied only to an *unprefixed* string primitive. For another, the combination of the lock and repeat prefixes could prevent other processors in the system from accessing memory for a relatively long time—the entire duration of the repeated string instruction.

The combination of any prefix with a repeat prefix will make it impossible to restart the string operation after being interrupted. To understand why, let's consider what happens when an interrupt occurs during the execution of a repeated string instruction. If the interrupt is forced to wait until all repetitions of the instruction are completed, it might have to wait a (relatively) long time. So the processor was designed to permit interrupts to be serviced after any repetition of a string instruction. While the repetitions are occurring, the instruction pointer contains the offset of the repeat prefix. If the instruction is interrupted, this is the offset that is saved, and this is the offset at which execution resumes after the interrupt processing is complete. If the instruction contains any prefixes prior to the repeat prefix, they will not be part of the instruction when it is reexecuted after being interrupted. (Note that the reexecuted string instruction does not redo what was done during the initial execution; the count in CX and string pointers in SI and DI were updated during each repetition prior to the interrupt, and the second execution starts with these updated values.) This problem would not exist if, during the repetitions, the instruction pointer contained the offset of the first prefix byte of the instruction. This is a flaw in the 8086 design!

Another instruction that has a potential problem with prefixes is WAIT. WAIT, like repeated string instructions, can be interrupted before it completes its task. And for the same reasons given above, WAIT will lose its prefixes if reexecuted after an interrupt. But the repeat prefix may not be used with WAIT, and both the lock prefix and the segment-overriding prefix have no effect on WAIT. So WAIT, with or without prefixes, will always restart properly after being interrupted.

Flag Settings

Throughout this chapter, references have been made to the flag settings following certain instructions. This section ties all that information together and completely describes the behavior of the flags.

The 8086 flags can be divided into two types: *status* flags and *control* flags. The former reflect properties of the results generated by certain instructions, and the latter control the operations of the processor. Table 3.11 shows the instructions whose results affect the status flags and the instructions that are used to establish the settings of the control flag. Let's attempt to explain the behavior of some of these flags.

Addition and subtraction instructions affect all status flags in the following manner: the overflow flag (OF) and carry flag (CF) indicate if the instruction resulted in a signed or unsigned result out of range; the auxiliary carry flag (AF) indicates if a correction is needed for decimal operations; and the sign flag (SF), zero flag (ZF), and parity flag (PF) indicate if the result is negative, zero, or contains an even number of 1's.

Grouped with the addition and subtraction instructions are the compare instructions (CMP, CMPS, SCAS) and the negation instruction (NEG). The compare instructions perform a subtraction, and the flags are set to reflect the result of this subtraction. The NEG instruction adds 1 (after complementing all bits), and the flags are set to reflect the result of this addition. The only time NEG sets the carry flag to 1 is when the value being "negated" is zero; the only times it sets the overflow flag to 1 is when the value being negated is -128 (eight bits) or -32768 (16 bits).

The increment and decrement instructions affect the status flags in the same manner as addition and subtraction instructions, except they do not affect the carry flag. This gives us the ability to write a loop that performs multiprecision arithmetic as follows:

Table 3.11 Flag Settings

A–STATUS FLAGS	OF	CF	AF	SF	ZF	PF
Addition & Subtraction						
ADD ADC SUB SBC	+	+	+	+	+	+
CMP NEG CMPS SCAS	+	+	+	+	+	+
Increment & Decrement						
INC DEC	+	–	+	+	+	+
Multiplication & Division						
MUL IMUL	+	+	?	?	?	?
DIV IDIV	?	?	?	?	?	?
Decimal Arithmetic						
DAA DAS	?	+	+	+	+	+
AAA AAS	?	+	+	?	?	?
AAM AAD	?	?	?	+	+	+
Boolean						
AND OR XOR TEST	0	0	?	+	+	+
Shift & Rotate						
SHL SHR (unit)	+	+	?	+	+	+
SHL SHR (variable)	?	+	?	+	+	+
SAR	0	+	?	+	+	+
ROL ROR RCL RCR (unit)	+	+	–	–	–	–
ROL ROR RCL RCR (variable)	?	+	–	–	–	–
Restore Flags						
POPF IRET	+	+	+	+	+	+
SAHF	–	+	+	+	+	+
Carry Flag Settings						
STC	–	1	–	–	–	–
CLC	–	0	–	–	–	–
CMC	–	*	–	–	–	–

B–CONTROL FLAGS	DF	IF	TF
Restore Flags			
POPF IRET	+	+	+
Interrupts			
INT INTO	–	0	0
Direction Flag Settings			
STD	1	–	–
CLD	0	–	–
Interrupt Flag Settings			
STI	–	1	–
CLI	–	0	–

Legend: + = affected   * = complemented
        1 = set to 1   ? = undefined
        0 = set to 0   – = unaffected

1. SI gets offset of least significant byte of first operand.
2. DI gets offset of least significant byte of second operand.
3. Clear carry (CLC).
4. Add-with-carry (ADC) byte pointed at by SI to byte pointed at by DI.
5. Increment (INC) SI so it points at next higher byte of first operand.
6. Increment (INC) DI so it points at next higher byte of second operand.
7. Jump back to step 4 if operands contain more bytes.

If the INC instructions in steps 5 and 6 affected the carry flag, the next executions of the ADC instruction in step 4 would not give the correct result.

Multiplication instructions generate double-length results and would therefore have to base the status flags on as many as 32-bits. Since no other instruction bases its flag settings on more than 16 bits, the processor would need a special flag-setting mechanism just for this one instruction. And it isn't clear what you would do with such flag settings anyway. To keep the processor simple, the values of most of the status flags are left undefined after a multiplication instruction. Undefined means the processor makes no attempt to set the flags in any particular manner (it just executes the instruction in the simplest way it can with total disregard for flag settings). Future versions of the processor might execute the instruction in a different manner and give different settings to the flags.

After a multiplication instruction is executed, it would be useful to know if the product can be considered as a single-length number without being out of range (the product considered as a double-length number is never out of range). This would enable us to do such things as multiply a byte by another byte and add the product to a third byte. For this reason, the overflow and carry flags are not left undefined; they indicate if the multiplication resulted in a signed or unsigned out-of-range result when considered as a single-length product.

For simplicity, all status flags are undefined after executing a division instruction.

The only status flag that is important after executing a decimal addition or subtraction adjustment is the carry flag (needed for multiple-precision arithmetic); all the other flags could have been left undefined. However, the 8080 has a DAA instruction (its only decimal instruction), and that instruction sets all five 8080 status flags (the 8080 doesn't have an overflow flag). So, for compatibility, the 8086 DAA instruction does the same. DAS, AAA, and AAS should also affect these five flags just to be consistent; DAS does, but implementation difficulties caused the sign flag, zero flag, and parity flag to be undefined after an AAA or AAS. It's not clear what carry and auxiliary carry mean with respect to the AAM and AAD instructions, so these were left undefined.

Since Boolean operations never produce results that are out of range, both the overflow and carry flags are set to zero after executing such instructions. The auxiliary carry flag has no utility following a Boolean instruction (its only purpose is for decimal arithmetic), so it is left undefined. The sign, zero, and parity flags are set to reflect the result of the instruction.

One Boolean instruction, NOT, is missing from the list of Boolean instructions that affect the flags. NOT does not affect the flags. This was the result of an oversight (I goofed!) when the processor was being defined.

Shift instructions are nothing more than multiplying or dividing by a power of 2. The status flags reflect the status of the result with the following two exceptions: the value of the auxiliary carry flag is undefined (we are not concerned with decimal arithmetic here), and the value of the overflow flag is undefined for variable shifts (the mechanism to detect overflow in this case was too complex). The arithmetic right shift (SAR) can never generate a signed result that is out of range, and therefore the overflow flag is set to 0 after executing such an instruction.

The rotate instructions were designed to be compatible with the 8080 rotate instructions and affect the flags in exactly the same way. For this reason, they affect the carry flag and do not affect the auxiliary carry flag, sign flag, zero flag, or parity flag. For consistency, it was decided that the rotate instructions should affect the overflow flag in the same way that the shift instructions do, even though it's not clear what overflow means in this case.

The flag restoring instructions restore the flags to some previously saved values. In particular, POPF and IRET restore all the flags (status as well as control) to values saved on the stack. SAHF is an odd instruction (it was included solely for compatibility with a similar instruction in the 8080) that restores the five 8080 status flags to values contained in AH.

All interrupts clear the interrupt-enable flag and the trap flag. If the interrupt-enable flag were not cleared, a "burst" of external interrupts could cause the processor to keep pushing CS and IP on the stack at an alarming rate, and the stack would immediately overflow. If the trap flag were not cleared, the processor would single-step through the debugger when the debugger was attempting to single-step through your program.

The behavior of the carry-flag instructions, direction-flag instructions, and interrupt-flag instructions is straightforward. They set, clear, or complement the one particular flag and do not affect any other flag.

4

8086
System Design

Before the advent of microprocessors, computer users were usually not concerned about system design; they would buy a complete system from a manufacturer. The system was often too big and expensive to be dedicated to a single application, so it was used as a general-purpose computing system to solve a wide variety of different problems. The small size and cost of the microprocessor makes it feasible to have a special-purpose system that is dedicated to a particular application. For example, a cash register could actually be controlled by a specially designed computer system that is built right into the cash register box. Since each application is different, the user no longer buys a complete system. Instead, he buys the components that make up a system and then puts the components together in a manner that would be suitable for his particular application. This is not unlike the hi-fi enthusiast putting together a set of audio components in a manner that satisfies his particular needs.

This chapter will present a *family* of components that can be used in an 8086 system and will show how these components can be put together to form a complete system. Very little knowledge of digital design is assumed other than a rudimentary understanding of the basic logic elements—AND gates, OR gates, and inverters.

This chapter does not apply to the 8088. System design for that processor is presented in the next chapter. These two system design chapters are presented in a parallel fashion so that either chapter can be read without reading the other.

Bus Structure

The 8086 is a microprocessor, not a microcomputer. The difference between the two is that a microprocessor does not contain any memory locations or input/output ports. To put it bluntly, a microprocessor can think but it can't remember, hear, or speak. Thus, additional units must be added to a microprocessor to make it into a usable microcomputer. Figure 4.1 illustrates a microcomputer system.

Fig. 4.1 A microcomputer system.

Fig. 4.2 A single data-bus system.

Fig. 4.3 Microcomputer system complete with address bus and data bus.

Information (data) is carried from one unit in a microcomputer system to another along paths called *data buses*. Typically, there is only one data bus, and it is shared by all the units in the system. The microprocessor generates control signals that permit the various units to take turns using the data bus. This is illustrated in Fig. 4.2.

It is not sufficient to tell a unit such as memory that its turn has come to use the data bus. The memory must be told which location within the memory is to be involved in the information transfer. The microprocessor generates the address of the memory location and places it on a second common bus called the *address bus*. A microprocessor system with a data bus, address bus, and control signals is shown in Fig. 4.3.

The data bus, address bus, and control signals all originate from the microprocessor itself. So let's take a closer look at the 8086 microprocessor to see what sort of buses and control signals it has. Since the 8086 is a 16-bit processor, it should have a data bus that is 16 bits wide so it can access an entire word in one memory reference. Furthermore, since it can address up to 2^{20} (approximately one million) bytes, it needs an address bus that is 20 bits wide. The 8086 is housed on a 40-pin chip, so there are only 40 connections that can be made between the processor and the other units in the system. If 36 of those connections were used up by the address and data buses, the remaining four would hardly be enough for all the necessary control signals and power and ground connections. To minimize the number of connections used by the address and data buses, these buses come out of the processor over a common set of pins, as illustrated in Fig. 4.4. This adds a slight degree of complexity to the rest of the system by requiring address latching (described in the next section).

Fig. 4.4 Shared address and data bus connections to 8086 chip.

Address Latching

Let's consider how data is sent from the processor to memory. At a certain instant, the processor sends the address of a specific memory location out on the address bus. At some later instant, the processor sends the data out on the data bus. But because these two buses share some of the same pins, the processor can no longer be sending out the address at the same time it is sending out the data. Therefore, unless someone had the forethought to jot down the address, it will be lost, and the data won't know where to go.

The 8086 family includes a chip called the *8282*. It is known as a *latch* and can be used to remember things that would otherwise get lost. It has eight data input pins and eight data output pins. When nudged to do so, it will memorize the data on its input pins. Nudging is done by placing a signal on one of its control pins, called STB (for strobe). Furthermore, placing a signal on its OE (output enable) control pin will cause the chip to make the memorized data available on its output pins. The chip is shown in Fig. 4.5.

Strictly speaking, the actual pin on the 8282 is labeled $\overline{\text{OE}}$ instead of OE. This means that the function of that pin is inverted. To get an OE signal, we must place no signal on pin $\overline{\text{OE}}$, and vice versa. For simplicity, such details will generally be omitted from this presentation (but not from the diagrams).

Fig. 4.5 Symbolic representation of 8282 latch chip.

Now the 8282 latch is just what we need to keep addresses from getting lost. At the time that the processor is putting out an address on the shared address/data bus, it is notifying everyone of this fact by putting out a control signal on its ALE (address latch enable) pin. This ALE signal provides just the nudging the 8282 needs in order to memorize an address. The connections between the 8086 and the 8282 are shown in Fig. 4.6.

We used three 8282 latches in Fig. 4.6 because an address is 20 bits, whereas a single 8282 can memorize only eight bits. In systems having limited amounts of memory, not all 20 address bits are used, and possibly one of the address latches could be eliminated. This is why one latch is shown dotted.

Data Amplifying

Address latching is necessary because the processor is no longer sending out the address when it comes time to read or write the data. But there is no need to latch the data. However, the processor is limited in how hard it can push out or pull in the data. For example, if there are too many units on the data bus, each

Fig. 4.6 Using a latch to separate the address from the shared address/data bus.

trying to receive the data, the 8086 might not have enough "oomph" (power) to get the data to all of them. (We would have a similar problem with addresses if we weren't using address latches.) The solution would be to use a data amplifier to receive the data, amplify it, and transmit it to anybody and everybody that asks for it. The only difficulty with such amplifying is that it must be bidirectional: data flows from the processor to the rest of the system and also from the rest of the system back to the processor. An amplifier that is able to *trans*mit and re*ceive* in either direction is called a *transceiver*.

The 8086 family includes the *8286* chip, which is a transceiver. It has eight pins that serve as data input pins and another eight that serve as data output pins. But the transceiver can interchange the roles of these two sets of pins so that the data can pass through the chip in either direction. The chip has two control pins—an OE (output enable) pin to tell it when to pass the data and a T (transmit) pin to tell it in which direction the data is to be transmitted through the chip. The chip is shown in Fig. 4.7.

The 8286 is just what we need to put more "oomph" on the data bus. At the time the 8086 is passing data on the shared address/data bus, it makes this known by putting out a control signal on its DEN (data enable) pin. And the 8086 puts out a control signal on its DT/R̄ (data transmit/receive) pin to indicate whether the data is going from the processor to the rest of the system or vice versa. The connections between the 8086 processor, the 8282 address latches, and the 8286 transceivers are shown in Fig. 4.8. The transceivers are shown dotted since they might not be necessary in small systems.

Fig. 4.7 Symbolic representation of 8286 transceiver.

Fig. 4.8 Using transceivers to boost up the data bus.

Measuring Time

Timing considerations are important for nearly every function performed by the 8086 processor. For example, let's look a little more closely at address latching. The 8086 processor places an address on the bus and notifies the 8282 latch of this fact by sending it an ALE signal. (What we are calling an ALE signal is really a transition on the ALE pin from a 1 to a 0, but let's not get bogged down in such details.) If the processor sends out the ALE signal and the address simultaneously, the latch might receive the ALE signal and attempt to memorize the address before all the address bits are on the bus and in stable form. Therefore, there must be some delay between the time the processor places the address on the bus and the time it sends out the ALE signal. This delay is undoubtedly short (considerably less than a millionth of a second) but nonetheless necessary to insure that the address is stable.

The processor measures delays in *clock pulses*. Clock pulses are signals received from a timing circuit called a *clock generator*. Just like the beats of a metronome, clock pulses provide a frame of reference for measuring time. If clock pulses arrive at the rate of one per second, a three clock pulse delay would be three seconds. But if a faster clock generator were used so that one million clock pulses arrive in a second, a three clock pulse delay would be only three millionths of a second. Thus the faster the clock, the shorter will be all delays until a point is reached where the delays are too short and the system will not function properly (the ALE signal comes before the address is stable). The fastest clock that will permit an 8086 system to still function properly is approximately eight million clock pulses per second.

The *8284A* clock generator is a chip that generates clock pulses. The rate at which the pulses occur is determined by a quartz crystal (like the ones used in electronic watches) that is wired to two pins of the 8284A. For reliability, the

Fig. 4.9 Connecting a clock generator to an 8086 system.

8284A will generate one clock pulse for every three pulses from the crystal. To generate eight million clock pulses per second, a 24 MHz (megacycles-per-second or megahertz) crystal is used. Figure 4.9 shows how an 8284A clock generator would be connected to an 8086 system.

Memory Units

Now that we've met the address bus and data bus, let's try to hook some memory onto the buses. There are two kinds of memories—those that never forget and those that do. The "unforgettable" variety are initially given information, which is burned into their memory cells. Everybody can read this information, but the memory will not let anybody overwrite it. Hence such memories are called *read-only memories* or ROMs (pronounced "roms") for short. The "forgettable" variety will allow anybody to read or overwrite its information and hence should be called *read write memories* or RWMs (pronounced "rwms") for short. Because of the pronunciation difficulties this presented, someone decided to call them *random access memories* or RAMS for short. Don't let this fool you; both kinds of memory can be accessed just as randomly!

As an example of a ROM, let us consider the *2716* memory chip. The chip contains 2^{11} (approximately 2,000) locations, each location containing eight bits. Hence it is sometimes designated as a 2K × 8 ROM chip. The chip contains 11 address pins and 8 data pins. On command, the chip will fetch the contents of the location specified by the address pins and place this information on the data pins. The command for doing this is a pair of control signals, one on the CE (chip enable) pin and one on the OE (output enable) pin of the 2716 chip. The chip is shown in Fig. 4.10.

Larger memories (more locations) can be obtained by combining several 2716 chips together. For example, a memory with a 2^{12} or approximately 4,000

Fig. 4.10 Symbolic representation of 2716 2Kx8 ROM chip.

Fig. 4.11 Combining two 2Kx8 memories to form a 4Kx8 memory.

locations, each location containing eight bits, would consist of two 2716 chips. An address is now 12 bits long. The 11 low-order bits of the address are sent to both chips. To prevent both of them from responding with data, only one of the chips will be enabled. The high-order bit of the address is used to determine which chip to enable. This is shown in Fig. 4.11. Still larger memories can be obtained by combining still more 2716 chips. In such cases, additional high-order address bits are used to determine which chip to select. This selection process is referred to as *address decoding*.

Memories can also be made wider (more bits per location) by adding more memory chips. In this case, more than one memory chip will be enabled for each address. For example, two 2716 chips were combined to form a 4K × 8 memory, whereas four such chips could have been combined to form a 4K × 16 memory. This is shown in Fig. 4.12.

As an example of a RAM, let us consider the *2142* memory chip. The chip contains 2^{10} (approximately 1,000) locations, each location containing four bits. Hence the chip is designated as a 1K × 4 RAM. The chip contains 10 address pins, four data pins, and several control pins. One of the control pins, CS (chip select), selects the chip. An unselected chip will do nothing. Another control pin, WE (write enable), causes the contents of the data pins to be placed in the location specified by the address pins. Still another control pin, OD (output disable), is used to determine whether or not to place the contents of the selected location onto the data pins. WE is used when writing to the chip; OD is used when reading from it. Figure 4.13 illustrates this chip.

Now we can put together a simple system consisting of an 8086, 4K of 16-bit ROM memory, and 4K of 16-bit RAM memory. This is shown in Fig.

Fig. 4.12 Combining four 2Kx8 memories to form a 4Kx16 memory.

Fig. 4.13 Symbolic representation of 2142 1Kx4 RAM chip.

4.14. Note that two new output control signals are shown on the 8086—namely RD (read) and WR (write). They indicate when the 8086 is about to read the contents of the data bus and when it is writing information onto the data bus. These signals are used to control the memories. One more control signal, BHE, will be explained shortly.

Now let's see what happens when the processor executes an instruction. Consider an instruction that moves the 8-bit contents of register AL to the byte at address 0AF0 (hexadecimal). Assume AX contains F307, which means that AL contains 07. First the processor places 0AF0 on the common address/data bus. Then the processor places a signal on its ALE (address latch enable) pin to tell the address latch to memorize that value. The latch does just that, and now the 0AF0

Fig. 4.14 8086 system with memory.

is on the address bus emanating from the right side of the latch. The processor can now remove the 0AF0 from the common bus and replace it with the F307. Next, the processor places a signal on its WR (write) pin to tell the memory to fetch the eight low-order bits of the common bus and place them into the byte whose address is on the address bus. The memory will do just that and place 07 into the byte at address 0AF0.

Now, you might ask, how did the memory know that the processor was executing a byte move and not a word move? Specifically, how did the memory know not to place the F3 into the byte at address 0AF1? The answer is simple: there is one more control signal that we didn't tell you about. That signal comes from a pin on the processor called BHE (bus high enable). It is issued by the processor at the same time the processor places the address on the common bus. And, like the address, it also goes to and is memorized by the address latch. The purpose of BHE is to tell the memory whether or not to access the eight high-order bits on the data bus. In the preceding example, there was no signal placed on the BHE pin.

The BHE signal is needed only when the processor writes to the memory. When the processor is reading memory, the memory doesn't have to know whether the processor is executing a byte or word instruction; the memory always returns a word, and the processor can decide how much of that word it wants to use. Thus it's unnecessary to send the BHE control signal to ROM memory as was seen in Fig. 4.14.

There is no need for a BLE (bus low enable) signal; the complement of the least significant address bit is used for that purpose. In other words, sending out an odd address will inhibit the memory from accessing the eight low-order bits on the data bus, whereas sending out an even address will not. Thus to transfer a byte to an odd address in memory, the processor must send out the odd address (disabling accesses to the low-order half of the data bus), send out a BHE signal (enabling accesses to the high-order half of the data bus), and send out the required data on the high-order half of the data bus. As we already saw in the preceding example, the processor transfers a byte to an even address in memory by sending out the even address (enabling accesses to the low-order half of the data bus), sending out no BHE signal (disabling accesses to the high-order half of the data bus), and sending out the required data on the low-order half of the data bus. The processor can transfer an entire word to an even address in memory by sending out the even address (enabling access to the low-order half of the data bus), sending out a BHE signal (enabling accesses to the high-order half of the data bus), and sending out the required data across both halves of the data bus.

And, finally, let's consider how the processor transfers an entire word to an odd address in memory. Two memory accesses are required to accomplish this. The first access consists of sending out the odd address (disabling access to the low-order half of the data bus), sending out a BHE signal (enabling access to the high-order half of the data bus), and sending out the low-order half of the word on the high-order half of the data bus (notice the byte juggling that just took place). After that memory access is completed, the processor sends out an even address obtained by adding 1 to the odd address (enabling access to the low-order half of the data bus), sending out no BHE signal (disabling access to the high-order half of the data bus), and sending out the high-order half of the word on the low-order half of the data bus (more byte juggling). Figure 4.15 shows the various ways of transferring information to memory.

(a) WRITING TO AN EVEN-ADDRESSED BYTE

Fig. 4.15 Writing bytes and words to even and odd addresses.

Fig. 4.15 Writing bytes and words to even and odd addresses (*cont.*).

The least significant address bit, like the BHE signal, need not be sent to
ROM Memory.

Input/Output Ports

It's time now to round out our system with some input and output. Once
that's done, our system will be able to communicate with the outside world.
Input and output ports hang on the address and data bus just like memory. That
means that the processor can select a particular port by sending its address out on
the address bus and can transfer data to or from the port by using the data bus. An
output control signal ($M/\overline{IO}$) from the 8086 can be used to distinguish memory
instructions, such as MOV, from the input/output instructions IN and OUT.
However, in small systems it's simpler to reserve certain memory addresses for
input or output ports and then talk to these ports with memory instructions instead
of input/output instructions. This is often referred to as *memory-mapped input/
output*.

As an example, let's consider an 8086 system that controls a pair of traffic
light units. Each traffic light unit consists of a red light, a yellow light, a green
light, and a left turn arrow. Thus there are four signals going from the 8086
system to each unit. We need an output port to control the traffic lights. An
output port is nothing more than a device for memorizing the last traffic light
settings that were sent to it and constantly feeding this information to the traffic
lights. Thus the 8282 latch seems like it would make a perfect output port. Let's
suppose that the memory in the system uses 2^{10} or 1024 memory addresses. In
other words, the lowest memory address is zero and the highest is 1023. Thus we
can place the output port at memory address 1024. We could incorporate circuitry that waits for 1024 ($A_{10} = 1$, other A's $= 0$) to be on the address bus and
then tells the output port to memorize what's on the data bus. However, in this
case it's much simpler to wait until address line $A_{10} = 1$ and ignore all the other
address lines. This has the effect of allowing the port to recognize all addresses
having $A_{10} = 1$ (approximately half a million of them); we can devote all these
addresses to one port since we have no other use for them. The system just
described is shown in Fig. 4.16.

Notice the AND gate connected to the STB (strobe) pin of the output port.
Its purpose is to send a signal to the STB pin if and only if address line $A_{10} = 1$
and the 8086 is sending out a WR signal. AND gates, OR gates, and inverters are
used to generate signals that are logical functions of other signals.

This example illustrates the use of memory-mapped output. The program
would use memory instructions to change the settings of the traffic light. For
example, an OR instruction designating memory address 1024 as the destination
operand could be used to change the settings of one of the traffic light units and
leave the other one unaltered. If we preferred to use the OUT instruction instead
(no memory-mapped output), we would need to invert the $M/\overline{IO}$ output signal
(not shown) and feed it into the AND gate.

Fig. 4.16 8086 system using memory-mapped input/output to control traffic light.

Fig. 4.17 Getting the processor's attention.

Fig. 4.18 8259A acting as an arbitrator.

Fig. 4.19 Handling more than eight external devices.

Fig. 4.20 8086 system with interrupt controller.

Interrupt Servicing

The 8086 processor chip has a couple of pins that can be used by external devices to get the processor's attention. One of these pins, INTR (normal interrupts), is used by the external device to say, "Will you give me a hand when you get a chance?" The other pin, NMI (non-maskable interrupt), is used to say, "Give me a hand now because later will be too late!" A more detailed description of these two different kinds of interrupts is found under Interrupt Instructions in Chap. 3.

Let's look at normal interrupts in more detail. The external device places a signal on the INTR pin of the 8086 when it wants help. As soon as the 8086 is able to respond (IF = 1 and processor is in between instructions), it will say to the external device, "OK, what can I do for you?" The 8086 says this by putting a signal on its INTA (interrupt acknowledge) pin. The external device then tells the 8086 what to do by placing a number between 0 and 255 on the data bus. This sequence is illustrated in Fig. 4.17.

All's fine as long as there is only one external device. But now consider what would happen if we had two or three or even more external devices, any of which might be asking for the processor's attention. If two of them both wanted help at precisely the same instant, they would both send signals simultaneously to the INTR pin of the 8086. The 8086 would eventually respond with its INTA signal, which both external devices would see. Then both devices would try to place a number on the data bus, and the 8086 would receive a confused mess.

What's needed is some sort of arbitrator (called an *interrupt controller*) to decide which external device is more important and pass its request on to the 8086. Such an arbitrator is the *8259A*. The external devices talk only to the 8259A and the 8259A talks to the 8086. This is shown in Fig. 4.18.

Fig. 4.21 A maximum-mode 8086 system.

More than eight external devices can be handled by using more than one 8259A. Figure 4.19 shows how we can handle up to 64 different external devices, each capable of interrupting the processor. One 8259A is at a higher level than the others; it is called the *master,* and the others are called *slaves.* Now the external devices talk only to the slaves; the slaves talk only to the master; and the master talks to the 8086.

In order for an 8259A to perform its duties, it must know what its external devices are. For one thing, it must know which are the more important external devices, so it can resolve disputes. For another, it must know what reason each device would have for generating an interrupt, so it can pass on the correct reason to the 8086 when that device's turn comes up. All of this information is actually "programmed" into the 8259A by the 8086. This means that the 8259A must also be a fairly sophisticated device; in fact, with the exception of the 8086 (and 8088), the 8259A is the most complex chip described in this text. The 8086 programs the 8259A by sending it information over the data bus; this is why the data bus is indicated as an input (as well as an output) to the 8259A. The actual details for programming the 8259A will not be presented here because that would require a chapter of its own.

Figure 4.20 shows how the 8259A fits together with all the other pieces we have seen so far.

Bigger Systems

The 8086 has one very severe limitation; it's trying to do a lot of things, but it only has 40 pins to do them with. In other words, the 8086 is too big for its britches. One way to solve this problem is to have the 8086 hold back and not do everything it's capable of, so it can fit into its pins. Another solution is to give the 8086 an additional set of pins and let it do everything it's capable of. The 8086 is actually schizophrenic and can behave either way depending on the system it's used in. Its mode of behavior is determined by an input control pin called MN/$\overline{\text{MX}}$ (minimum/maximum), which in a given system is either permanently on or permanently off. When there is a signal on this pin, the 8086 holds back and is said to be behaving in its minimum mode. No signal on MN/$\overline{\text{MX}}$ tells the 8086 that there's another set of pins available.

The extra set of pins is actually a chip called the 8288 *bus controller*. It performs some of the functions that were using up precious pins on the 8086 chip, leaving the 8086 free to perform some of its other functions over those pins. For example, the ALE signal (address latch enable) is generated by the 8288, thereby permitting the 8086 to use its ALE pin to perform a function that it previously had to keep hidden. An example of a signal that the 8086 is able to send out in maximum mode but must keep hidden in minimum mode is a LOCK signal (discussed in Chap. 3), which permits several processors to execute at the same time over the same buses without stepping on each other's toes.

Figure 4.21 shows an example of a maximum mode 8086 system. The 8086 uses pins S_0, S_1, and S_2 to let the 8288 know what's going on. Notice the ALE, DT/R, DEN, and INTA signals that came off the 8086 in minimum mode now come off the 8288. Furthermore, the M/$\overline{\text{IO}}$, RD, and WR signals that came off the 8086 have been functionally replaced with the MRDC (memory read command), MWTC (memory write command), IORC (input/output read command), and IOWC (input/output write command). This separation of memory read and write signals from input/output read and write signals makes it easier to distinguish between a memory instruction and an input/output instruction. You will recall that in Fig. 4.16 we avoided making that distinction by using memory-mapped I/O.

The output of the 8284A clock generator is fed into the 8288. This makes it possible for the 8288 to generate such signals as ALE or DEN at the correct number of clock pulses after the address or data has been placed on the bus. The S_0, and S_1, and S_2 signals let the 8288 know when such things are placed on the bus.

The data transceivers and the third address latch are usually not optional in maximum systems and hence were not drawn dotted in Fig. 4.21.

Summary

This chapter has shown how the 8086 can be combined with other circuit components to form a complete system. The components described here have been designed to be used together with a minimum of interconnecting circuitry. Additional components in the 8086 family are described in the *Intel MCS-86 User's Manual*.

Once a system has been designed and built, it must be programmed. This is the topic of Chaps. 6 through 8.

5

8088

System Design

Before the advent of microprocessors, computer users were usually not concerned about system design; they would buy a complete system from a manufacturer. The system was often too big and expensive to be dedicated to a single application, so it was used as a general-purpose computing system to solve a wide variety of different problems. The small size and cost of the microprocessor makes it feasible to have a special-purpose system that is dedicated to a particular application. For example, a cash register could actually be controlled by a specially designed computer system that is built right into the cash register box. Since each application is different, the user no longer buys a complete system. Instead, he buys the components that make up a system and then puts the components together in a manner that would be suitable for his particular application. This is not unlike the hi-fi enthusiast putting together a set of audio components in a manner that satisfies his particular needs.

This chapter will present a *family* of components that can be used in an 8088 system and will show how these components can be put together to form a complete system. Very little knowledge of digital design is assumed other than a rudimentary understanding of the basic logic elements—AND gates, OR gates, and inverters.

This chapter does not apply to the 8086. System design for that processor appears in the previous chapter. These two system design chapters are presented in a parallel fashion so that either chapter can be read without reading the other.

Bus Structure

The 8088 is a microprocessor, not a microcomputer. The difference between the two is that a microprocessor does not contain any memory locations or input/output ports. To put it bluntly, a microprocessor can think but it can't remember, hear, or speak. Thus, additional units must be added to a microprocessor to make it into a usable microcomputer. Figure 5.1 illustrates a microcomputer system.

Fig. 5.1 A microcomputer system.

Fig. 5.2 A single data-bus system.

Fig. 5.3 Microcomputer system complete with address bus and data bus.

Information (data) is carried from one unit in a microcomputer system to another along paths called *data buses*. Typically, there is only one data bus, and it is shared by all the units in the system. The microprocessor generates control signals that permit the various units to take turns using the data bus. This is illustrated in Fig. 5.2.

It is not sufficient to tell a unit such as memory that its turn has come to use the data bus. The memory must be told which location within the memory is to be involved in the information transfer. The microprocessor generates the address of the memory location and places it on a second common bus called the *address bus*. A microprocessor system with a data bus, address bus, and control signal is shown in Fig. 5.3.

The data bus, address bus, and control signals all originate from the microprocessor itself. So let's take a closer look at the 8088 microprocessor to see what sort of buses and control signals it has. Since the 8088 is an 8-bit processor, it should have a data bus that is 8 bits wide so it can access an entire byte in one memory reference. Furthermore, since it can address up to 2^{20} (approximately one million) bytes, it needs an address bus that is 20 bits wide. The 8088 is housed on a 40-pin chip, so there are only 40 connections that can be made between the processor and the other units in the system. If 28 of those connections were used up by the address and data buses, the remaining 12 would hardly be enough for all the necessary control signals and power and ground connections. To minimize the number of connections used by the address and data buses, these buses come out of the processor over a common set of pins, as illustrated in Fig. 5.4. This adds a slight degree of complexity to the rest of the system by requiring address latching (described in the next section).

Fig. 5.4 Shared address and data bus connections to 8088 chip.

Address Latching

Let's consider how data is sent from the processor to memory. At a certain instant, the processor sends the address of a specific memory location out on the address bus. At some later instant, the processor sends the data out on the data bus. But because these two buses share some of the same pins, the processor can no longer be sending out the address at the same time it is sending out the data. Therefore, unless someone had the forethought to jot down the address, it will be lost, and the data won't know where to go.

The 8088 family includes a chip called the *8282*. It is known as a *latch* and can be used to remember things that would otherwise get lost. It has eight data input pins and eight data output pins. When nudged to do so, it will memorize the data on its input pins. Nudging is done by placing a signal on one of its control pins, called STB (for strobe). Furthermore, placing a signal on its OE (output enable) control pin will cause the chip to make the memorized data available on its output pins. The chip is shown in Fig. 5.5

Strictly speaking, the actual pin in the 8282 is labeled $\overline{\text{OE}}$ instead of OE. This means that the function of that pin is inverted. To get an OE signal, we must place no signal on pin $\overline{\text{OE}}$, and vice versa. For simplicity, such details will generally be omitted from this presentation (but not from the diagrams).

Fig. 5.5 Symbolic representation of 8282 latch chip.

Now the 8282 latch is just what we need to keep addresses from getting lost. At the time that the processor is putting out an address on the shared address/data bus, it is notifying everyone of this fact by putting out a control signal on its ALE (address latch enable) pin. This ALE signal provides just the nudging the 8282 needs in order to memorize an address. The connections between the 8088 and the 8282 are shown in Fig. 5.6.

We used three 8282 latches in Fig. 5.6 because an address is 20 bits, whereas a single 8282 can memorize only eight bits. In systems having limited amounts of memory, not all 20 address bits are used, and possibly one of the address latches could be eliminated. This is why one latch is shown dotted.

Data Amplifying

Address latching is necessary because the processor is no longer sending out the address when it comes time to read or write the data. But there is no need to latch the data. However, the processor is limited in how hard it can push out or pull in the data. For example, if there are too many units on the data bus,

Fig. 5.6 Using a latch to separate the address from the shared address/data bus.

each trying to receive the data, the 8088 might not have enough "oomph" (power) to get the data to all of them. (We would have a similar problem with addresses if we weren't using address latches.) The solution would be to use a data amplifier to receive the data, amplify it, and transmit it to anybody and everybody that asks for it. The only difficulty with such amplifying is that it must be bidirectional: data flows from the processor to the rest of the system and also from the rest of the system back to the processor. An amplifier that is able to *trans*mit and re*ceive* in either direction is called a *transceiver.*

The 8088 family includes the *8286* chip, which is a transceiver. It has eight pins that serve as data input pins and another eight that serve as data output pins. But the transceiver can interchange the roles of these two sets of pins so that the data can pass through the chip in either direction. The chip has two control pins—an OE (output enable) pin to tell it when to pass the data and a T (transmit) pin to tell it in which direction the data is to be transmitted through the chip. The chip is shown in Fig. 5.7.

The 8286 is just what we need to put more "oomph" on the data bus. At the time the 8088 is passing data on the shared address/data bus, it makes this known by putting out a control signal on its DEN (data enable) pin. And the 8088 puts out a control signal in its DT/$\overline{\text{R}}$ (data transmit/receive) pin to indicate whether the data is going from the processor to the rest of the system or vice versa. The connections between the 8088 processor, the 8282 address latches, and the 8286 transceiver is shown in Fig. 5.8. The transceiver is shown dotted since it might not be necessary in small systems.

Fig. 5.7 Symbolic representation of 8286 transceiver.

Fig. 5.8 Using transceivers to boost up the data bus.

Measuring Time

Timing considerations are important for nearly every function performed by the 8088 processor. For example, let's look a little more closely at address latching. The 8088 processor places an address on the bus and notifies the 8282 latch of this fact by sending it an ALE signal. (What we are calling an ALE signal is really a transition on the ALE pin from a 1 to a 0, but let's not get bogged down in such details.) If the processor sends out the ALE signal and the address simultaneously, the latch might receive the ALE signal and attempt to memorize the address before all the address bits are on the bus and in stable form. Therefore, there must be some delay between the time the processor places the address on the bus and the time it sends out the ALE signal. This delay is undoubtedly short (considerably less than a millionth of a second) but nonetheless necessary to insure that the address is stable.

The processor measures delays in *clock pulses*. Clock pulses are signals received from a timing circuit called a *clock generator*. Just like the beats of a metronome, clock pulses provide a frame of reference for measuring time. If clock pulses arrive at the rate of one per second, a three clock pulse delay would be three seconds. But if a faster clock generator were used so that one million clock pulses arrive in a second, a three clock pulse delay would be only three millionths of a second. Thus the faster the clock, the shorter will be all delays until a point is reached where the delays are too short and the system will not function properly (the ALE signal comes before the address is stable). The fastest clock that will permit an 8088 system to still function properly is approximately eight million clock pulses per second.

The *8284A* clock generator is a chip that generates clock pulses. The rate at which the pulses occur is determined by a quartz crystal (like the ones used in electronic watches) that is wired to two pins of the 8284A. For reliability, the

Fig. 5.9 Connecting a clock generator to an 8088 system.

8284A will generate one clock pulse for every three pulses from the crystal. To generate eight million clock pulses per second, a 24 MHz (megacycles-per-second or megahertz) crystal is used. Figure 5.9 shows how an 8284A clock generator would be connected to an 8088 system.

Memory Units

Now that we've met the address bus and data bus, let's try to hook some memory onto the buses. There are two kinds of memories—those that never forget and those that do. The "unforgettable" variety are initially given information, which is burned into their memory cells. Everybody can read this information, but the memory will not let anybody overwrite it. Hence such memories are called *read-only memories* or ROMs (pronounced "roms") for short. The "forgettable" variety will allow anybody to read or overwrite its information and hence should be called *read write memories* or RWMs (pronounced "rwms") for short. Because of the pronunciation difficulties this presented, someone decided to call them *random access memories* or RAMS for short. Don't let this fool you; both kinds of memory can be accessed just as randomly!

As an example of a ROM, let us consider the *2716* memory chip. The chip contains 2^{11} (approximately 2,000) locations, each location containing eight bits. Hence it is sometimes designated as a 2K × 8 ROM chip. The chip contains 11 address pins and 8 data pins. On command, the chip will fetch the contents of the location specified by the address pins and place this information on the data pins. The command for doing this is a pair of control signals, one on the CE (chip enable) pin and one on the OE (output enable) pin of the 2716 chip. The chip is shown in Fig. 5.10.

Larger memories (more locations) can be obtained by combining several 2716 chips together. For example, a memory with a 2^{12} or approximately 4,000

Fig. 5.10 Symbolic representation of 2716 2K x 8 ROM chip.

Fig. 5.11 Combining two 2K x 8 memories to form a 4K x 8 memory.

locations, each location containing eight bits, would consist of two 2716 chips. An address is now 12 bits long. The 11 low-order bits of the address are sent to both chips. To prevent both of them from responding with data, only one of the chips will be enabled. The high-order bit of the address is used to determine which chip to enable. This is shown in Fig. 5.11. Still larger memories can be obtained by combining still more 2716 chips. In such cases, additional high-order address bits are used to determine which chip to select. This selection process is referred to as *address decoding*.

As an example of a RAM, let us consider the *2142* memory chip. The chip contains 2^{10} (approximately 1,000) locations, each location containing four bits. Hence the chip is designated as a 1K $\times$ 4 RAM. The chip contains 10 address pins, four data pins, and several control pins. One of the control pins, CS (chip select), selects the chip. An unselected chip will do nothing. Another control pin, WE (write enable), causes the contents of the data pins to be placed in the location specified by the address pins. Still another control pin, OD (output disable), is used to determine whether or not to place the contents of the selected location onto the data pins. WE is used when writing to the chip; OD is used when reading from it. Figure 5.12 illustrates this chip.

Fig. 5.12 Symbolic representation of 2142 1K x 4 RAM chip.

Fig. 5.13 8088 system with memory.

Now we can put together a simple system consisting of an 8088, 4K of 8-bit ROM memory, and 4K of 8-bit RAM memory. This is shown in Fig. 5.13. Note that two new output control signals are shown on the 8088—namely RD (read) and WR (write). They indicate when the 8086 is about to read the contents of the data bus and when it is writing information onto the data bus. These signals are used to control the memories.

Now let's see what happens when the processor executes an instruction. Consider an instruction that moves the 8-bit contents of register AL to the byte at address 0AF0 (hexadecimal). Assume AL contains 07. First the processor places 0AF0 on the common address/data bus. Then the processor places a signal on its ALE (address latch enable) pin to tell the address latch to memorize that value. The latch does just that, and now the 0AF0 is on the address bus emanating from the right side of the latch. The processor can now remove the 0AF0 from the common bus and replace it with the 07. Next, the processor places a signal on its WR (write) pin to tell the memory to fetch the eight low-order bits of the common bus and place them into the byte whose address is on the address bus. The memory will do just that and place 07 into the byte at address 0AF0.

Next let's consider how the processor transfers an entire word to memory. Two memory accesses are required to accomplish this. The first access consists of sending out the lower memory address along with the low-order half of the word. After that memory access is completed, the processor sends out the higher memory address along with the high-order half of the word.

Input/Output Ports

It's time now to round out our system with some input and output. Once that's done, our system will be able to communicate with the outside world. Input and output ports hang on the address and data bus just like memory. That means that the processor can select a particular port by sending its address out on the address bus and can transfer data to or from the port by using the data bus. An output control signal (IO/$\overline{\text{M}}$) from the 8088 can be used to distinguish memory instructions, such as MOV, from the input/output instructions IN and OUT. However, in small systems it's simpler to reserve certain memory addresses for input or output ports and then talk to these ports with memory instructions instead of input/output instructions. This is often referred to as *memory-mapped input/ output*.

As an example, let's consider an 8088 system that controls a pair of traffic light units. Each traffic light unit consists of a red light, a yellow light, a green light, and a left turn arrow. Thus there are four signals going from the 8088 system to each unit. We need an output port to control the traffic lights. An *output port* is nothing more than a device for memorizing the last traffic light settings that were sent to it and constantly feeding this information to the traffic lights. Thus the 8282 latch seems like it would make a perfect output port. Let's suppose that the memory in the system uses 2^{10} or 1024 memory addresses. In other words, the lowest memory address is zero and the highest is 1023. Thus we can place

Fig. 5.14 8088 system using memory-mapped input/output to control traffic light.

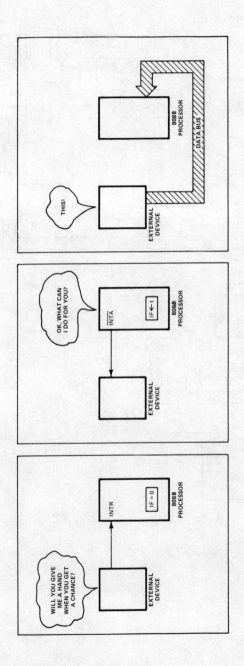

Fig. 5.15 Getting the processor's attention.

Fig. 5.16 8259A acting as an arbitrator.

Fig. 5.17 Handling more than eight external devices.

Fig. 5.18 8088 system with interrupt controller.

the output port at memory address 1024. We could incorporate circuitry that waits for 1024 ($A_{10} = 1$, other A's = 0) to be on the address bus and then tells the output port to memorize what's on the data bus. However, in this case it's much simpler to wait until address line $A_{10} = 1$ and ignore all the other address lines. This has the effect of allowing the port to recognize all addresses having $A_{10} = 1$ (approximately half a million of them); we can devote all these addresses to one port since we have no other use for them. The system just described is shown in Fig. 5.14.

Notice the AND gate connected to the STB (strobe) pin of the output port. Its purpose is to send a signal to the STB pin if and only if address line $A_{10} = 1$ *and* the 8088 is sending out a WR signal. AND gates, OR gates, and inverters are used to generate signals that are logical functions of other signals.

This example illustrates the use of memory-mapped output. The program would use memory instructions to change the settings of the traffic light. For example, an OR instruction designating memory address 1024 as the destination operand could be used to change the settings of one of the traffic light units and leave the other one unaltered. If we preferred to use the OUT instruction instead (no memory-mapped output), we would need to feed the IO/$\overline{\text{M}}$ output signal (not shown) into the AND gate.

Interrupt Servicing

The 8088 processor chip has a couple of pins that can be used by external devices to get the processor's attention. One of these pins, INTR (normal interrupts), is used by the external device to say, "Will you give me a hand when you get a chance?" The other pin, NMI (non-maskable interrupt), is used to say, "Give me a hand now because later will be too late!" A more detailed description of these two different kinds of interrupts is found under Interrupt Instructions in Chap. 3.

Let's look at normal interrupts in more detail. The external device places a signal on the INTR pin of the 8088 when it wants help. As soon as the 8088 is able to respond (IF = 1 and processor is in between instructions), it will say to the external device, "OK, what can I do for you?" The 8088 says this by putting a signal on its INTA (interrupt acknowledge) pin. The external device then tells the 8088 what to do by placing a number between 0 and 255 on the data bus. This sequence is illustrated in Fig. 5.15.

All's fine as long as there is only one external device. But now consider what would happen if we had two or three or even more external devices, any of which might be asking for the processor's attention. If two of them both wanted help at precisely the same instant, they would both send signals simultaneously to the INTR pin of the 8088. The 8088 would eventually respond with its INTA

Fig. 5.19 A maximum-mode 8088 system.

signal, which both external devices would see. Then both devices would try to place a number on the data bus, and the 8088 would receive a confused mess.

What's needed is some sort of arbitrator (called an *interrupt controller*) to decide which external device is more important and pass its request on to the 8088. Such an arbitrator is the *8259A*. The external devices talk only to the 8259A and the 8259A talks to the 8088. This is shown in Fig. 5.16.

More than eight external devices can be handled by using more than one 8259A. Figure 5.17 shows how we can handle up to 64 different external devices, each capable of interrupting the processor. One 8259A is at a higher level than the others; it is called the *master,* and the others are called *slaves.* Now the external devices talk only to the slaves; the slaves talk only to the master; and the master talks to the 8088.

In order for an 8259A to perform its duties, it must know what its external devices are. For one thing, it must know which are the more important external devices, so it can resolve disputes. For another, it must know what reason each device would have for generating an interrupt, so it can pass on the correct reason to the 8088 when that device's turn comes up. All of this information is actually "programmed" into the 8259A by the 8088. This means that the 8259A must also be a fairly sophisticated device; in fact, with the exception of the 8088 (and 8086), the 8259A is the most complex chip described in this text. The 8088 programs the 8259A by sending it information over the data bus; this is why the data bus is indicated as an input (as well as an output) to the 8259A. The actual details for programming the 8259A will not be presented here because that would require a chapter of its own.

Figure 5.18 shows how the 8259A fits together with all the other pieces we have seen so far.

Bigger Systems

The 8088 has one very severe limitation; it's trying to do a lot of things, but it only has 40 pins to do them with. In other words, the 8088 is too big for its britches. One way to solve this problem is to have the 8088 hold back and not do everything it's capable of, so it can fit into its pins. Another solution is to give the 8088 an additional set of pins and let it do everything it's capable of. The 8088 is actually schizophrenic and can behave either way depending on the system it's used in. Its mode of behavior is determined by an input control pin called $\overline{\text{MN/MX}}$ (minimum/maximum), which in a given system is either permanently on or permanently off. When there is a signal on this pin, the 8088 holds back and is said to be behaving in its minimum mode. No signal on MN/$\overline{\text{MX}}$ tells the 8088 that there's another set of pins available.

The extra set of pins is actually a chip called the 8288 *bus controller*. It performs some of the functions that were using up precious pins on the 8088 chip, leaving the 8088 free to perform some of its other functions over those pins. For example, the ALE signal (address latch enable) is generated by the 8288, thereby permitting the 8088 to use its ALE pin to perform a function that it previously had to keep hidden. An example of a signal that the 8088 is able to send out in maximum mode but must keep hidden in minimum mode is a LOCK signal (discussed in Chap. 3), which permits several processors to execute at the same time over the same buses without stepping on each other's toes.

Figure 5.19 shows an example of a maximum mode 8088 system. The 8088 uses pins S_0, S_1, and S_2 to let the 8288 know what's going on. Notice the ALE, DT/R, DEN, and INTA signals that came off the 8088 in minimum mode now come off the 8288. Furthermore, the IO/$\overline{\text{M}}$, RD, and WR signals that came off the 8088 have been functionally replaced with the MRDC (memory read command), MWTC (memory write command), IORC (input/output read command), and IOWC (input/output write command). This separation of memory read and write signals from input/output read and write signals makes it easier to distinguish between a memory instruction and an input/output instruction. You will recall that in Fig. 5.14 we avoided making that distinction by using memory-mapped I/O.

The output of the 8284A clock generator is fed into the 8288. This makes it possible for the 8288 to generate such signals as ALE or DEN at the correct number of clock pulses after the address or data has been placed on the bus. The S_0, and S_1, and S_2 signals let the 8288 know when such things are placed on the bus.

The data transceiver and the third address latch are usually not optional in maximum systems and hence were not drawn dotted in Fig. 5.19.

Summary

This chapter has shown how the 8088 can be combined with other circuit components to form a complete system. The components described here have been designed to be used together with a minimum of interconnecting circuitry. Additional components in the 8088 family are desribed in the *Intel MCS-86 User's Manual*.

Once a system has been designed and built, it must be programmed. This is the topic of the next three chapters.

6

8086
Assembly-Language
Programming

In the previous chapters we learned what an 8086 is composed of and how an 8086 can be put together with other components to form a complete system. But now that we have such a system, we need to be able to write a program that such a system will execute. The remainder of this book will show how to write such programs.

Object Code and Source Code

Let's start by considering a very simple program. All the program does is read in word values from input port 5, increment each value read, and write the results to output port 2. The program is as follows:

Memory Address (Hexadecimal)	Memory Contents (Binary)	Comments
00000	11100101	read word into AX . . .
00001	00000101	. . . from input port 5
00002	01000000	increment AX
00003	11100111	write word from AX. . .
00004	00000010	. . . to output port 2
00005	11101011	repeat by jumping . . .
00006	11111001	. . . back seven bytes
00007	. . .	

The first two columns specify the address and contents of each relevant memory location and, as such, constitute the only form of the program comprehensible to the processor. This is often referred to as *object code,* and the language of 1's and 0's in which the object code is written is called *machine language.* Once we have the program in object code form, we can place it in memory and then have the 8086 execute it.

All the information needed to write the 8086 object code of any program is found in Chaps. 2 and 3. This information is the format of each instruction and

Fig. 6.1 The translation process.

Fig. 6.2 Assemblers and compilers.

the encodings that go into each field of each instruction. So, in theory at least, we could end the discussion of programming right here.

Practically speaking, writing a program in terms of 1's and 0's is a tedious, repetitive, error-prone task. Ironically, these are the kinds of tasks that computers are very good at performing. So, instead of trying to write the program in the language of the machine, it makes more sense to write the program in a language more familiar to us and then use a computer to translate it into the 8086's language. A program written in this more familiar language is called *source code*, and the computer program that translates source code into object code is called a *translator*. This is illustrated in Fig. 6.1.

There are two distinct kinds of languages in which we could write our source code. These are called *assembly languages* and *high-level languages* and are described below. The corresponding translators are called *assemblers* and *compilers* as illustrated in Fig. 6.2.

The process of translation might involve performing some final cleanup activities before the output is truly machine code. These cleanup activities are part of the translation process but, unfortunately, have been given distinctive names like *relocation* and *linkage*. Throughout this text, references to the translation process (assembling, compiling) will imply all necessary cleanup activities as well.

A program written in assembly language is a symbolic representation of the machine-language program. The relation between the statements in an assembly-language program and the resulting object code is usually very obvious. A high-level language, on the other hand, is a formalized, unambiguous dialect of some so-called natural language (typically English). The relation between statements in a high-level language and the resulting object code is often not obvious. Assembly language gives you complete control over the resulting object code and thereby allows you to generate very efficient object code (providing you're a very efficient programmer). A high-level language frees you from having to think about the resulting object code and allows you to concentrate on the task you are trying to program. You are at the mercy of the compiler as far as generating efficient object code is concerned. But a very good compiler can sometimes generate more efficient object code than you could have done by writing in assembly language, especially if you're not skilled at generating efficient code (it's nothing to be ashamed of; most of us aren't).

The remainder of this chapter describes ASM-86, an assembly language for the 8086. Chapters 7 and 8 describe two high-level languages available for the 8086—namely PL/M-86 and Pascal. These three chapters are presented in a parallel fashion, using the same organization of material as much as possible. The chapters were written to be independent of each other so that any one could be read first.

Symbolic Names

The primary advantage of using assembly language instead of machine language is the ability to use symbolic names. Let's illustrate this point by rewriting the example of the previous section, this time using assembly-language source code.

```
CYCLE:    IN       AX,5        ;read word from port 5 into AX
          INC      AX          ;increment AX
          OUT      2,AX        ;write result to port 2
          JMP      CYCLE       ;keep repeating
```

The above program is simpler to read and understand because it uses symbolic names instead of numbers as much as possible. For example, the opcodes of the four instructions are 1110010-, 01000---, 1110011-, and 11101011 in the object code, whereas they are IN, INC, OUT, and JMP in the assembly-language source code. Such symbolic names for opcodes are called *instruction mnemonics*. The symbolic opcode names introduced in Chap. 3 and used throughout this book are, in fact, the instruction mnemonics of ASM-86. The ASM-86 assembler can recognize these instruction mnemonics and generate the corresponding bit patterns in the object code.

Besides the opcode fields, there are other fields in the object code. The contents of each of these fields must somehow be specified in the assembly-language source code so that the assembler can generate the appropriate bit patterns in the object code. For example, the INC instruction has a 3-bit **reg** field, indicating which register is to be incremented when the instruction is executed. The contents of this **reg** field are specified in the source code by indicating the symbolic name of the register, as in "INC AX." The symbolic register names used in ASM-86 are the names that have been used for the registers throughout this book—namely AX, BX, CX, DX, AL, BL, CL, DL, AH, BH, CH, DH, BP, SP, SI, DI, CS, DS, ES, and SS.

Both the IN and OUT instructions have a 1-bit **w** field and an 8-bit port-number field. The port numbers are specified in the source code in a very straightforward manner by "IN AX,5" and "OUT 2,AX." The **w** field is specified in a more subtle manner by the presence of the AX in "IN AX,5" and "OUT 2,AX." Recall that input and output always use the accumulator and, in particular, use AX when words are involved and AL when bytes are involved. So the appearance of AX instead of AL in the IN and OUT instructions indicates that the **w** field is a 1. (The ASM-86 convention is to place the destination before the source; hence AX precedes port number on the IN instruction and follows it on the OUT instruction.)

Another example of a symbolic name in the above program is the label CYCLE on the IN instruction. This permits the JMP instruction to refer to the location of the IN instruction by name as in "JUMP CYCLE." The assembler now has enough information to determine that this is a jump backwards of seven bytes and can generate a −7 in the appropriate field of the JMP instruction.

A Complete Program

In the previous section, we wrote a fragment of an ASM-86 program. To make that fragment into a complete program, we need to add some additional statements:

1. IN_AND_OUT	SEGMENT		;start of segment
2.	ASSUME	CS: IN_AND_OUT	;that's what's in CS
3. CYCLE:	IN	AX,5	
4.	INC	AX	
5.	OUT	2,AX	
6.	JMP	CYCLE	
7. IN_AND_OUT	ENDS		;end of segment
8.	END	CYCLE	;end of assembly

This entire program will reside in a single segment in the 8086 memory. During the assembly process, we don't know (nor do we care) where that segment will be located. That decision will be made later, before the segment is actually loaded into memory and the code executed. During the assembly process, we will be content to refer to the starting address of the segment by the symbolic name IN_AND_OUT. Lines 1 and 7 delimit the extent of the segment; line 1 introduces the segment named IN_AND_OUT, and line 7 marks the *end* of the segment (ENDS).

Line 8 flags the end of the source program, thereby telling the assembler that there are no more lines to assemble. Furthermore, it indicates that when the program is executed, it should start with the instruction labeled CYCLE (line 3). The object code generated by the assembler, besides containing the contents of all the relevant memory locations, also contains this starting address.

The ASSUME statement on line 2 is a bit harder to explain. I wish I could give you a good reason for having it. Unfortunately, I can't. Instead, I'll just state the following rule: prior to or at the very beginning of any segment containing code, we must tell the assembler what it should assume will be in the CS register when that code is executed. As far as we're concerned, this will always be the starting address (without the last four "0" bits) of the segment, and so we must include the statement:

ASSUME   CS: Name—of—segment

It is beyond the scope of this book to explain (1) why the assembler needs to know this and (2) why the assembler can't just look at the beginning of the segment and see the name.

Structure of ASM-86 Programs

Let's now consider a more detailed ASM-86 program and then try to deduce the structure of such programs in general. This program will be referred to as the "sample program" throughout this chapter.

```
 1. MY—DATA      SEGMENT                                    ;data segment
 2. SUM          DB          ?                              ;reserve a byte for SUM
 3. MY—DATA      ENDS
 4. MY—CODE      SEGMENT                                    ;code segment
 5.              ASSUME      CS:MY—CODE, DS:MY—DATA
                                                            ;contents of CS and DS
 6. PORT—VAL     EQU         3                              ;symbolic name for port number
 7. GO:          MOV         AX,MY—DATA                     ;initialize DS to MY—DATA
 8.              MOV         DS,AX
 9.              MOV         SUM,0                           ;clear sum
10. CYCLE:       CMP         SUM,100                         ;if SUM exceeds 100
11.              JNA         NOT—DONE
12.              MOV         AL,SUM                          ;. . . then output SUM to port 3
13.              OUT         PORT—VAL,AL
14.              HLT                                         ;. . . and stop execution
15. NOT—DONE:    IN          AL,PORT—VAL                     ;otherwise add next input
16.              ADD         SUM,AL
17.              JMP         CYCLE                           ;and repeat the test
18. MY—CODE      ENDS
19.              END         GO                              ;end of assembly
```

Line 1 introduces a segment somewhere in the 8086 memory (we don't care where) and gives it the name MY—DATA. Line 3 ends the segment. The only thing in the segment is SUM, which is defined to be a *byte* (DB) of data. The question mark on line 2 indicates that the generated object code needs to reserve a place in memory for SUM, but it need not specify any particular intitial contents for that location. MY—DATA is apparently going to be used as a data segment.

Line 4 introduces another segment and gives it the name MY—CODE. This segment extends all the way to line 18. An examination of lines 7 to 17 reveals that the segment contains instructions, so we apparently intend to use it as a code segment. Line 19 flags the end of the source program and indicates that, when the program is executed, execution should start with the instruction labeled GO (line 7).

The ASSUME statement on line 5 tells the assembler what it should assume will be in the CS and DS register when the segment of code is executed. We've already discussed the need for the assumption on CS. The need for making an assumption about what's in DS is more believable. Since some assembly-language instructions in the code segment access data directly (in particular, the byte SUM), the assembler must generate machine-language instructions that address SUM using the direct addressing mode (remember the operand-addressing modes introduced in Chap. 2?). These generated instructions must specify (1) the offset of SUM and (2) some segment register, typically DS, containing the starting address of the segment (namely MY—DATA) containing SUM. The assembler needs to know which segment registers (if any) will contain MY—DATA's starting address at the time these instructions are executed. With this information, the assembler can determine if a segment-overriding prefix is required on these instructions (as would be the case if, for example, MY—DATA's starting address were contained only in ES) and, if so, which segment register should be specified by the prefix. Furthermore, if none of the registers will contain MY—DATA's starting address at instruction-execution time, the assembler knows that it cannot generate any instructions capable of accessing SUM and will be able to report this error to us at instruction-assembly time.

So now we know why we had to assume that some segment register would contain MY—DATA's starting address at instruction-execution time (so that SUM can be accessed) and why it is nice to assume that DS would be the one (so no segment-overriding prefix is necessary). But now we need to make sure that this assumption is satisfied. We insure this by executing certain instructions (lines 7 and 8) prior to the first access to SUM.

Line 6 specifies that PORT—VAL is *equi*valent to the constant 3. This permits PORT—VAL to be used in place of 3 on succeeding lines. The intent here is to make PORT—VAL a symbolic name for port 3 and refer to PORT—VAL whenever port 3 is wanted. Now if we decide to rewrite the program next month so that it uses port 4 instead, we have to make only one change—namely line 6 is changed to:

PORT—VAL EQU 4

The instructions on lines 7 through 17 will keep adding inputs from port 3 until the sum exceeds 100 and will then output that sum to port 3 and halt. On a line-by-line basis, this is accomplished as follows. The instruction on line 7 puts (the 16 most significant bits of) the starting address of segment MY—DATA into register AX, and on line 8 this value is moved from AX to DS. This will make SUM accessible in succeeding instructions. The instruction on line 9 initializes SUM to 0. Observe that on lines 7, 8, and 9, the destinations (such as SUM on line 9) are always written before the sources (such as 0 on line 9). Line 10 compares (CMP) the value in SUM to 100 and sets the processor flags to indicate the result of the comparison. Line 11 tests the flags and *jumps* if SUM was *not above* 100 (JNA). The target of the jump is the instruction labeled NOT—DONE (line 15). If the jump on line 11 is not taken (SUM exceeds 100), the SUM will be moved into AL (line 12), the contents of AL will be sent to output port 3 (line 13), and the processor will halt (line 14). If the jump on line 11 is taken (SUM does not exceed 100), the value on input port 3 will be sent to AL (line 15), added to SUM (line 16), and the jump on line 17 will transfer control back to line 10.

Now, from the above example, let's try to generalize about the structure of an ASM-86 program. It consists of one or more segment blocks followed by an END statement. Each segment block starts with a SEGMENT statement and ends with an ENDS (end-of-segment) statement. Between the SEGMENT and ENDS statements is a sequence of other statements. Each statement normally occupies one line (if succeeding lines are needed, they start with "&"). The structure of an ASM-86 program is shown below:

```
NAME1        SEGMENT
             statement
                .
                .
                .
             statement
NAME1        ENDS
NAME2        SEGMENT
             statement
                .
                .
                .
             statement
NAME2        ENDS

                .
                .
                .
             END
```

The programs presented here all display a consistent tabular pattern. Such tabulation is not part of the program structure. It is purely optional as far as the assembler is concerned but is highly recommended to make the programs easier for us to read and understand. As an example of this point, consider the following untabulated version of the IN__AND__OUT program. It would present no additional difficulty to the assembler (in fact it would assemble faster) but would be much less comprehensible to us.

```
IN__AND__OUT SEGMENT ;start of segment
ASSUME CS:IN__AND__OUT ;that's what's in CS
CYCLE:IN AX,5
INC AX
OUT 2,AX
JUMP CYCLE
IN__AND__OUT ENDS ;end of segment
END CYCLE ;end of assembly
```

Tokens

Before examining the kinds of statements from which ASM-86 programs are built, we must become familiar with the building blocks of statements. Statements are composed of such things as *identifiers, reserved words, delim-*

Table 6.1 Reserved words in ASM-86

A. Instruction Mnemonics

AAA	CLD	ESC	JAE	JNA	JNP	LDS	MOV	POPF	RET	STC
AAD	CLI	HLT	JB	JNAE	JNS	LEA	MOVS	PUSH	ROL	STD
AAM	CMC	IDIV	JBE	JNB	JNZ	LES	MUL	PUSHF	ROR	STI
AAS	CMP	IMUL	JCXZ	JNBE	JO	LOCK	NEG	RCL	SAHF	STOS
ADC	CMPS	IN	JE	JNE	JP	LODS	NIL	RCR	SAL	SUB
ADD	CWD	INC	JG	JNG	JPE	LOOP	NOP	REP	SAR	TEST
AND	DAA	INT	JGE	JNGE	JPO	LOOPE	NOT	REPE	SBB	WAIT
CALL	DAS	INTO	JL	JNL	JS	LOOPNE	OR	REPNE	SCAS	XCHG
CBW	DEC	IRET	JLE	JNLE	JZ	LOOPNZ	OUT	REPNZ	SHL	XLAT
CLC	DIV	JA	JMP	JNO	LAHF	LOOPZ	POP	REPZ	SHR	XOR

B. Register Names

AH	BL	CL	DI	ES
AL	BP	CS	DL	SI
AX	BX	CX	DS	SP
BH	CH	DH	DX	SS

C. Directives

ASSUME	END	EXTRN	NOSEGFIX	PUBLIC
CODEMACRO	ENDM	GROUP	ORG	PURGE
DB	ENDP	LABEL	PROC	RECORD
DD	ENDS	MODRM	RELB	SEGFIX
DW	EQU	NAME	RELW	SEGMENT

D. Miscellaneous

ABS	EQ	INPAGE	MASK	NOTHING	PROCLEN	STACK
AT	FAR	LE	MEMORY	OFFSET	PTR	THIS
BYTE	GE	LENGTH	MOD	PAGE	SEG	TYPE
COMMON	GT	LOW	NE	PARA	SHORT	WIDTH
DUP	HIGH	LT	NEAR	PREFIX	SIZE	

iters, constants, and *comments.* These building blocks are sometimes called *tokens.*

Identifiers   Identifiers are names that you, the programmer, are free to make up. Examples of identifiers in the sample program are SUM, CYCLE, and PORT_VAL. An identifier is a sequence of letters, numbers, and underscore characters (_) but may not start with a number. An identifier may be up to 31 characters long, which means that, for all practical purposes, the length is unlimited. Examples of identifiers are given below:

```
X
GAMMA
JACK5
THIS_NODE
THISNODE
```

The last two examples are indeed different identifiers.

Reserved Words   Reserved words look like identifiers, but they have a special meaning in the language, and you may not use them as identifier names. In our sample program, we saw such reserved words as SEGMENT, MOV, EQU, and AL. Thus it would be perfectly acceptable for us to make up a name like EQUAL as in

```
EQUAL    DB    ?
```

but it would be improper for us to write

```
EQU    DB    ?
```

A complete list of ASM-86 reserved words is given in Table 6.1.

Delimiters   Delimiters are the non-alphanumeric characters that have special meaning in the 8086 assembly language. In our sample program, we saw such delimiters as : and ;. In this chapter we will become exposed to many of the delimiters. A complete list of delimiters in ASM-86 is given in Table 6.2.

Constants   Constants are the fixed values appearing in ASM-86 programs. In our sample program we saw such constants as 0, 3, and 100. These are *whole-number constants.* The assembly language also allows for *string constants.*

A whole-number constant can be any non-fractional number between 0 and 65535 (that is $2^{16} - 1$). It is normally written as a decimal number but can also be written in binary (ending with a B), octal (ending with a Q), or hexadecimal

Table 6.2 Delimiters in ASM-86

'	;	<	$	*
,	:	>	=	/
(	.	[	–	?
)	&	]	+	

(ending with an H). To avoid confusion with identifiers, a hexadecimal constant must start with a numeric digit; a leading zero would suffice. Examples of whole-number constants are 15, 1010B, 27Q, 3A0H, and 0BFA3H.

A string constant is a sequence of one or two characters enclosed within apostrophes. (Strings of more than two characters are permitted in very restricted cases and will not be discussed in this text.) An apostrophe itself may be included in a string constant by writing it as two consecutive apostrophes. Examples of string constants are 'A', 'AB', and ''''. The last example is the string consisting of the apostrophe character. The value of a string constant is the ASCII code of the character(s) in the string (see Appendix C for the ASCII codes). For example, the value of 'A' is the same as 41H (both have the value 65), and the value of 'AB' is the same as 4142H. Thus string constants and whole-number constants can be used interchangeably.

Comments Comments are any sequence of characters following a semicolon (;) up to the end of the line. They have no meaning to the assembler but should be used generously in your program to keep reminding you of what you are doing. For although comments like

```
INC     CX      ;increment CS
```

convey little information, comments like

```
INC     CX      ;prepare count for next iteration
```

go a long way to making a program more readable.

Expressions

One more building block, namely expressions, must be introduced before we can build statements. Expressions are built up from some of the tokens just described.

Loosely speaking, an expression is a sequence of *operands* and *operators* that can be combined to produce a value at the time the program is being assembled. So now we must introduce both operands and operators and indicate how they are combined to produce the value of an expression.

Operands An operand is something that has a value. There are two kinds of values that an operand might have—a numeric value and a memory address value.

Operands that have numeric values are constants or are identifiers that represent constants. Some numeric-valued operands appearing in our sample program are 100 and PORT_VAL. The permissible range of values for such operands is from −65,535 to +65,535.

Note that the value of an operand may be negative, but a constant is never negative. A minus sign can be written in front of a constant but is never considered as part of the constant; it is an arithmetic operator.

Memory-address operands are frequently identifiers such as SUM and CYCLE in the sample program. The value of a memory address is not simply a number; it is a set of components, each component generally being a number. One component is the 16 most significant bits of the starting address of the segment in which the memory address is contained (the four least significant bits of a segment starting address are always zeros). Another component is the offset of the memory address within the segment. These two components are referred to as the *segment* and *offset* of the memory-address operand.

Another operand is an expression itself, perhaps enclosed in parentheses, and used in some bigger expression such as in 3*(PORT__VAL + 5).

Operators An operator takes the value of one or more operands and produces a new value. There are five kinds of operators in ASM-86—*arithmetic operators, logical operators, relational operators, analytic operators,* and *synthetic operators.*

Arithmetic operators are nothing more than the familiar addition operator (+), subtraction operator (−), multiplication operator (*), and division operator(/). Another arithmetic operator, MOD, produces the remainder that results after doing a division. Thus 19/7 is 2, whereas 19 MOD 7 is 5.

Arithmetic operators may always be applied to a pair of numeric operands, and the result will be a numeric value. The rules for applying arithmetic operators on memory-addressing operands are quite a bit more restrictive. These rules can be summarized by saying that such operations are valid only if the result has a meaningful physical interpretation. For example, the product of two memory addresses has no meaningful interpretation (what segment would it be in? what offset would it have?) and hence is a prohibited operation. The difference of two memory addresses in the same segment, on the other hand, is meaningfully interpreted as the distance between them (difference in their offsets) and is simply a numeric value. The only other meaningful arithmetic operation involving a memory address is adding or subtracting a numeric value to or from it. The result is another memory address having the same segment but whose offset is the original offset increased or decreased by the numeric value. Thus SUM+2, CYCLE-5, and NOT__DONE-GO would all be valid expressions in our sample program, whereas SUM-CYCLE would not (they are in different segments). It should be emphasized that the value of SUM+2 is a memory address two bytes beyond SUM in the MY__DATA segment; it is *not* the numeric value that is 2 plus the contents of location SUM (such contents would not be known until the program is executed, whereas expressions are evaluated when the program is assembled).

The logical operators are the usual bit-by-bit AND, OR, XOR (exclusive-or), and NOT. The operands of logical operators must be numeric (memory-address operands are not allowed), and the result will be numeric. For example,

```
1010101010101010B AND 1100110011001100B is 1000100010001000B;
1100110011001100B OR 1111000011110000B is 1100000011000000B;
NOT 1111111111111111B is 0000000000000000B;
```
and
```
1111000011110000B XOR SUM is invalid.
```

As an example of logical operators, consider the following statements:

```
IN          AL,PORT__VAL
OUT         PORT__VAL AND 0FEH,AL
```

Execution of the IN instruction will fetch input from port PORT__VAL, wherever that is. Execution of the OUT instruction will send output to port PORT__VAL AND 0FEH, which is either the same port (if PORT__VAL is even) or the next lower-numbered port (if PORT__VAL is odd). The actual value of the port of the OUT instruction is determined when the instruction is assembled, not when it is executed.

Observe that AND, OR, XOR, and NOT are instruction mnemonics as well as ASM-86 operators. As ASM-86 operators, they cause a value to be computed when the program is being assembled. As instruction mnemonics, they perform their roles when the program is being executed. For example,

```
AND         DX,PORT__VAL AND 0FEH
```

will cause the assembler to compute the value of PORT__VAL AND 0FEH and then generate an AND-immediate instruction containing that value in its data field. When this instruction is later executed, it will cause the contents of the DX register to be ANDed with that value and the result placed in the DX register.

The relational operators are equal (EQ), not-equal (NE), less-than (LT), greater-than (GT), less-than-or-equal (LE), greater-than-or-equal (GE). An example would be PORT__VAL LT 5. The two operands must both be numeric or must both be memory addresses in the same segment. The result is always a numeric value and will be 0 if the relationship is false and 0FFFFH (16 bits of 1's) if the relationship is true.

An example of using a relational operator is shown:

```
MOV         BX,PORT__VAL LT 5
```

The assembler will assemble the instruction for

```
MOV         BX,0FFFFH
```

if the value of PORT__VAL is less than 5; otherwise the assembler will assemble the instruction for

```
MOV         BX,0
```

At first it may appear that there isn't much utility for relational operators because it's not often that you would want to generate an instruction with a field that contains either 0 or 0FFFFH and no other choices. However, by combining the relational operators with the logical operators, the two relational results of 0 and 0FFFFH can be molded into any numeric values you desire. For example,

```
MOV         BX,((PORT__VAL LT 5) AND 20) OR ((PORT__VAL GE 5) AND 30)
```

will assemble into

```
MOV         BX,20
```

if PORT__VAL is less than 5, and into

```
MOV      BX,30
```

otherwise. Note the generous use of parentheses to force the order in which the operators are applied. If you're always using parentheses to make the ordering explicit, you'll never have to memorize a bunch of "silly" rules about which operators get evaluated first.

The analytic operators are used to decompose memory-address operands into their components, and the synthetic operators are used to build memory-address operands from their components. A discussion of these operators will be presented after we learn more about memory-address operands.

Statements

There are two kinds of statements that can appear in an ASM-86 program—namely *instruction statements* (MOV, ADD, JMP, etc.) and *directive statements* (DB, SEGMENT, EQU, etc.). Each instruction statement causes the assembler to generate an instruction in the resulting object code. The directive statements tell the assembler what kind of code to generate for succeeding instruction statements. For example, the directive statement

```
MY__PLACE      DB      ?
```

tells the assembler that MY__PLACE is defined to be a byte. The assembler allocates a memory address for MY__PLACE. Later, when the assembler encounters the instruction statement

```
INC      MY__PLACE
```

it will generate an instruction in the object code to increment the contents of MY__PLACE. Because of the previously encountered directive statement, the assembler will know to place a '0' (to indicate a byte) in the w field of the increment instruction.

The formats of the two kinds of statements are similar. The instruction statements are of the form

```
label:     mnemonic     argument,...,argument     ;comment
```

whereas the directive statements are of the form

```
name     directive     argument,...,argument     ;comment
```

Observe that the label in an instruction statement is followed by a colon whereas the name in a directive statement is not. This highlights the difference between the two kinds of statements. A label associates a symbolic name with the location of an instruction and can be used as an operand in some jump or call instruction. The name in a directive statement has no relation to an instruction location and can never be jumped to. Labels in instruction statements are always optional; names in directive statements can be mandatory, optional, or prohibited depending on the particular directive.

Mnemonics in instruction statements and directives in directive statements specify the purpose of the statement. The instruction mnemonics correspond to the set of approximately 100 opcodes available in the 8086, and the directives correspond to the set of some 20 functions provided by the ASM-86 assembler (see Table 5.1). The particular mnemonic or directive may require that additional information be provided to define its purpose completely. This information is provided by a sequence of *arguments*.

Comments in statements are used to make the program more readable. Comments are always optional, but when present, they must be preceded by a semicolon for identification purposes.

Directive Statements

The various directive statements in ASM-86 are *symbol-definition statements*, *data-definition statements*, *segmentation-definition statements*, *procedure-definition statements*, and *termination statements*. Each of these statements will be described in this section.

Symbol-Definition Statements
The EQU statement provides a means for defining symbolic names to represent values or other symbolic names. The two forms of the EQU statement are illustrated:

```
name          EQU        expression
new_name      EQU        old_name
```

Some examples are as follows:

```
BOILING_POINT        EQU        212
BUFFER_SIZE          EQU        32
NEW_PORT             EQU        PORT_VAL+1
COUNT                EQU        CX
```

The last example differs from the other three in that COUNT does not represent a value; it is a synonym for the CX register.

A symbolic name can be "undefined" by a PURGE statement so that it may later be used to represent something entirely different.

```
PURGE        BUFFER_SIZE
```

Data-Definition Statements
A data-definition statement allocates memory for a data item, associates a symbolic name with that memory address, and optionally supplies an initial value for the data. Symbolic names associated with data items are called *variables*. Examples of data-definition statements are as follows:

```
THING              DB     ?        ;defines a byte
BIGGER_THING       DW     ?        ;defines a word (2 bytes)
BIGGEST_THING      DD     ?        ;defines a doubleword (4 bytes)
```

In the above examples, THING is a symbolic name associated with a byte in memory, BIGGER_THING with two consecutive bytes in memory, and BIGGEST_THING with four consecutive bytes in memory.

Before we can discuss the question marks (?), we need to introduce the concept of initial values of data items. The object code produced by the assembler contains the 1's and 0's that make up each instruction and the memory address at which each instruction should reside. After the object code is produced, the instructions are loaded into memory at the indicated addresses and then executed. At the time the instructions are loaded, initial values for data items could also be loaded into memory. This means that the object code, besides containing instructions and their addresses, would also contain initial values for data items and their addresses. These initial values are specified to the assembler in the data definition statements. The following statement will cause the assembler to produce object code that, when loaded into memory, will result in a 25 being placed in the memory address allocated to THING:

```
THING     DB      25       ;byte initially contains 25
```

A question mark in place of an initial value means that we do not choose to specify an initial value for that data item; we will be satisfied with whatever initially appears in the corresponding memory location. When the assembler sees the question mark, it still allocates memory for the data item, but it is not required to produce object code to initialize the memory location (although it may very well do so).

In general, the initial value could be specified by an expression since expressions are evaluated at the time the program is assembled. So we can write statements like:

```
IN_PORT      DB      PORT_VAL
OUT_PORT     DB      PORT_VAL+1
```

You will recall that expressions come in two varieties—numeric and memory address. It is certainly meaningful to initialize either a byte or a word with a numeric value. But what about a memory-address value? It will never fit into a byte, so forget about that. But the offset component will fit nicely into a word, and both the offset and segment components will fit into a double word. So we can write initialization statements like:

```
LITTLE_CYCLE     DW      CYCLE       ;offset of CYCLE
BIG_CYCLE        DD      CYCLE       ;offset and segment of CYCLE
         .
         .
         .
CYCLE:           MOV     BX,AX
```

The above initialization on LITTLE_CYCLE would permit an indirect intrasegment jump or call to use the data item named LITTLE_CYCLE in order to transfer control to the label named CYCLE. Similarly, an intersegment jump or call could transfer control to CYCLE by using the data item named BIG_CYCLE.

So far we have used data-definition statements to define a single byte (or word or double word) at a time. We frequently have occasions to deal with tables of bytes (or words or double words). For example, the 8086 XLAT instruction uses a table of bytes to translate an encoded value into the same value under a different encoding. The 8086 interrupt mechanism uses a table of double words starting at memory location 0 to point to the starting addresses of the interrupt service routines. And the 8086 string instructions operate on tables of bytes or words containing the string elements.

A table is defined by placing several initial values on a data-definition statement. The following statement defines a table of bytes containing powers of 2:

```
POWERS__2      DB        1,2,4,8,16
```

The byte at the memory address corresponding to POWERS__2 will be initialized to 1 (when the object code is loaded into memory), and the next four bytes will be initialized to 2, 4, 8, and 16 respectively. A table of bytes, all initialized to zero, can be defined by

```
ALL__ZERO      DB        0,0,0,0,0,0
```

or by the shorthand notation

```
ALL__ZERO      DB        6 DUP (0)
```

And, finally, an uninitialized table can be defined by either of the following equivalent statements:

```
DONT__CARE     DB        ?,?,?,?,?,?,?,?
DONT__CARE     DB        8 DUP (?)
```

Types of Memory Locations   ASM-86 associates a *type* with every memory location referred to in the program. The assembler, by being constantly aware of the type of each memory location, can generate the correct code when it encounters an instruction that accesses a memory location. For example, the data-definition statement

```
SUM      DB      ?
```

informs the assembler that the memory location SUM is of type BYTE. Later, when the assembler encounters an instruction statement such as

```
INC      SUM
```

the assembler will know to generate a byte-increment instruction rather than a word-increment instruction.

A memory location can be one of the following types:

1. BYTE of data, as in:

```
SUM                 DB        ?        ;defining a byte
```

2. WORD of data (two consecutive bytes), as in:

```
BIGGER__SUM         DW        ?        ;defining a word
```

3. DWORD of data (four consecutive bytes), as in:

    BIGGEST__SUM   DD   ?   ;defining a doubleword

4. NEAR instruction location, as in:

    CYCLE: CMP   SUM,100

5. FAR instruction location:
    (means of defining such locations will be discussed shortly)

An instruction location can appear in a jump or call instruction statement. The assembler will generate an intrasegment jump or call if the type of the location is NEAR and an intersegment jump or call if it is FAR. For example, the labeled instruction statement

CYCLE: CMP   SUM,100

informs the assembler that the memory location CYCLE is of type NEAR. (We will see shortly how the synthetic operators PTR and THIS can be used to define a memory location of type FAR.) Later, when the assembler encounters an instruction such as

JMP   CYCLE

the assembler will know to generate an intrasegment jump instruction rather than an intersegment jump instruction.

A memory address built by adding or subtracting a numeric value to or from some other memory address has the same type as the original memory address. For example, SUM+2 is another BYTE, BIGGER__SUM−3 a WORD, and CYCLE+1 a NEAR instruction location.

Analytic and Synthetic Operators   We now know enough about memory addresses to finish up the discussion of operators. The analytic operators are used to decompose memory-address operands into their components. These operators are SEG, OFFSET, TYPE, SIZE, and LENGTH.

The SEG operator returns the segment component of the memory-address operand, and the OFFSET operator returns the offset component. Both of these components are generally numeric values.

The TYPE operator returns a numeric value, which is the type component of the memory-address operand. The value of the type component for the various memory-address operands is as follows:

Memory-Address Operand	Type Component
BYTE of data	1
WORD of data	2
DWORD of data	4
NEAR instruction location	−1
FAR instruction location	−2

Notice that the type component for bytes, words, and double words corresponds to the number of bytes that each occupies. The value of the type component for instruction locations does not have a physical interpretation.

The LENGTH and SIZE operators are applicable only with data-memory-address operands (BYTE, WORD, or DWORD). The LENGTH operator returns a numeric value, which is the number of units (bytes, words, or double words) associated with the memory-address operand. The SIZE operator returns a numeric value, which is the total number of bytes allocated for the memory-address operand. For example, if MULTI__WORDS is defined by

```
MULTI__WORDS        DW        50 DUP (0)
```

then LENGTH MULTI__WORDS is 50 and SIZE MULTI__WORDS is 100. Notice that SIZE X is equal to (LENGTH X) * (TYPE X).

The synthetic operators are used to build memory-address operands from their components. These operators are PTR and THIS.

The PTR operator builds a memory-address operand that has the same segment and offset of some other memory-address operand but has a different type. Unlike a data-definition statement, the PTR operator does not allocate any memory; it merely gives another meaning to previously allocated memory. For example, if TWO__BYTE were defined by

```
TWO__BYTE        DW        ?
```

then we could give a name to the first byte in the word as follows:

```
ONE__BYTE        EQU        BYTE PTR TWO__BYTE
```

In this example, the PTR operator has created a new memory-address operand having the same segment and offset components as TWO__BYTE but having a type component of BYTE. We can name the second byte of TWO__BYTE either as

```
OTHER__BYTE        EQU        BYTE PTR (TWO__BYTE+1)
```

or more simply as

```
OTHER__BYTE        EQU        ONE__BYTE+1
```

The PTR operator can also be used to create words and double words as illustrated below:

```
MANY__BYTES          DB      100 DUP (?)              ;an array of 100 bytes
FIRST__WORD          EQU     WORD PTR MANY__BYTES
SECOND__DOUBLE       EQU     DWORD PTR (MANY__BYTES+4)
```

And, furthermore, the PTR operator can be used to create locations of instructions as illustrated below:

```
INCHES:     CMP     SUM,100                    ;type of INCHES is NEAR
            .
            .
            .
```

```
        JMP     INCHES                  ;intrasegment jump
                  .
                  .
                  .
MILES   EQU     FAR PTR INCHES          ;type of MILES is FAR
        JMP     MILES                   ;intersegment jump
```

Notice that the above examples illustrate ways to build new memory-address operands from old ones by (1) using the PTR operator as in BYTE PTR TWO__BYTE, (2) using arithmetic operators as in ONE__BYTE + 1, and (3) using a combination of PTR and arithmetic operators as in BYTE PTR (TWO__BYTE + 1). Arithmetic operators are useful when we wish to change the offset component but leave the type component unchanged. The PTR operator is useful when we wish to change the type component but leave the offset component unchanged. Neither arithmetic operators nor PTR changes the segment component. And the new memory-address operand, created by either arithmetic operators or PTR, will have a length component of 1 (providing it's not an instruction location).

The synthetic operator THIS, like PTR, builds a memory-address operand of a specified type without allocating any memory for it. The segment and offset component of the new memory-address operand is the segment and offset of the next memory location available for allocation. For example,

```
                  .
                  .
                  .
MY__BYTE        EQU     THIS BYTE
MY__WORD        DW      ?
                  .
                  .
                  .
```

would create MY__BYTE with type component of BYTE and with the same segment and offset components as MY__WORD. In this example, MY__BYTE could have been built with the PTR operator instead as follows:

```
MY__BYTE        EQU     BYTE PTR MY__WORD
```

The THIS operator is very convenient for defining FAR instruction locations as in the following:

```
MILES   EQU     THIS FAR
        CMP     SUM,100
          .
          .
          .
        JMP     MILES
```

Note that the use of the THIS operator in the above example made it unnecesssary to have a NEAR instruction location with the same segment and offset as MILES. If we were to use the PTR operator instead of the THIS operator, such a NEAR instruction would have been necessary.

Segmentation-Definition Statements   The segmentation-definition
statements allow us to organize our program so that it uses the 8086 memory
segments. These directives are SEGMENT, ENDS, ASSUME, and ORG.

The SEGMENT and ENDS statements subdivide the assembly-language
source program into segments. Such segments correspond to the memory segments into which the resulting object code will eventually be loaded. The assembler is concerned with program segmentation for the following reasons:

1. Intrasegment jump and call instructions contain only the offset (16 bits)
   of the new location. Intersegment jump and call instructions must contain the segment (another 16 bits) in addition to the offset.
2. Data-accessing instructions that use the current data segment and current stack segment in the manner most optimal for the 8086 architecture
   contain only the offset (16 bits) of the data location. Any other instruction that accesses a data location within one of the four currently-
   addressable segments must contain a segment-overriding prefix
   (another eight bits) in addition to the offset. (''Current'' refers to when
   the instruction is executed, not assembled.)

Therefore, in order to assemble the correct object code, the assembler must be
aware not only of the segment structure of the program but also of which segments will be addressable (pointed at by segment registers) when various instructions are executed. This information is supplied by the ASSUME directive.

The following example shows how the SEGMENT, ENDS, and ASSUME
directives can be used to define a code, data, extra, and stack segment:

```
MY__DATA    SEGMENT
X           DB          ?
Y           DW          ?
Z           DD          ?
MY__DATA    ENDS

MY__EXTRA   SEGMENT
ALPHA       DB          ?
BETA        DW          ?
GAMMA       DD          ?
MY__EXTRA   ENDS

MY__STACK   SEGMENT
            DW          100 DUP (?)                    ;this is the stack
TOP         EQU         THIS WORD
MY__STACK   ENDS

MY__CODE    SEGMENT
            ASSUME      CS:MY__CODE,DX:MY__DATA
            ASSUME      ES:MY__EXTRA,SS:MY__STACK
START:      MOV         AX, MY__DATA                   ;initializes DX
            MOV         DS,AX
            MOV         AX,MY__EXTRA                   ;initializes ES
            MOV         ES,AX
```

```
        MOV     AX,MY__STACK                    ;initializes SS
        MOV     SS,AX
        MOV     SP,OFFSET TOP                   ;initializes SP
        .
        .
        .
MY__CODE    ENDS

        END     START
```

Observe that the code at the head of the MY__CODE segment will, at the time the program is executed, initialize the various segment registers to point to the appropriate segments (and will initialize the stack pointer to point to the end of the stack segment). The ASSUME statement makes the assembler aware of the values that will be in segment registers at the time the code is executed.

To illustrate the purpose of the ASSUME statement, let's consider code (within SEGMENT MY__CODE) that moves the contents of byte X to byte ALPHA. To do this, we need an instruction that moves the contents of X into a register, say BX, and an instruction that moves the contents of the register into ALPHA. How about:

```
MOV     BX,X            ;from X to BX
MOV     ALPHA,BX        ;from BX to ALPHA.
```

During the execution of such MOV instructions, the 8086 processor would normally look in the DS register to find the starting address of the segment in which the specified item (X or ALPHA) is located. This will work fine when accessing X (the first instruction) because DS will indeed contain the starting address of segment MY__DATA in which X is located. But this will not work when accessing ALPHA (the second instruction) because the starting address of segment MY__EXTRA in which ALPHA is located will not be contained in DS. The ASSUME statement has made the assembler aware that the first instruction will execute properly. The assembler is also aware (thanks to the ASSUME statement) that the starting address of MY__EXTRA, although not in DS, will be in one of the other segment registers—namely ES. The assembler, therefore, generates a segment-overriding prefix for the second instruction so that it too will execute properly.

It's not always possible for us to know what will be in the segment registers when a particular instruction will be executed. Consider the following example:

```
OLD__DATA   SEGMENT
OLD__BYTE   DB          ?
OLD__DATA   ENDS

NEW__DATA   SEGMENT
NEW__BYTE   DB          ?
NEW__DATA   ENDS
```

```
MORE__CODE    SEGMENT
              ASSUME    CS:MORE__CODE
              MOV       AX,OLD__DATA              ;put OLD__DATA into
              MOV       DS,AX                     ;. . .DS and
              MOV       ES,AX                     ;. . .ES
              ASSUME    DS:OLD__DATA,ES:OLD__DATA
                  .
                  .
                  .
CYCLE:        INC       OLD__BYTE                 ;what's in DS now?
                  .
                  .
                  .
              MOV       AX,NEW__DATA              ;put NEW__DATA
              MOV       DS,AX                     ;. . .into DS
              JMP       CYCLE
                  .
                  .
                  .
MORE__CODE    ENDS
```

The first time the INC instruction is executed, DS will contain OLD__DATA and the indicated assumption on DS will be correct. But then DS will become changed to NEW__DATA, and the same INC instruction will be executed a second time. Therefore, it would be wrong for the assembler to make any assumptions about the contents of DS when the INC instruction is executed; the assembler must generate a segment-override prefix (specifying the extra segment) on the INC instruction even though this prefix would be unnecessary on the first execution of INC. In order to tell the assembler not to make any assumptions about DS, we must place the following assumption just before the INC instruction:

```
                  .
                  .
                  .
              ASSUME    DS:NOTHING
CYCLE:        INC       OLD__BYTE
                  .
                  .
                  .
```

Prior to or at the very beginning of any segment containing code, we must tell the assembler (via an ASSUME statement) what it should assume will be in the CS register when that segment of code is executed. It is beyond the scope of this book to explain why ASM-86 requires this.

It is not absolutely essential to use an ASSUME statement to tell the assembler what will be in DS, ES, and SS. Instead, we could tell the assembler which segment register should be used for the execution of each instruction. For example, the move of X to ALPHA in the previous example could be written as:

```
MOV       BX, DS:X
MOV       ES:ALPHA,BX
```

This says that DS should be used when X is accessed, and ES should be used when ALPHA is accessed. Since the processor would normally use DS when executing these instructions, the assembler produces a segment-overriding prefix when generating object code for the second instruction but not for the first instruction.

Now let's look at one of the shortcomings of memory segments and see how we can get around it. Memory segments always start on 16-byte boundaries (remember that the last four bits of segment starting addresses are zero). A segment can be up to 2^{16} bytes long. If a segment doesn't use all of its approximately 65,000 bytes, some other segment can start just beyond the last byte used by the first segment. But the second segment must also start on a 16-byte boundary and, therefore, may not be able to start immediately after the last byte used by the first segment. This means there could be up to 15 bytes wasted between segments.

As an example, suppose the first segment starts at address 10000 (hexadecimal) and uses only 6D (hexadecimal) bytes. So the last byte used is at address 1006C. The earliest the second segment could start would be at address 10070, thereby wasting the bytes at 1006D, 1006E, and 1006F.

Now, instead of starting the second segment at the lowest 16-byte boundary beyond the last byte used by the first segment, we could start the second segment at the highest 16-byte boundary that does not cause any bytes to be wasted. So, in the previous example, we could start the second segment at address 10060. This will result in the last few bytes (13 to be exact) used by the first segment to be also in the second segment. But the second segment would then simply not use its first few bytes, and everybody would be happy. So, if the second segment starts at 10060, the bytes in the second segment below offset 000D would simply not be used by the second segment. Therefore, no bytes are wasted.

We usually don't care where in memory our segments are located, so we let the translator make that choice for us. However, we might want to give the translator some constraints such as "don't overlap this segment with any other segment," "make sure the first byte used by this segment is at an even address (so that word accesses can be done in a single memory reference)," or "start this segment at the following address." We can write these constraints into the source program as follows:

1. Don't overlap. First usable byte in segment is on a 16-byte boundary and has an offset of 0000.

```
MY_SEG      SEGMENT      ;this is the normal case
              .
              .
              .
MY_SEG      ENDS
```

2. Overlap if you must, but first usable byte must be on a word boundary.

```
MY_SEG      SEGMENT     WORD            ;word aligned
              .
              .
              .
MY_SEG      ENDS
```

3. Overlap if you must, and place first usable byte anywhere you like.

```
MY_SEG      SEGMENT     BYTE            ;byte aligned
              .
              .
              .
MY_SEG      ENDS
```

4. Start segment at specified 16-byte boundary. First usable byte is at specified offset

```
MY_SEG      SEGMENT     AT 1A2BH        ;address 1A2B0
            ORG         0003H           ;address 1A2B3
              .
              .
              .
MY_SEG      ENDS
```

The last example introduced another statement, namely ORG (for *ori*gin). It specifies the next offset to be used in the segment.

Procedure-Definition Statements   Procedures are sections of code that are called into execution from various places in the program. Each time a procedure is called upon, the instructions that make up the procedure are executed, and then control is returned back to the place from which the procedure was originally called.

The 8086 instructions for calling to and returning from a procedure are CALL and RET. You will recall that these instructions come in two flavors— intrasegment and intersegment. The intersegment ones push (CALL) and pop (RET) both the segment and the offset of the place to which the procedure should return. The intrasegment ones push and pop only the offset.

Procedures that are called with intrasegment CALLs must return with intrasegment RETurns. Such procedures are known as *NEAR* procedures. Similarly, procedures that are called with intersegment CALLs must return with intersegment RETurns and are known as *FAR* procedures.

The procedure-definition statements, PROC and ENDP (*end p*rocedure), delimit a procedure and indicate whether it is a NEAR or FAR procedure. This helps the assembler in two ways:

1. When assembling CALL instructions to that procedure, the assembler will know which kind of CALL to assemble.

2. When assembling RET instructions within that procedure, the assembler will know which kind of RET to assemble.

The following example illustrates this:

```
MY_CODE      SEGMENT
UP_COUNT     PROC       NEAR
             ADD        CX,1
             RET
UP_COUNT     ENDP
START:       .
             .
             .
             CALL       UPCOUNT
             .
             .
             .
             CALL       UPCOUNT
             .
             .
             .
             HLT
MY_CODE      ENDS
             END        START
```

Since UP_COUNT is declared to be a NEAR procedure, all CALLs to it are assembled as intrasegment CALLs, and all RETurns within it are assembled as intrasegment returns.

The above example points out some similarities between the RET instructions and the HLT instruction. There may be more than one RET in a procedure just as there may be more than one HLT in a program. The last instruction in a procedure (program) need not be a RET (HLT); but, if it is not, that instruction should be a jump back to somewhere within the procedure (program). The END (ENDP) tells the assembler where the procedure (program) ends but does not cause the assembler to generate a RET (HLT) instruction.

Termination Statements   With one exception, each terminating statement is paired up with some beginning statement. For example, SEGMENT and ENDS, PROC and ENDP. These terminating statements are described together with their corresponding beginning statements.

The one exception is END, which flags the end of the source program. It tells the assembler that there are no more instructions to assemble. The form of the END statement is

END   expression

where the expression must yield a memory-address value. That address is the address of the first instruction to be executed when the program is executed.

The following example illustrates the use of the END statement:

START:
       .
       .
       .

       END   START

Instruction Statements

The instruction statements, for the most part, correspond to the instructions of the 8086 processor. Each instruction statement causes the assembler to generate one 8086 instruction. An 8086 instruction consists of an **opcode** field as well as fields specifying the operand-addressing mode (**mod** field, **r/m** field, **reg** field). So the instruction statements in ASM-86 must contain an instruction mnemonic as well as sufficient addressing information to permit the assembler to generate the instruction.

    Instruction Mnemonics   Most of the instruction mnemonics are precisely those symbolic opcode names introduced in Chap. 3 for the 8086 instructions. Some additional instruction mnemonics, NIL and NOP, were added to make the assembly language more versatile.

The instruction mnemonic NOP (no-operation) causes the assembler to generate the 1-byte instruction that exchanges the contents of the AX register with the contents of the AX register (hexadecimal **opcode** 90). Not only doesn't this instruction do anything, it doesn't waste any time not doing it since it doesn't make any memory accesses. Although it seems strange to waste precious memory locations on instructions that do nothing, sometimes there are good reasons for wanting to do this. The NOPs might serve as placeholders for instructions that will be filled in later, possibly when the program is executing (a popular trick in earlier years). They might also be used to slow down a portion of the program where precise timing relationships are important.

NIL is the only instruction mnemonic that does not cause the assembler to generate any instructions. In contrast to NOP, which causes the assembler to generate an instruction that does nothing when executed, NIL doesn't.even cause an instruction to be generated. The NIL instruction statement serves as a convenient placeholder for labels in the assembly-language program. This is illustrated by the following instruction statements:

```
CYCLE:     NIL
           INC        AX
```

Although this is equivalent to

```
CYCLE:     INC        AX
```

the NIL makes it much easier to insert instructions ahead of the INC instruction in the source program if the need arises later.

Instruction Prefixes The 8086 instruction set permits instructions to start off with one or more prefix bytes. There are three possible prefixes—segment-override, repeat, and lock.

ASM-86 permits the following prefixes to be included along with the instruction mnemonic:

```
LOCK
REP        (repeat
REPE       (repeat while equal)
REPNE      (repeat while not equal)
REPZ       (repeat while zero)
REPNZ      (repeat while non-zero)
```

An example of an instruction statement using a prefix is given:

```
CYCLE:    LOCK DEC      COUNT
```

The segment-overriding prefix is generated automatically by the assembler whenever the assembler realizes that a memory access requires such a prefix. The assembler makes this decision in two steps. First, it selects a segment register that will make the instruction execute properly. The assembler selects the segment register based on the information it received from previous ASSUME statements. However, we could force the assembler to select a particular segment register by including that register in the instruction as in:

```
MOV       BX,ES:SUM
```

Second, the assembler determines, from its knowledge of the 8086 processor, if a segment-overriding prefix is necessary to force the execution of the instruction to use the selected segment register.

Operand-Addressing Modes The 8086 processor provides various operand-addressing modes. ASM-86 must therefore provide a means of expressing each such mode when writing instruction statements. These will be illustrated by examples:

1. Immediate:
```
    MOV       AX,15      ;15 is an immediate operand
```

2. Register:
```
    MOV       AX,15      AX is a register operand
```

3. Direct:
```
    SUM       DB      ?
              .
              .
              .
    MOV       SUM,15     ;SUM is a direct memory operand
```

4. Indirect through base register:

```
MOV        AX,[BX]
MOV        AX,[BP]
```

5. Indirect through index register:

```
MOV        AX,[SI]
MOV        AX,[DI]
```

6. Indirect through base register plus index register:

```
MOV        AX,[BX] [SI]
MOV        AX,[BX] [DI]
MOV        AX,[BP] [SI]
MOV        AX,[BP] [DI]
```

7. Indirect through base or index register plus offset:

```
MANY_BYTES        DB        100 DUP (?)
                  .
                  .
                  .
         MOV      AX,MANY_BYTES[BX]
         MOV      AX,MANY_BYTES[BP]
         MOV      AX,MANY_BYTES[SI]
         MOV      AX,MANY_BYTES[DI]
```

8. Indirect through base register plus index register plus offset:

```
MANY_BYTES        DB        100 DUP (?)
                  .
                  .
                  .
         MOV      AX,MANY_BYTES[BX][SI]
         MOV      AX,MANY_BYTES[BX][DI]
         MOV      AX,MANY_BYTES[BP][SI]
         MOV      AX,MANY_BYTES[BP][DI]
```

You will recall that the assembler uses its knowledge about a memory location's type when generating instructions that reference that memory location. For example, the assembler would generate a byte-increment when encountering the following:

```
SUM        DB        ?              ;type is BYTE
           .
           .
           .
           INC      SUM       ; a byte increment
```

However, with indirect operand-addressing modes, it is not always possible for the assembler to know the type of the memory location, as illustrated by

```
MOV      AL,[BX]
```

Even though the assembler does not know the type of the source operand in the above instruction, it does know that the type of the destination operand, AL, is

BYTE. So the assembler assumes that [BX] is also of type BYTE and generates a byte-move instruction. But now consider the statement:

```
INC     [BX]
```

There is no second operand here to help the assembler determine the type of [BX]. So the assembler cannot decide whether to generate a byte-increment instruction or a word-increment instruction. The above statement must therefore be written as either

```
INC     BYTE PTR [BX]      ;a byte-increment
```

or

```
INC     WORD PTR [BX]      ;a word-increment
```

so that the assembler can determine the type.

String Instructions   The assembler can usually determine the type of an operand (and hence know what kind of code to generate for accessing that operand) from its declaration. However, we have just seen that when using an indirect-addressing mode we might have to supply the assembler with additional information so it can determine the type.

String instructions are another example of when such additional information is necessary. Consider the string instruction MOVS. This instruction moves the contents of the memory address whose offset is in SI into the memory address whose offset is in DI. We should not need to specify any operands since the instruction has no choice as to which items to move and where. However, the instruction could move either a byte or a word; the assembler must know which is being moved so it can generate the correct instruction. For this reason, the ASM-86 statement for the MOVS instruction must specify the items that have been moved into SI and DI.

For example, consider the following:

```
ALPHA     DB       ?
BETA      DB       ?
                   .
                   .
                   .
          MOV      SI,OFFSET ALPHA
          MOV      DI, OFFSET BETA
          MOVS     BETA,ALPHA
```

The presence of BETA and ALPHA on the MOVS statement informs the assembler to generate a MOVS instruction that moves bytes (because the TYPE components of both BETA and ALPHA are BYTE). Furthermore, from the SEG components of BETA and ALPHA, the assembler is able to determine if the operands of the MOVS instruction are in accessible segments. The OFFSET components of ALPHA and BETA are ignored.

Like MOVS, the other four string primitives contain operands; MOVS and CMPS have two operands while SCAS, LODS, and STOS have one. For example:

```
CMPS      BETA,ALPHA
SCAS      ALPHA
LODS      ALPHA
STOS      BETA
```

XLAT also requires an operand—namely the item that was moved into BX to serve as the translation table. The SEG component of this operand enables the assembler to determine if the translation table is in a currently accessible segment; the OFFSET component is ignored. An example of an XLAT statement is as follows:

```
MOV       BX,OFFSET TABLE
XLAT      TABLE
```

Examples

The following examples illustrate some of the details of ASM-86:

1. Translate the values from input port 1 into a Gray code and send the result to output port 1.

```
MY_DATA   SEGMENT
GRAY      DB        18H,34H,05H,06H,09H,0AH,0CH,11H,12H,14H
MY_DATA   ENDS

MY_CODE   SEGMENT
          ASSUME    CS:MY_CODE, DS:MY_DATA
GO:       MOV       AX,MY_DATA              ;establish data segment
          MOV       DS,AX
          MOV       BX,OFFSET GRAY          ;translation table into BX
CYCLE:    IN        AL,1                    ;read in next value
          XLAT      GRAY                    ;translate it
          OUT       1,AL                    ;output it
          JMP       CYCLE                   ;and repeat
MY_CODE   ENDS
          END       GO
```

2. Add two unpacked BCD (ASCII) strings together.

```
MY_DATA   SEGMENT
STRING_1  DB        '1','7','5','2'         ;value is 2571
STRING_2  DB        '3','8','1','4'         ;value is 4183
MY_DATA   ENDS

MY_CODE   SEGMENT
          ASSUME    CS:MY_CODE, DS:MY_DATA, ES:MY_DATA
GO:       MOV       AX,MY_DATA              ;establish data segment
          MOV       DS,AX
          MOV       ES,AX                   ;LODS,STOS use ES
          CLC                               ;no carry initially
          CLD                               ;forward strings
          MOV       SI,OFFSET STRING_1      ;establish string pointers
          MOV       DI,OFFSET STRING_2
```

```
CYCLE:      LODS      STRING__1          ;get STRING__1 element
            ADC       AL,[DI]            ;add STRING__2 element
            AAA                          ;correct for ASCII
            STOS      STRING__2          ;result into STRING__2
            JCXZ      CYCLE              ;repeat for entire string
            HLT
MY__CODE    ENDS
            END       GO
```

3. Decimal multiplication algorithm of Fig. 3.32

```
MY__DATA    SEGMENT
A           DB        '3','7','5','4','9'
B           DB        '6'
C           DB        LENGTH (A) DUP (?)
MY__DATA    ENDS

MY__CODE    SEGMENT
            ASSUME    CS:MY__CODE,DS:MY__DATA, ES:MY__DATA
GO:         MOV       AX,MY__DATA        ;establish data segment
            MOV       DS,AX
            MOV       ES,AX              ;LODS,STOS use ES
            CLD                          ;forward strings
            MOV       SI,OFFSET A        ;establish pointers
            MOV       DI,OFFSET C
            MOV       CX,LENGTH A        ;establish count
            AND       B,0FH              ;clear upper half of b
            MOV       BYTE PTR [SI],0    ;clear c[I]
CYCLE:      LODS      A                  ;get a[i]
            AND       AL,0FH             ;clear its high-order bits
            MUL       AL,B               ;multiply by b
            AAM                          ;correct for ASCII
            ADD       AL,[DI]            ;add c[i]
            AAA                          ;adjust for ASCII
            STOS      C                  ;store in c[i]
            MOV       [DI],AH            ;. . . and c[i+1]
            JCXZ      CYCLE              :repeat for entire string
            HLT
MY__CODE    ENDS
            END       GO
```

4. Move 50 bytes between two overlapping strings.

```
MY__DATA    SEGMENT
STRING      DB        1000 DUP (?)
STRING__1   EQU       STRING+7
STRING__2   EQU       STRING+25
MY__DATA    ENDS

MY__CODE    SEGMENT
            ASSUME    CS:MY__CODE, DS:MY__DATA, ES:MY__DATA
STRING__SIZE EQU      50                 ;number of bytes to move
GO:         MOV       AX,MY__DATA        ;establish data segment
            MOV       DS,AX
            MOV       ES,AX              ;MOVS uses ES
            MOV       CX,STRING__SIZE
```

```
            MOV        SI,OFFSET STRING_1    ;source string
            MOV        DI, OFFSET STRING_2   ;destination string
            CLD                              ;assume a forward move
            CMP        SI,DI                 ;if source string comes first
            JLT        OK
            STD                              ;...we need backwards move
            ADD        SI,STRING_SIZE-1      ;set SI and DI to
            ADD        DI,STRING_SIZE-1      ;...end of strings
OK:         REPEAT MOVS STRING_2,STRING_1    ;move the string
            HLT
MY_CODE     ENDS
            END        GO
```

In Conclusion

This chapter was not meant to be a compendium of all the features and rules of ASM-86 (the *Intel MCS-86 Assembly Language Reference Manual* does that very well). Instead, it attempted to present most of the features of the language in a form that was easy to digest and to convey enough information to enable you to write meaningful programs. What was not covered were many of the more advanced features, so that attention could be focused on the underlying concepts of the language.

7

8086
High-Level-Language
Programming (PL/M)

Who Needs High-Level Languages?

Writing programs for the 8086 can be done in a laborious way by figuring out the binary encodings for each instruction, in an endurable way by thinking about the instructions conceptually and using an assembler to generate the binary, or in an effortless way by thinking about the problem we want to solve and using a compiler to transform our high level solution into instructions and eventually into binary. This is not to imply that there aren't assembly-language programmers who don't enjoy what they're doing; certainly there must be a lot of pleasure in reducing a 1025-byte program to fit into 1024 bytes. Such programmers are in big demand when programs don't fit into the amount of memory that's been allocated for them. But there are often times when writing and debugging large programs as quickly as possible is more important than doing it in as few bytes as possible. It's at those times that high-level languages and compilers prove indispensable.

Other adjectives often used by the advocates of high-level language programs are the following:

1. High reliability—good chance the program will do what's expected of it.
2. Ease of maintainability—future changes can be made with little difficulty.
3. Self-documenting—easy to read and understand.

To illustrate these points, let's write a program that finds the smallest number divisible by three that is greater than 100. The answer, of course, is 102; but let's see how the 8086 can be used to figure it out.

One way to solve the problem would be to start with zero and keep adding three until the result exceeds 100. More specifically, start with a byte X being zero and, while X is less than or equal to 100, add three to X.

A high-level programming language would let you write down the program directly from the verbal description of the solution. In the programming language called PL/M-86, this would look like:

```
DECLARE X BYTE;
X = 0;
DO WHILE X < = 100;
    X = X+3;
END;
```

Notice that the above program could be written without giving any thought to the instruction set of the 8086. The program would be fed into a compiler, which generates the 8086 instructions for us.

Now let's try to write an assembly-language program to find the result. We need to convert the description of the solution into a sequence of steps corresponding to 8086 instructions.

1. Reserve a byte in memory for X.
2. Move a zero into that byte.
3. Compare the value in X to 100.
4. If the comparison indicates X exceeds 100, jump to the end of the program.
5. Add three to X.
6. Jump back to step 3.
7. This is the end of the program, so halt.

From these steps, we can write the program in ASM-86, an assembly language for the 8086.

```
1.    X           DB        ?
2.                MOV       X,0
3.    CYCLE:      CMP       X,100
4.                J..       DONE
5.                ADD       X,3
6.                JMP       CYCLE
7.    DONE:       HLT
```

The fourth step was left incomplete because we're not too sure what it should be. We want to jump if X exceeds 100, and we just compared X to 100. Since comparing means subtracting 100 from X, that means that if X exceeds 100 we get a number greater than zero after doing the subtraction. It looks like we want to do a JG (jump on greater) instruction. Or, on the other hand, is X subtracted from 100 so we get a number less than zero if X exceeds 100? Maybe we want a JL (jump on less) instruction? Well, at least there's a 50–50 chance of getting it right. Notice that we didn't have to worry about doing it wrong in the high-level language program. (Actually, the best instruction for step 4 is JA.)

In all fairness to assembly-language programming, let's see what can be done to shorten our program. For one thing, the first time step 4 is executed, the jump will not be taken. So let's move steps 3 and 4 to the end of the loop and remove step 6, thereby saving one instruction.

```
1.       X          DB      ?
2.                  MOV     X,0
3.       CYCLE:     ADD     X,3
4.                  CMP     X,100
5.                  JNA     CYCLE
6.
7.                  HLT
```

Another thing we could do is use the AL register instead of the memory byte X. This would shorten the instructions in steps 2, 3, and 4 by one byte each and also free up the byte dedicated to X.

```
1.
2.                  MOV     AL,0
3.       CYCLE:     ADD     AL,3
4.                  CMP     AL,100
5.                  JNA     CYCLE
6.
7.                  HLT
```

Now suppose we don't own either a compiler or an assembler. Then we must write all the instructions in binary. As an example, let's consider the instruction in step 5. The JNA CYCLE instruction is a 2-byte instruction with the first byte containing 0111 0110. The second byte has to tell the number of bytes to jump over to get to CYCLE. This means we must know how long each instruction is and then count the number of bytes between the instruction in step 3 and the instruction in step 6. This is left as an exercise for those readers who enjoy binary programming.

Now that you've read the three approaches to programming the 8086, it's up to you to make a choice. If you still believe in binary or assembly-language programming exclusively, the remainder of this chapter would be of little interest to you. However, if you believe you may have some use for high-level languages, read on.

Probably the most popular high-level languages are COBOL, BASIC, and FORTRAN. COBOL is a popular language in commercial data-processing applications. FORTRAN is used frequently in applications involving numerical computations. BASIC is a favorite language among microcomputer hobbyists because of its simplicity and its interactive nature; BASIC programs are often executed directly without first being compiled into machine-language instructions. PASCAL, a language designed to be used for teaching purposes, has been gaining in popularity recently as a high-level language.

Intel's proprietary language PL/M was the first high-level language intended primarily for microprocessor applications and was the first programming language available for the 8086 (even before 8086 assembly language). PL/M-86, the 8086 dialect of PL/M, is discussed in detail in this chapter.

Structure of PL/M-86 Programs

Let's not waste time introducing our first PL/M-86 program.

```
1.      PROG:
2.                      DO;     /* add inputs divided by 2 until total exceeds 100 */

3.                              DECLARE SUM BYTE:
4.                              SUM = 0;

5.                              DO WHILE SUM < =100;
6.                                  SUM = SUM+INPUT(3)/2;
7.                              END;

8.                              OUTPUT(3) = SUM;
9.                      END PROG;
```

Without knowing a thing about PL/M-86, you can read and almost understand the program above. Line 1 seems to be telling us that the name of the program is PROG, and line 9 seems to confirm this. Line 2 seems to be saying that we're about to DO something, and line 9 must be saying that we've just ENDed doing it. Furthermore, line 2 contains some English, which is telling us what we're about to do. Line 3 must be reserving a byte in memory, probably in a data segment, and naming it SUM. So far no instructions have been generated. Line 4 looks like the first instruction—moving zero into SUM. Lines 5 through 7 seem to be related; they are grouped together and start off with DO and finish with END. They seem to be repeatedly reading in values from input port 3, dividing them by 2, and adding the result to SUM until SUM exceeds 100. This is just what the comment in line 2 promised we would do. Finally, line 8 looks like it's writing out the SUM to output port 3.

From this example, let's try to generalize about the structure of a PL/M-86 program. It starts off with a name and ends with the same name. The program itself is bounded by the words DO and END (although more DO - END pairs may appear within the program). The program consists of a sequence of statements, some of which are declarative statements (DECLARE SUM BYTE) and the others are executable statements (SUM = SUM+INPUT(3)/2). Semicolons are used profusely; they indicate the end of each statement. The structure of a PL/M-86 program is shown below:

```
name:
    DO;
                statement;
                statement;
                    .                       declarative statements
                    .
                    .
                statement;
                statement;
                    .                       executable statements
                    .
                    .
                statement;
    END name;
```

The programs presented here all display a consistent indentation pattern. Such indentation is not part of the program structure. It is purely optional as far as the PL/M-86 compiler is concerned but is highly recommended to make the programs easier for us to read and understand. As an extreme example of this point, consider the following unindented version of the preceding program. It would present no additional difficulty to the PL/M-86 compiler (in fact, it would compile faster) but would be much less comprehensible to us.

```
PROG: DO:/* add inputs until total exceeds 100 */
DECLARE SUM BYTE;SUM=0;DO WHILE SUM< =100;
SUM=SUM+INPUT(3)/2;END;OUTPUT(3)=SUM;END PROG;
```

Tokens
Before examining the kinds of statements from which PL/M-86 programs are built, we must become familiar with the building blocks of statements. Statements are composed of such things as *identifiers, reserved words, delimiters, constants,* and *comments.* These building blocks are sometimes called *tokens.*

Identifiers   Identifiers are names that you, the programmer, are free to make up. An example of an identifier in the sample program already discussed is SUM. An identifier is a sequence of letters and numbers starting with a letter. An identifier can be up to 31 characters long which means that, for all practical purposes, the length is unlimited. In order to improve readability, you can embed dollar signs ($) arbitrarily in an identifier. For instance, the identifier NEWS-TEAM could be written as either NEW$STEAM or NEWS$TEAM depending on which meaning was intended. Examples of identifiers are the following:

> X
> GAMMA
> JACK5
> THIS$NODE

Reserved Words   Reserved words look like identifiers, but they have special meaning in the language, and you may not use them as identifier names. In our sample program, we saw such reserved words as DO, END, DECLARE, BYTE, and WHILE. Thus it would be perfectly acceptable for us to make up a name like ENDING as in

DECLARE ENDING BYTE;

but it would be improper for us to write

DECLARE END BYTE;

A complete list of PL/M-86 reserved words is given in Table 7.1.

Delimiters   Delimiters are the non-alphanumeric character sequences appearing in PL/M-86 programs. In our sample program we saw such delimiters as < = and ;. Each delimiter has a special meaning in the language, and we will become exposed to most of them in this chapter. A complete list of delimiters in PL/M-86 is given in Table 7.2.

Table 7.1 Reserved Words in PL/M-86

ADDRESS	CASE	END	INITIAL	NOT	REENTRANT
AND	DATA	EOF	INTEGER	OR	RETURN
AT	DECLARE	EXTERNAL	INTERRUPT	PLUS	STRUCTURE
BASED	DISABLE	GO	LABEL	POINTER	THEN
BY	DO	GOTO	LITERALLY	PROCEDURE	TO
BYTE	ELSE	HALT	MINUS	PUBLIC	WHILE
CALL	ENABLE	IF	MOD	REAL	WORD
					XOR

Table 7.2 Delimiters in PL/M-86

$	.	+	<	< >	/*
=	/	−	>	:	*/
:=	(	'	< =	;	
@	)	*	> =	,	

Constants   Constants are the fixed values appearing in PL/M-86 programs. In our sample program, we saw such constants as 0, 3, and 100. These are *whole-number constants;* PL/M-86 also allows for *floating-point constants* and *string constants.*

A *whole-number constant* can be any non-fractional value between 0 and 65535 (that is $2^{16} - 1$). It is normally written as a decimal number but can also be written in binary (ending with a B), octal (ending with a Q), or hexadecimal (ending with an H). To avoid confusion with identifiers, a hexadecimal constant must start with a numeric digit; a leading zero would suffice. Examples of whole-number constants are 15, 1010B, 27Q, 3A0H, and 0BFA3H.

A *floating-point constant* is a non-negative number with a decimal point. It may also end with an E followed by a number to indicate multiplication by a power of 10. Examples of floating-point constants are 15.6, 138., 7.0E3, and 1.32E−7.

A *string constant* is a sequence of one or two characters enclosed within apostrophes. (Strings of more than two characters are permitted in very restricted cases and will not be discussed in this text.) An apostrophe itself may be included in a string constant by writing it as two consecutive apostrophes. Examples of string constants are 'A', 'AB', and ''''. The last example is the string consisting of the apostrophe character. The value of a string constant is the ASCII code of the character(s) in the string (see Appendix C for the ASCII codes). For example, the value of 'A' is the same as 41H (both have the value 65), and the value of 'AB' is the same as 4142H. Thus string constants and whole-number constants can be used interchangeably.

Note that a constant is never negative. More will be said about this later.

Comments   Comments are sequences of characters enclosed within the delimiters /* and */. They have no meaning to the compiler but should be used generously in your program to keep reminding you of what you are doing. Although comments like

```
I = 0;      /* I equals zero */
```

would be absurd, comments like

```
I = 0;      /* initialize array index prior to first iteration */
```

go a long way to making a program more readable.

Expressions

One more building block, namely expressions, must be introduced before we can build statements. The expression itself is built up from some of the tokens just described.

Loosely speaking, an expression is a sequence of operands and operators that can be combined to produce a value. So now we must introduce both operands and operators and indicate how they are combined to produce the value of an expression.

If you have read and understood the section in Chap. 5 on expressions in assembly-language programming, you might find the following analogy interesting. In assembly-language programming, the instruction mnemonics (not the expressions) correspond to the items that get executed (instructions) when the program is run. In high-level languages, there are no instruction mnemonics; the expressions represent sequences of instructions that get executed when the program is run. Assembly-language expressions are evaluated at the time the program is being assembled; high-level language expressions are evaluated when the program is run.

Operands An operand is something that has a value. The simplest kind of operand is a constant. Thus 15, 2.7E5, and ¹UG¹ are all operands. Another kind of operand is a variable representing a single numeric value. Frequently, this is simply an identifier, such as SUM in the sample program. Unlike a constant, the value represented by a variable is not known until you execute the program and will usually take on different values at different times during the execution. Another operand is an expression itself, perhaps enclosed in parentheses, and used in some bigger expression such as in 3*(SUM+2).

Note that the value of an operand may be negative, but a constant is never negative. A minus sign can be written in front of a constant but is never considered as part of the constant; it is an arithmetic operator.

Operators An operator takes the values of one or more operands and produces a new value. There are three kinds of operators in PL/M-86—*arithmetic operators, relational operators,* and *logical operators.*

Arithmetic operators are nothing more than the familiar addition operator (+), subtraction operator(−), multiplication operator (*), and division operator

Table 7.3 The 'type' of a Constant

Constant	Type
0 <=WHOLE-NUMBER <=255	BYTE OR INTEGER
255 < WHOLE-NUMBER <=32767	WORD OR INTEGER
32767 < WHOLE-NUMBER <=65535	WORD
ONE-CHARACTER STRING	BYTE
TWO-CHARACTER STRING	WORD
FLOATING-POINT	REAL

(/). Another arithmetic operator, MOD, produces the remainder that results after doing a division. Thus 19/7 is 2, whereas 19 MOD 7 is 5.

Now for some restrictions on arithmetic operators. PL/M-86 permits only certain operand combinations and not others. For example, PL/M-86 lets you write 15 + 2 as well as 15.3E7 + 2.1E3. But it prohibits hybrids like 15 + 2.1E3. In order to understand which combinations are permitted, we need to classify the operands into various *types*. Variables can be classified as BYTE, WORD, INTEGER, or REAL. (A variable's type is specified when the variable is declared.) A variable of type BYTE can take on any non-fractional value from 0 to 255, type WORD from 0 to 65535, and type INTEGER from −32768 to +32767. In other words, a BYTE is an unsigned 8-bit binary number; a WORD is an unsigned 16-bit binary number; and an INTEGER is a signed 16-bit binary number. A variable of type REAL can take on the value of any real (fractional or non-fractional) number within certain limits.

We can extend this notion of types to include constants as well as variables. We have already seen that a constant can be a one- or two-character string constant, a floating-point constant, or a whole-number constant. A one-character string constant is of type BYTE, two-character string constant of type WORD, and a floating-point constant of type REAL. A whole-number constant can be of type BYTE, WORD, or INTEGER depending on the value of the constant. This is summarized in Table 6.3. Note that this table shows the range for integers as being between 0 and 32767; this is the range of constants that can be treated as integers, not the range of integer values (−32768 to 32767).

Now that we have classified the operands (constants and variables) into types, we can state the rule for valid operand combinations for arithmetic operators. The rule is simple. It states that both operands must be of the same type. In most cases, the result will also be of that type. For example, you may not add an INTEGER operand (variable or constant) to a REAL operand (variable or constant); nor may you add apples to oranges. One exception is permitted: one operand may be of type BYTE and the other type WORD; the result will be of type WORD (OK, you can add nickels and dimes).

Such restrictions might appear to make the language harder to learn by giving us more rules to memorize. On the contrary, they make the language easier because we only have to remember one general rule—"you can't mix types"—rather than having to memorize a bunch of rules like "if you mix this type with that type you get some other type." And besides, you probably didn't mean to mix types anyhow, so the compiler can help prevent you from making certain kinds of errors. But, if you're persistent and really want to mix types, the language provides routines (not described here) that let you change types.

The relational operators are equal $(=)$, not-equal $(< >)$, less-than $(<)$, greater-than $(>)$, less-than-or-equal $(< =)$, and greater-than-or-equal $(> =)$. In case you're puzzled how we get not-equal from $< >$, consider not-equal as the combination of less-than-or-greater-than. Now $< >$ makes sense (of course $\neq$ would have made more sense, but it doesn't exist on standard keyboards).

The valid operand combinations for relational operators are the same as for arithmetic operators. Thus we can compare two BYTEs, two WORDs, two INTEGERs, or a BYTE and a WORD. The result of the comparison is always a BYTE, and the value of that BYTE is 0FFH if the comparison is true and 00H if the comparison is false. For example, $6 > 5$ yields 0FFH; $1.5 = 2.1$ yields 00H; and $7 > 2.3$ is an invalid comparison.

The result of a relational operator (true or false) is useful for making tests, such as in an IF statement. An example of such a test is given:

IF X<10 THEN X = X+1;

The result of $X < 10$ would be either 0FFH (if true) or 00H (if false), and it is this result that determines whether or not $X = X+1$ gets executed.

The logical operators are the usual bit-by-bit AND, OR, XOR (exclusive-or), and NOT. The operands of logical operators must be either of type BYTE (result will be of type BYTE), of type WORD (result will be of type WORD), or one of each (result will be of type WORD). For example,

```
10101010B AND 11001100B is 10001000B;
1100110011001100B OR 1111000011110000B is 1100000011000000B;
NOT 11111111B is 00000000B;
```
and
```
11110000B XOR 1.7 is invalid.
```

An interesting thing happens when the operands of a logical operator are the true or false results of relational operators: the result of the bit-by-bit logical operation is a BYTE with a meaningful true (0FFH) or false (00H) value. For example:

(1<2) AND (4>3)	yields	0FFH AND 0FFH	yields 0FFH (true)
(6=5) OR (1<>0)	yields	00H OR 0FFH	yields 0FFH (true)
NOT (1=1)	yields	NOT 0FFH	yields 00H (false)

This permits us to construct useful combinations of relations as in:

DO WHILE (A>3) AND (A<10);

Statements

There are two kinds of statements in PL/M-86—declarative statements and executable statements. Declarative statements are typically associated with data, while executable statements are associated with code.

A *declarative statement* introduces an object, associates a name with that object, and allocates memory for it if necessary. For example:

DECLARE COST BYTE;

This declaration introduces a variable, gives it the name COST, and allocates a byte of memory for it.

Declarative statements generate no code. Rather, they tell the compiler what kind of code to generate for succeeding executable statements.

An *executable statement* describes code to be generated. For example:

PRICE = COST+3;

The code the compiler will generate will probably contain an instruction that moves the contents of COST into a register. The previous declarative statement has told the compiler that such a move instruction is to be a byte-move instruction and not a word-move instruction.

Executable Statements

The various executable statements in PL/M-86 are *assignment statements, selective statements, repetitive statements,* and some additional miscellaneous statements. Each of these statements will be described in this section.

Assignment Statements   The simplest kind of executable statement is the assignment statement. It causes the value of an expression to be assigned to a variable. The format of an assignment statement is as follows:

VARIABLE = EXPRESSION;

Some examples of assignment statements are below:

LENGTH = 5;
WIDTH = 2*LENGTH;

Just as PL/M-86 keeps us from adding apples to oranges, it also prohibits us from assigning apples to oranges. In other words, both the expression being assigned and the variable it is assigned to must be of the same type. Thus we can write

DECLARE COUNT BYTE;
COUNT = 117;

but we cannot write

DECLARE COUNT BYTE;
COUNT = 6.5;

One exception: we can assign byte expressions to word variables. So we can write:

DECLARE COUNT WORD;
COUNT = 117;

To simplify assigning the same value to several variables, an assignment statement can be written as:

VARIABLE, VARIABLE, ..., VARIABLE = EXPRESSION;

This is illustrated by:

LEFT, RIGHT = INIT−1;

And assignments can be embedded inside an assignment statement (using a special assignment operator :=) as in:

VOLUME = HEIGHT *(AREA:=LENGTH*WIDTH);

The following program is an example that uses assignment statements:

```
FACTORIAL:
    DO; and for!* compute 1!, 2!, 3!, and 4! */
        DECLARE FACT1 BYTE;
        DECLARE FACT2 BYTE;
        DECLARE FACT3 BYTE;
        DECLARE FACT4 BYTE;
        FACT1 = 1;
        FACT2 = 2*FACT1;
        FACT3 = 3*FACT2;
        FACT4 = 4*FACT3;
    END FACTORIAL;
```

The following program is identical to the previous one, except it uses embedded assignments. It also declares all four bytes with one declaration.

```
FACTORIAL:
    DO; /* compute 1!, 2!, 3!, and 4! */
        DECLARE (FACT1,FACT2,FACT3,FACT4) BYTE;
        FACT4 = 4*(FACT3:=3*(FACT2:=2*(FACT1:=1) ) );
    END FACTORIAL;
```

Selective Statements   If assignment statements were the only executable statements, programmers would get bored quickly. So, to make programming more interesting, the selective statement was invented. There are two kinds of selective statements—the *IF statement* and the *CASE statement*.

The IF statement has the form:

IF expression THEN statement;

An example of an IF statement is given:

IF SPEED>55 THEN FINE = 25;

The IF statement tells what to do if the expression is true. A natural question to ask is, "If not, then what?" The answer is nothing, unless we're told what ELSE to do as in the following ELSE statement:

IF HEIGHT<6 THEN CLEARANCE = 6−HEIGHT;
ELSE CLEARANCE = 0;

The following program illustrates the use of the IF statement in computing income taxes:

```
TAX:
      DO;
            DECLARE (SALARY,TAX) INTEGER;
            DECLARE (AGE, EXEMPTIONS) BYTE;
            SALARY = ...;                                    /* insert salary here */
            AGE = ...;                                       /* insert age here*/
            EXEMPTIONS= 1;
            IF AGE>65 THEN EXEMPTIONS = EXEMPTIONS +1;
            SALARY = SALARY-750*EXEMPTIONS;
            IF SALARY<1000 THEN TAX = 14*SALARY/100;
            ELSE TAX = 140+20*(SALARY-1000)/100;
      END TAX:
```

The IF statement permits specifying only one statement after the THEN. But any collection of statements starting with a DO statement and ending with an END statement behaves like a single statement. Such a collection of statements is called a *simple-DO block*.

```
DO:
      statement;
      statement;
         .
         .
         .
      statement;
END;
```

Now a more complicated IF statement would look like this:

```
IF MINUTES>=60 THEN
      DO;
            HOURS = HOURS +1;
            MINUTES = MINUTES-60;
      END;
```

The IF statement has the ability to select one or the other of two statements to be executed depending on the truth or falsity of an expression. The CASE statement is a more general selective statement. The CASE statement selects one out of a set of statements based on the value of an expression. It has the form:

```
DO CASE expression;
```

A block starting with a CASE statement and ending with a matching END is called a *DO-CASE block*. For example:

```
DO CASE DAY$OF$CHRISTMAS;
      GO TO ERROR;                                                      /* zeroeth day */
      PATRIDGE$IN$A$PEAR$TREE = PARTRIDGE$IN$A$PEAR$TREE+1;  /* first day */
      TURTLE$DOVES = TURTLE$DOVES+2;                                    /* second day */
      FRENCH$HENS = FRENCH$HENS+3;                                      /* third day */
      CALLING$BIRDS = CALLING$BIRDS+4;                                  /* fourth day */
      GOLDEN$RINGS = GOLDEN$RINGS+5;                                    /* fifth day */
```

```
          GEESE$A$LAYING = GEESE$A$LAYING+6;              /* sixth day */
          SWANS$A$SWIMMING = SWANS$A$SWIMMING+7;          /* seventh day */
          MAIDS$A$MILKING = MAIDS$A$MILKING+8;            /* eighth day */
          DRUMMERS$DRUMMING = DRUMMERS$DRUMMING+9;  /* ninth day */
          PIPERS$PIPING = PIPERS$PIPING+10;               /* tenth day */
          LADIES$DANCING = LADIES$DANCING+11;             /* eleventh day */
          LORDS$A$LEAPING = LORDS$A$LEAPING+12;           /* twelfth day */
END;
```

If, in the above example, the value of DAYOFCHRISTMAS is 7, the only statement in the block that is executed is:

```
SWANS$A$SWIMMING = SWANS$A$SWIMMING+7;
```

The entire DO-CASE block is equivalent to the following collection of IF statements:

```
IF DAY$OF$CHRISTMAS=0 THEN
     GO TO ERROR;
ELSE IF DAY$OF$CHRISTMAS=1 THEN
     PARTRIDGE$IN$A$PEAR$TREE = PARTRIDGE$IN$A$PEAR$TREE+1;
ELSE IF DAY$OF$CHRISTMAS=2 THEN
     TURTLE$DOVES = TURTLE$DOVES+2;
ELSE IF DAY$OF$CHRISTMAS=3 THEN
     FRENCH$HENS = FRENCH$HENS+3;
ELSE IF DAY$OF$CHRISTMAS=4 THEN
     CALLING$BIRDS = CALLING$BIRDS+4;
ELSE IF DAY$OF$CHRISTMAS=5 THEN
     GOLDEN$RINGS = GOLDEN$RINGS+5;
ELSE IF DAY$OF$CHRISTMAS=6 THEN
     GEESE$A$LAYING = GEESE$A$LAYING+6;
ELSE IF DAY$OF$CHRISTMAS=7 THEN
     SWANS$A$SWIMMING = SWANS$A$SWIMMING+7;
ELSE IF DAY$OF$CHRISTMAS=8 THEN
     MAIDS$A$MILKING = MAIDS$A$MILKING+8;
ELSE IF DAY$OF$CHRISTMAS=9 THEN
     DRUMMERS$DRUMMING = DRUMMERS$DRUMMING+9;
ELSE IF DAY$OF$CHRISTMAS=10 THEN
     PIPERS$PIPING = PIPERS$PIPING+10;
ELSE IF DAY$OF$CHRISTMAS=11 THEN
     LADIES$DANCING = LADIES$DANCING+11;
ELSE IF DAY$OF$CHRISTMAS=12 THEN
     LORDS$A$LEAPING = LORDS$A$LEAPING+12;
```

The CASE statement was not really necessary; we can always use a bunch of IF statements as just illustrated. However, when the CASE statement is appropriate, it makes the program simpler.

Repetitive Statements   So far, we have seen how to write a program that executes statements in sequence, one after another. We also want the ability to execute one or more statements repeatedly. PL/M-86 provides the ability to repeat for a given number of times (*iterative-DO statement*) or for as long as a given condition is satisfied (*DO-WHILE statements*). Repetitions can also be accomplished using the more elementary *GOTO statement*.

The GOTO statement has the form:

```
GO TO label;
```

GOTO is a single reserved word that, for readability, may be written as the two words GO TO. The following example illustrates the use of the GOTO statement:

```
JAIL:
          .
          .
          .
          GO TO JAIL;          /* go directly -- do not pass go */
```

The iterative-DO statement has the form:

```
DO variable = expression TO expression BY expression;
```

A block starting with an iterative-DO statement and ending with a matching END is called an *iterative-DO block*. For example:

```
DO DAYS = 1 TO 365 BY 7;
     WEEKS = WEEKS+1;
END;
```

The effect of the above example is to assign values of 1, 8, 15, . . ., 365 to DAYS, and after each assignment execute the statement:

```
WEEKS = WEEKS+1;
```

This is equivalent to:

```
     DAYS = 1;
CYCLE:
     IF DAYS>=365 THEN
          DO;
               WEEKS = WEEKS+1;
               DAYS = DAYS+7;
               GO TO CYCLE;
          END;
```

The following program illustrates how the iterative-DO statement is used to compute the number of leap years in the twenty-first century:

```
LEAPS:
     DO;
          DECLARE YEARS WORD;
          DECLARE LEAP$YEARS BYTE;

          LEAP$YEARS = 0;
          DO YEARS = 2000 to 2099 BY 4;
               LEAP$YEARS = LEAP$YEARS+1;
          END;

     END LEAPS;
```

Iterative-DO statements are frequently incremented by 1. In such cases, the "BY 1" can be left off. The following program illustrates this point. The program computes the sum of the first 10 integers:

```
ADD10:
    DO;
        DECLARE I BYTE;
        DECLARE SUM BYTE;
        SUM = 0;
            DO I = 1 TO 10;
                SUM = SUM+I;
            END;
    END ADD10;
```

A DO-WHILE statement has the form:

```
DO WHILE expression;
```

A block starting with a DO-WHILE statement and ending with a matching END is called a *DO-WHILE block*. An example is the following:

```
DO WHILE DEMAND>SUPPLY;
    PRICE = PRICE+1;
END;
```

The effect of the above example is to repeatedly execute the statement as long as the value of DEMAND is greater than the value of SUPPLY. This is equivalent to:

```
CYCLE:
    IF DEMAND>SUPPLY THEN
        DO;
            PRICE = PRICE+1;
            GO TO CYCLE;
        END;
```

Miscellaneous Executable Statements Some final exectable statements are shown:

```
HALT;
ENABLE;
DISABLE;
```

They generate the obvious 8086 instructions that (1) halt the processor, (2) enable interrupts, and (3) disable interrupts.

Declarative Statements

Scalars The simplest kind of declarative statement is the *scalar declaration*. Such a declaration defines a variable representing a single numeric value. Examples of such declarations are below:

```
DECLARE LITTLE$THINGS BYTE;          /* an 8-bit unsigned value */
DECLARE BIG$THINGS WORD;             /* a 16-bit unsigned value */
DECLARE SIGNED$THINGS INTEGER;       /* a signed value */
DECLARE FRACTIONAL$THINGS REAL:      /* a real value */
```

In these examples LITTLE$THINGS may be assigned any whole number between 0 and 255, BIG$THINGS any whole number between 0 and 65535,

SIGNED$THINGS any whole number between −32768 and +32767, and FRACTIONAL$THINGS any floating-point number within certain limits. Here are some examples of using the variables just declared:

```
LITTLE$THINGS = 57;
BIG$THINGS = 43195;
SIGNED$THINGS = −14216;
FRACTIONAL$THINGS = 27.148;
```

You know that you have to declare your variables, but how do you know what to declare them to be? Should they be BYTEs, or WORDs, or INTEGERs, or REALs? To answer that, you have to think about each variable and decide what range of values will be assigned to it when the program runs. If the variable is something like NUMBEROFWIVES, or BALL$SCORE, or any other variable that will never be negative, or fractional, or exceed 255, you can declare it to be a BYTE. If it can get bigger than 255 but not bigger than 65535—such as PAGESINBOOK, NUMBEROFEMPLOYEES (in a medium-sized company), or GRAINSOFSAND (in a small sandbox)—then declare it to be a WORD. If it can be negative as well—such as CHECK$BOOK$BALANCE— use INTEGER. REALs can be used in two different situations. They are used for things that get REALLY big, like WEALTH or DESCENDANTSOFADAM. They are also used for things that occur in the REAL world and are therefore "measured" instead of "counted," such as MILESPERGALLON or SPECIFIC$GRAVITY. Of course, REALs can be used for things that are both big and measurable, such as SPACE$MILES or SECONDS$SINCE$CREA-TION. If you're not sure what range of values your variable might take on when the program runs, you should anticipate the worst and declare it to be REAL; similarly, if your variable can take on positive whole number values that may only occasionally get slightly bigger than 255, you must declare it to be a WORD. By erring on the side of caution like this, your program will still be able to execute properly; although your code size might be larger than necessary, and your program might run slower than necessary. If you erred in the other direction, your program would either die completely or (worse yet) give incorrect results.

Related Items   So far we have seen only scalar declarations. They introduce variables that can have only one value at a time, and they show no relationships among any of the values in a program. But frequently values are related, and programs can be simplified by grouping the related values together. For example, consider a program that reads in the age (to the nearest year) of 10 people and then determines how many of them are over 40. The following is the hard way to solve the problem:

```
OVER$40$THE$HARD$WAY:
    DO;
          ·  DECLARE AGE$0 BYTE;
             DECLARE AGE$1 BYTE;
             DECLARE AGE$2 BYTE;
             DECLARE AGE$3 BYTE;
```

```
DECLARE AGE$4 BYTE;
DECLARE AGE$5 BYTE;
DECLARE AGE$6 BYTE;
DECLARE AGE$7 BYTE;
DECLARE AGE$8 BYTE;
DECLARE AGE$9 BYTE;
DECLARE OVER$40 BYTE;
```

```
                              .                 /* read in the ages */
                              .
OVER$40 = 0;                                    /* initialize the count */
IF AGE$0 > 40 THEN OVER$40 = OVER$40 + 1;
IF AGE$1 > 40 THEN OVER$40 = OVER$40 + 1;
IF AGE$2 > 40 THEN OVER$40 = OVER$40 + 1;
IF AGE$3 > 40 THEN OVER$40 = OVER$40 + 1;
IF AGE$4 > 40 THEN OVER$40 = OVER$40 + 1;
IF AGE$5 > 40 THEN OVER$40 = OVER$40 + 1;
IF AGE$6 > 40 THEN OVER$40 = OVER$40 + 1;
IF AGE$7 > 40 THEN OVER$40 = OVER$40 + 1;
IF AGE$8 > 40 THEN OVER$40 = OVER$40 + 1;
IF AGE$9 > 40 THEN OVER$40 = OVER$40 + 1;
                                                /* do something with result */
```

```
END OVER$40$THE$HARD$WAY;
```

Obviously, the variables AGE$0, AGE$1, . . ., AGE$9 are related to each other in the sense that all of them are ages. PL/M-86 allows such related variables to be grouped together as one variable with 10 byte values. Such a variable, AGE, would be declared by:

```
DECLARE AGE (10) BYTE;
```

Such a multivalued variable is called an *array*. The individual components (called *elements)* in the array AGE can be referred to as AGE(0), AGE(1), . . ., AGE(9). Now the previous program can be rewritten as follows:

```
OVER$40$THE$EASY$WAY:
    DO;
            DECLARE AGE (10) BYTE;
            DECLARE OVER$40 BYTE;
            DECLARE I BYTE;

                                                /* read in the ages */
                              .
OVER$40 = 0;                                    /* initialize the count */
DO I = 0 to 9;
IF AGE(I) > 40 THEN OVER$40 = OVER$40 + 1;
END;

                                                /* do something with result */
```

```
END OVER$40$THE$EASY$WAY;
```

Arrays may be of types other than BYTE as shown by the following examples:

```
DECLARE LOTS$OF$LITTLE$THINGS (100) BYTE;
DECLARE LOTS$OF$BIG$THINGS (25) WORD;
```

```
DECLARE LOTS$OF$SIGNED$THINGS (50) INTEGER;
DECLARE LOTS$OF$FRACTIONAL$THINGS (10) REAL;
```

Another method of grouping related variables together is the *structure*. An example of a structure is

```
DECLARE RELATED$THINGS STRUCTURE
    (LITTLE$THING BYTE, BIG$THING WORD);
```

and the individual components (called *members*) in the structure can be referred to as RELATED$THINGS.LITTLE$THING and RELATED$THINGS. BIG$THING. There are several obvious differences between structures and arrays:

1. The components of an array are called elements; the components of a structure are called members.
2. The elements of an array are all of the same type, while the members of a structure may be of differing types.
3. An element in an array is referred to by its position in the array (which may be the value of a variable). A member in a structure is referred to by its name (which is fixed in the program).

The members of a structure can be scalars or arrays. An example of a structure member being an array is as follows:

```
DECLARE PERSON STRUCTURE (NAME (15) BYTE,
    AGE BYTE, HEIGHT REAL, WEIGHT REAL);
```

The individual members in this structure can be referred to as PERSON.NAME (0), PERSON.NAME (1), . . ., PERSON.NAME (14), PERSON.AGE, PER-SON.HEIGHT, and PERSON.WEIGHT. Other examples of structure members being arrays are shown:

```
DECLARE PAYCHECK STRUCTURE (NAME (15) BYTE, SALARY WORD);
DECLARE AUTOMOBILE STRUCTURE (CHASSIS$NUMBER WORD,
    CYLINDERS BYTE, TIRE$PRESSURE (4) REAL);
```

Now that we've seen arrays inside of structures, let's take a look at structures within arrays. For example:

```
DECLARE PLAYING$CARD (52) STRUCTURE (SUIT BYTE, VALUE BYTE);
```

Some of the components in this array of structures are PLAYING$CARD (7). SUIT and PLAYING$CARD (25).VALUE. Let's go one step further and look at arrays within structures within arrays such as:

```
DECLARE PAYCHECK (100) STRUCTURE (NAME (15) BYTE, SALARY WORD);
```

Some of the components here are PAYCHECK (38).NAME (7) and PAYCHECK (70).SALARY. You may be wondering where this will all end. Don't worry; it just did. PL/M-86 prohibits structures within structures, so an array of structures containing arrays is the most complex thing we can declare.

It's time for us to look at an example involving structures. Consider a company that keeps all its payroll information in a computer file. Every payday the company runs its payroll program, which reads this file and prints the paychecks. But now it's raise time, and the company wants to give everybody a $200 raise. So it executes the following program:

```
RAISES:
    DO;
        DECLARE PAYCHECK (100) STRUCTURE
            (NAME (15) BYTE, SALARY WORD);
        DECLARE I BYTE;

        .
        .                    /* read in the payroll file */
        .

        DO I = 0 to 99;      /* increase everyone's salary */
            PAYCHECK(I).SALARY = PAYCHECK(I).SALARY+200;
        END;

        .
        .                    /* write out the updated file */
        .

    END RAISES;
```

Memory Locations   When we write a declaration such as,

```
DECLARE MY$SPECIAL$BYTE BYTE;
```

in our program, we are telling the compiler to pick some unused byte in memory and reserve it for MY$SPECIAL$BYTE. Usually we don't care where in memory that byte is located. But every so often we must assert ourselves so that we can feel we are the masters over the machine. To cater to our needs, PL/M-86 allows us to specify the location explicitly as follows:

```
DECLARE MY$SPECIAL$BYTE BYTE AT (3000H);
```

Such explicit control is useful if certain locations have very specialized meanings. For example, we may have wired up our processor so that location 3000H does not refer to a memory location but refers to an input port instead. As we saw in Chap. 4, this is called *memory-mapped I/O*. In that case, it would be very important that the variable MY$SPECIAL$BYTE refer to location 3000H and to nowhere else.

Even when we don't tell the compiler where to locate a variable, there are times when we need to know which location the compiler picked. That location is a constant (it doesn't ever change during the execution of our program), and we might want to use that constant in our program. PL/M-86 lets us express that constant without telling us what the constant is. This is done by writing @MY$SPECIAL$BYTE in the program whenever we want to refer to the location of MY$SPECIAL$BYTE. Such constants are called *reference-location constants*.

One thing we might want to do with a reference-location constant is specify the location of one variable in terms of the location of some other variable. For example:

```
DECLARE FLOOR (20) WORD;
DECLARE LOBBY AT WORD (@FLOOR(0));
```

Thus we can refer to the ground floor either by FLOOR(0) or by its nickname LOBBY.

Another thing we might want to do with a reference-location constant is assign it to some other variable. For example, we might want to write:

```
MY$SPECIAL$LOCATION = @MY$SPECIAL$BYTE;
```

But before we write such an assignment, let's make sure we're not assigning apples to oranges. To determine this, we need to know the type of @MY$SPE-CIAL$BYTE. It can't be of type BYTE, WORD, or INTEGER because there can be more than one million values that @MY$SPECIAL$BYTE could have. And it would be strange for PL/M-86 to consider @MY$SPECIAL$BYTE as being of type REAL since locations in memory are never fractional values. So PL/M-86 has a special type called POINTER, which it uses to refer to locations in memory. Reference-location constants are of type POINTER. Also, whole-number constants can be of type POINTER instead of type BYTE, or WORD, or INTEGER, depending on where they're used. The following are examples of valid PL/M-86 assignments involving pointers:

```
DECLARE OZ REAL;
DECLARE YELLOW$BRICK$ROAD POINTER;
YELLOW$BRICK$ROAD = @OZ;

DECLARE DATA$PNTR POINTER;
DATA$PNTR = 3A07H;
```

Pointers are very restrictive in terms of where they can be used. They may not be used with arithmetic or logical operators. For example, the statement

```
DATA$PNTR = DATA$PNTR+1;
```

is invalid. The only operators that can be applied to pointers are the relational operators. Thus the following is valid:

```
IF DATA$PNTR=YELLOW$BRICK$ROAD THEN ...;
```

So if all we can do with pointers is compare them and assign to them, are they really useful? The answer to that question lies in the fact that we really don't want to do much with pointers but want to do a lot with the things they're pointing to. We want some way to refer to the thing being pointed at and use that just like any other variable in our program. We can assign a name to the thing being pointed at as follows:

```
DECLARE ITEM$PNTR POINTER;
DECLARE ITEM BASED ITEM$PNTR BYTE;
```

In this example, ITEM is declared to be the name of the byte that ITEM$PNTR points at. The location of ITEM is not fixed; it changes whenever a new value is assigned to ITEM$PNTR. ITEM is called a *based variable;* it is "based" on ITEM$PNTR.

An example of a program that uses a based variable would certainly be helpful now. The following program zeros the largest value in an array of words. First, we'll do it without based variables and then with based variables so you can compare them.

```
WITHOUT$BASED$VARIABLES:
    DO;
            DECLARE ITEM (50) WORD;              /* the array of words */
            DECLARE BIG$ITEM$INDEX BYTE;         /* index into array for
                                                    biggest value */
            DECLARE I BYTE;                      /* a running index into
                                                    array */

                    .
                    .                            /* read in the 50 values */
                    .
            BIG$ITEM$INDEX = 0;                  /* initialize the index */
            DO I = 1 TO 49;                      /* find the biggest item */
              IF ITEM(I)>ITEM(BIG$ITEM$INDEX)
                THEN BIG$ITEM$INDEX = I;
            END;
            ITEM(BIG$ITEM$INDEX) = 0;            /* zero out the biggest
                                                    item */

                    .                            /* write out the 50 values */
                    .
                    .
    END WITHOUT$BASED$VARIABLES;

WITH$BASED$VARIABLES:
    DO;
            DECLARE ITEM (50) WORD;              /* the array of words */
            DECLARE BIG$ITEM$PNTR POINTER;       /* pointer to biggest value */
            DECLARE BIG$ITEM BASED BIG$ITEM$PNTR
              WORD;                              /* this is the biggest item */
            DECLARE I BYTE;                      /* a running index into array */
                    .
                    .                            /* read in the 50 values */
                    .
            BIG$ITEM$PNTR = @ITEM(0);            /* initialize the pointer */
            DO I = 1 TO 49;                      /* find the biggest item */
              IF ITEM (I)>BIG$ITEM
                THEN BIG$ITEM$PNTR = @ITEM(I);
            END;
            BIG$ITEM = 0;                        /* zero out the biggest item */

                    .                            /* write out the 50 values */
                    .
                    .
    END WITH$BASED$VARIABLES;
```

Literal Declarations   As a convenience feature, PL/M-86 lets us assign a name to a sequence of characters. For example:

```
DECLARE PI LITERALLY '3.14159';
```

Then we can use PI later on in the program as a shorthand for 3.14159. Another use for such a declaration is to declare a constant that we might want to change next week (or next month, or next year). Rather than use that constant throughout the program, we give the constant a name like

```
DECLARE BUFFER$SIZE LITERALLY '32';
```

and use BUFFER$SIZE throughout the program. Now we need only make the change in one place. Things like PI and BUFFER$SIZE that are declared with LITERALLY are called *macros*.

Some programmers have discovered that they can even use LITERALLY to create synonyms for the reserved words in PL/M-86. Using this trick, they have shown how easy it is to write unreadable programs such as:

```
DECLARE LTL LITERALLY 'LITERALLY';
DECLARE DCL LTL 'DECLARE';
DCL WRD LTL 'WORD';
DCL MQP WRD;                              /* huh? */
```

You're free to use this trick if you wish, bt dnt cm 2 me whn u gt n trbl.

Fortunately, the name of a macro must be an identifier. Otherwise, think of the fun we could have by defining and using such macros as:

```
DECLARE ? LITERALLY ';';       /* no good */
```

Procedures

A very important concept in programming is the subroutine or procedure. It provides the ability to execute a section of code at several different places in the program without having to repeat the code at each of these places. Consider, for example, the problem of making change for a dollar:

```
MAKING$CHANGE:
     DO;
          DECLARE COINS (8) BYTE;            /* this is the result */
          DECLARE CHANGE BYTE;               /* number to be converted */
          DECLARE I BYTE;                    /* index into COINS array */
          CHANGE = 100-...;                  /* write the cost here */
          I = 0;                             /* initialize the index */
          DO WHILE CHANGE>=50;               /* half dollars */
               COINS(I) = 50;
               I = I+1;
               CHANGE = CHANGE-50;
          END;
          DO WHILE CHANGE>=25;               /* quarters */
               COINS(I) = 25;
               I = I+1;
               CHANGE = CHANGE-25;
          END;
          DO WHILE CHANGE>=10;               /* dimes */
               COINS(I) = 10;
               I = I+1;
               CHANGE = CHANGE-10;
          END;
          DO WHILE CHANGE>=5;                /* nickels */
               COINS(I) = 5;
               I = I+1;
               CHANGE = CHANGE-5;
```

```
        END;
        DO WHILE CHANGE >=1;                    /* pennies */
            COINS(I) = 1;
            I = I+1;
            CHANGE = CHANGE-1;
        END;
        DO WHILE I<8;                           /* zero out rest of coins */
            COINS(I) = 0;
            I = I+1;
        END;
    END MAKING$CHANGE;
```

Notice that the sequence of code

```
COINS(I) = X;
I = I+1;
CHANGE = CHANGE-X;
```

for different values of X occurs in several places. It sure would simplify the program if we could write this code only once and then call upon it from different places in the program. PL/M-86 lets us do just that by declaring the code to be a procedure as follows:

```
MAKING$CHANGE$WITH$PROCEDURES:
    DO;
                DECLARE COINS (8) BYTE;        /* this is the result*/
                DECLARE CHANGE BYTE;           /* number to be converted */
                DECLARE I BYTE;                /* index into COINS array */

                NEXT$COIN:                     /* this is a procedure
                    PROCEDURE (X);                declaration */
                        DECLARE X BYTE;        /* X is specified when procedure
                        COINS(I) = X;             is called */
                        I = I+1;
                        CHANGE = CHANGE-X;
                    END NEXT$COIN;

                CHANGE = 100-...;              /* write the cost here */
                I = 0;                         /* initialize the index */
                DO WHILE CHANGE >=50;          /* half dollar */
                    CALL NEXT$COIN(50);
                END;
                DO WHILE CHANGE >=25;          /* quarters */
                    CALL NEXT$COIN(25);
                END;
                DO WHILE CHANGE >=10;          /* dimes */
                    CALL NEXT$COIN(10);
                END;
                DO WHILE CHANGE >=5;           /* nickels */
                    CALL NEXT$COIN (5);
                END;
                DO WHILE CHANGE >=1;           /* pennies */
                    CALL NEXT$COIN(1);
                END;
                DO WHILE I<8;                  /* zero out rest of coins */
                    CALL NEXT$COIN(0);
                END;
    END MAKING$CHANGE$WITH$PROCEDURES;
```

This previous example has illustrated the fact that a procedure is a section of code that is declared rather than executed. It appears along with the other declarative statements of the program. It can be called into execution from other parts of the program by using CALL statements.

Passing Information   In many applications, we need to send input information to a procedure and receive output information (results) back. The simplest method of sending information to a procedure is by placing the information in a specific variable (or variables) before calling the procedure. The procedure knows to look in that variable. The same variable is used every time the procedure is called. The procedure can use this method for returning its results as well. An example of transferring information through specific variables is the following:

Declaration	*Call*

UP$COUNT:
     PROCEDURE;
         COUNT = COUNT+1;
     END UP$COUNT;
	CALL UP$COUNT;

In this example, COUNT is the specific variable used both for sending information to the procedure and for receiving information from the procedure.

Another method of sending information to a procedure is by specifying the information every time the procedure is called. Information specified in this manner is called a *parameter*. An example of a parameter is the 50 in

CALL NEXT$COIN(50);

Within the procedure, there is a variable corresponding to each parameter. Each time the procedure is called, the values of the parameters are placed in the corresponding variables. An example of using parameters is shown below:

Declaration	*Call*
	DECLARE MAX BYTE;
CHECK$SIZE:	DECLARE MIN BYTE;
PROCEDURE (I,J);	
DECLARE I BYTE;	CALL CHECK$SIZE(MAX,
DECLARE J BYTE;	MIN);
IF I<J THEN COUNT = COUNT+1;	
END CHECK$SIZE;	

In this example, the values (not the locations) of MAX and MIN are passed to CHECK$SIZE and become the values of its parameters I and J. CHECK$SIZE does not know where MAX and MIN are located and therefore cannot change their values.

If a parameter contained the location of a value instead of the value itself, the procedure could either fetch a value from that location or place a result in that location or both. This is illustrated in the following example:

Declaration	*Call*

```
                                          DECLARE FIRST BYTE;
SWITCH:                                    DECLARE LAST BYTE;
    PROCEDURE (I,J);
        DECLARE I POINTER;                 CALL SWITCH(@FIRST,
        DECLARE J POINTER;                     @LAST);
        DECLARE VAL$I BASED I BYTE;
        DECLARE VAL$J BASED J BYTE;
        DECLARE TEMP BYTE;
        TEMP = VAL$I;
        VAL$I = VAL$J;
        VAL$J = TEMP;
    END SWITCH;
```

Notice that what was passed to the procedure was not the value of FIRST and LAST but rather their *locations*—namely @FIRST and @LAST. Thus the values in I and J are the locations of FIRST and LAST. Now we need variables within the procedure that correspond to FIRST and LAST. But this is exactly what we get when we declare variables VAL$I and VAL$J that are based on I and J. So within the procedure, we can talk about VAL$I and VAL$J as if they were the variables FIRST AND LAST.

There is one more way a result can be returned from a procedure. But before looking at this final method, let's introduce the RETURN statement. Up to this point, we have been assuming that the procedure returns when it gets to its END statement. In fact, we could make this explicit by writing a RETURN statement just before the END statement as shown below:

```
UPCOUNT:
    PROCEDURE;
        COUNT = COUNT+1;
        RETURN;                      /* this statement is optional */
    END UPCOUNT;
```

Such a RETURN statement is not necessary since the compiler understands that it must do a return whenever it gets to the end of a procedure. However, some procedures might want to return before the end is reached. In such cases, an explicit RETURN statement is necessary. The following procedure illustrates this:

```
UPCOUNT:
    PROCEDURE;
        IF COUNT=10 THEN RETURN;
        COUNT = COUNT+1;
        RETURN;                      /* this statement is optional */
    END UPCOUNT;
```

Now we can look at the final way a result can be received from a procedure—in the procedure's name. The procedure is not called into execution with a CALL statement; instead, it is called by using the name of the procedure as an operand in an expression. Let's look at the following example:

Declaration

```
PHONE$BILL:
     PROCEDURE (NUMBER$OF$CALLS) WORD;
          DECLARE NUMBER$OF$CALLS BYTE;
          RETURN 500+5*NUMBER$OF$CALLS;
     END PHONE$BILL;
```

Use

```
EXPENSES = PHONE$BILL(78)+ELECTRIC$BILL(113)+...;
```

Procedures that return results on their own name are distinguished from other procedures in two ways. First, the RETURN statement(s) specify the value of the result to be returned (and thus the RETURN statement before the END statement is no longer optional). Second, the procedure specifies the type (WORD in the PHONE$BILL example) of the result to be returned. Such procedures are called *typed procedures*.

Thus we have seen three ways of sending information to procedures and three ways of receiving information back. These ways are summarized below:

Sending to Procedure	*Receiving from Procedure*
specified variables	specified variables
value parameters	location parameters
location parameters	typed procedures

Interrupt Procedures The interrupt mechanism of the 8086 was described in Chap. 3. Briefly summarizing it, an external device can interrupt the processor by sending the processor an interrupt signal and a number between 0 and 255. The processor responds to the interrupt signal by executing an interrupt routine corresponding to the number. PL/M-86 allows you to specify interrupt routines by declaring procedures that include interrupt numbers. Such procedures are called *interrupt procedures*. Unlike conventional procedures that are called into execution with CALL statements, an interrupt procedure is called into execution automatically when the processor responds to an interrupt. The following procedure would be called into execution when interrupt type 75 occurs:

```
KEY$PRESS:
     PROCEDURE INTERRUPT 75;
          CHARACTER = INPUT(1);
     END KEY$PRESS;
```

Reentrant Procedures It is sometimes, although not often, desirable to have a procedure call itself. As an example, we might want to write a procedure that calculates factorials (remember factorials?—things like 7! = 7*6*5*4*3*2*1 and things like 100! = a-very-big-number). One way to calculate 7! (pronounced seven factorial) would be to calculate 6! and multiply the result by 7. So the factorial procedure that is asked for the factorial of X could call upon the factorial procedure (which means calling upon itself) to calculate the factorial of X−1 and then multiply that result by X. But if we're not careful, this may never end. So to make sure this sequence of procedure calls terminates, the factorial procedure, when asked for the factorial of 1, could simply return the result 1 without calling on any other procedures. An example of the factorial procedure written in PL/M-86 is shown below:

```
FACTORIAL:
    PROCEDURE (X) WORD REENTRANT;
        DECLARE X BYTE;
        IF X=1 THEN RETURN 1;
        RETURN X*FACTORIAL(X-1);
    END FACTORIAL;
```

The FACTORIAL procedure contains something we haven't seen before—namely the designation REENTRANT in the procedure declaration. This tells the compiler that the procedure might be entered at least once more before it finishes and returns the answer it was initially asked for. The compiler has to know this so that it can preserve any information (such as the value of X) associated with the intitial entry. Let's see what would happen if the compiler didn't preserve this information. When the FACTORIAL procedure is called from a statement such as

```
ANSWER = 1+FACTORIAL(7);
```

the value of variable X is 7. The FACTORIAL procedure will then call on FACTORIAL(7−1). Now the FACTORIAL procedure will be reentered with X having a value of 6. The original value of X, namely 7, has been lost. But with that value of X lost, the initial call on FACTORIAL(7) will no longer be able to return the correct result for X*FACTORIAL(7−1). What saves the day is the designation REENTRANT; it causes the compiler to use a different memory location for X each time the procedure is entered.

A procedure calling itself is only one way a procedure might be reentered. Another way is for a procedure to call on a second procedure, and that second procedure in turn to call on the original procedure. Both of these forms of reentrancy are called *recursion*. A procedure can also be reentered if an interrupt occurs while the procedure is being executed and, during the interrupt processing, the procedure is called again. Such popular (?) procedures as INVERSE$HYPERBOLIC$COSECANT might very well be called upon during the main stream of processing and also during the servicing of an interrupt.

Any procedures that might be entered more than once before returning must be designated as REENTRANT if they are to execute correctly. If in doubt about any procedures, you can always designate them as REENTRANT, and they will execute correctly. The only penalty you pay for designating a procedure as REENTRANT is that the procedure can't put a value into a variable local to the procedure and expect to find that same value the next time the procedure is called.

Indirect Procedure Calls
To end this section with a bit of confusion, let's assume we want to call on a procedure, but we don't know which one. And we won't know which one until the program is in execution. For example, we

want to convert 50 into a sequence of digits, but the kind of conversion varies depending on what came before. This can be done as follows:

```
DECLARE A$CONVERSION$ROUTINE POINTER;
             .
             .
             .
A$CONVERSION$ROUTINE = @CONVERT$TO$BINARY;
GO TO COMMON$PLACE;
             .
             .
             .
A$CONVERSION$ROUTINE = @CONVERT$TO$OCTAL;
GO TO COMMON$PLACE;
             .
             .
             .
A$CONVERSION$ROUTINE = @CONVERT$TO$HEXADECIMAL;
GO TO COMMON$PLACE;
             .
             .
             .
A$CONVERSION$ROUTINE = @CONVERT$TO$ROMAN$NUMERALS;
GO TO COMMON$PLACE;
             .
             .
             .
COMMON$PLACE:
CALL A$CONVERSION$ROUTINE (50);
```

At various places throughout this program, we assign the location of some conversion routine to A$CONVERSION$ROUTINE. Then, when we get to COMMON$PLACE, we can call on a conversion routine indirectly and even pass a parameter to it as shown above.

Block Structure and Scope

So far we have seen how to declare objects (variables, procedures, labels, macros) in one part of a program and use them somewhere else in the program. But we've never said just where in the program we can refer to objects once they are declared. The portions of a program in which the name of an object is recognized is called the *scope* of the object.

Before we can talk about scope, we must introduce the concept of a block. A *block* is a sequence of statements starting with either DO or PROCEDURE and ending with the matching END. An entire PL/M-86 program is a block.

Other kinds of blocks in PL/M-86 are as follows:

1. Procedure declaration
2. Simple-DO block
3. DO-WHILE block
4. Iterative-DO block
5. DO-CASE block

We have already seen that objects can be declared at the beginning of a procedure declaration. They may also be declared at the beginning of any simple-DO block.

Now we can define the scope of an object. The scope is specified by the following equation:

scope = block in which object is declared
    + all nested blocks
    − those nested blocks that redeclare the same identifier

One restriction is that objects must be declared before they are used (this makes the compiler's life much simpler) with the exception of reentrant procedures (the compiler has agreed to work overtime for us here). But since labels are objects, we have to say what we mean by "the declaration of a label." A label is considered to be declared at the head of the smallest block of any kind enclosing the "label:." Let's clarify and motivate these scope rules with some examples:

Example 1: Scope includes block in which object is declared.

```
DO;
      DECLARE X BYTE;
      X = X+1;                    /* of course this is within the scope of X */
END;
```

Example 2: Scope includes nested blocks as well.

```
DO;
      DECLARE X BYTE;
      DO;
            DECLARE Y BYTE;
            X = Y+1;             /* this is also within the scope of X */
            END;
END;
```

Example 3: Scope does not include nested blocks in which same identifier is redeclared.

```
DO;
      DECLARE X BYTE;
      DO;
      DECLARE X (5) BYTE;
      X = X+1;                    /* error since this is outside the
                                     scope of scaler X */
      X(3) = X(2)+1;              /* however, this is within the
                                     scope of array X */

      END;
      X = X+1;                    /* and this is within the scope of
                                     scaler X */
END;
```

Example 4: Scope does not include outer block.

```
DO;
      DO;
            DECLARE X BYTE;
      END;
      X = X+1;                    /* error since this is outside the scope of X */
END;
```

Example 5: Objects must be declared before being used.

```
DO;
    A:
            PROCEDURE;
        X = X+1;                    /* error since X not yet declared */
        END A;
        DECLARE X BYTE;
END;
```

Example 6: Labels can be forward referenced.

```
DO;
        ...                         /*declaration of L considered as being here */
        GO TO L;                    /* OK since L already declared */
        L:                          /* this is not the declaration */
END;
```

Example 7: Label scope includes inner blocks as well.

```
DO;
        ...                         /* declaration of L considered here */
        DO;
                GO TO L;
        END;
        L:                          /* this is not the declaration*/
END;
```

Example 8: Reentrant procedures can be called before being declared.

```
DO;

    A:
            PROCEDURE REENTRANT;
                CALL B;
            END A;
    B:
            PROCEDURE REENTRANT;
                CALL A;
            END B;
END;
```

In this case, it would be impossible to declare both procedures (A and B) before either one is referenced since each one refers to the other. This explains why REENTRANT procedures are exceptions to the "declare before using" rule.

Input and Output

No discussion of a programming language would be complete without a description of how to get data into the program and how to get answers out. In our early example, we saw how to get data in with

```
SUM = SUM+INPUT(3);
```

and how to get answers out with

```
OUTPUT(3) = SUM;
```

In general, a byte of data can be read from any input port i by using INPUT(i) as
an operand in an expression, and a byte of data can be written to any output port j
by using OUTPUT(j) on the left side of an assignment statement. Furthermore, a
word of data can be read from or written to a port by using INWORD(i) or
OUTWORD(j). An example of a program that reads 16-bit data values from the
first 100 input ports and writes them out to the corresponding output ports is as
follows:

```
IN$ONE$PORT$AND$OUT$THE$OTHER:
    DO;
        DECLARE I BYTE;
        DO I = 0 TO 99;
            OUTWORD(I) = INWORD(I);
        END;
    END IN$ONE$PORT$AND$OUT$THE$OTHER;
```

Modular Programming

So far we have been calling the block of code starting with "NAME: DO;"
and ending with "END NAME;" a program. In truth, this is only a *module;* a
program is a collection of one or more modules. Each module is compiled
independently of the other modules. This enables a program to be subdivided
among several programmers. It also permits a single programmer to partition his
program into small, easily comprehended sections.

Let's review the structure of a module. It takes the following form:

```
NAME:
    DO;
        statement;
        statement

          .
          .
          .

        statement;
    END NAME;
```

The above statements can be either declarative statements or executable
statements (with declarative statements coming first). Any of the statements may
be blocks (procedure declarations, DO-WHILE blocks, etc.) with other
statements included in them. We need to distinguish those statements explicitly
mentioned in the form above from any statements that may be included in those
statements. Thus we will use the term *statements on the outermost level* to refer
to those statements explicitly shown above.

One of the modules that comprises a program is given the name *main
program*. Actually, main module would have been a better name, but it's too late
now to change history. The main program consists of (possibly) declarative
statements and (certainly) executable statements on the outermost level. In fact,
the main program could be the complete program by itself. However, it sometimes lacks the declarations of some of the objects referred to in its executable
statements. These declarations are to be found in the other modules. The other

modules are distinguishable from the main program because they contain only declarative statements on the outermost level.

So now a technique for using modules emerges. We might subdivide a program into the task of reading or writing the data from some complex data structure (such as might be found in an airline reservation system) and the task of manipulating the data that was read or is to be written. The procedure declarations of those procedures that read or write the data, along with the declaration of the data itself, could be written into one module. The actual manipulations on the data (the booking of the reservations) would go into the main program and might even be written by a different person.

We have previously made the point that declarative statements conveyed information to the compiler so that it would know what kind of code to generate for the executable statements. For example,

DECLARE THIS$HERE$THING WORD;

lets the compiler know that when it encounters

THIS$HERE$THING = 0;

it must generate code to zero out two bytes of memory rather than just one byte. Furthermore, the DECLARE statement caused the compiler to reserve a specific pair of bytes for THIS$HERE$THING. Thus, the compiler knew which two bytes had to be zeroed when the assignment statement was encountered.

Now if the declaration for THIS$HERE$THING is in some other module, the compiler is stymied when it sees the assignment statement involving THIS$HERE$THING. It could possibly do without the location of THIS$HERE$THING by generating code that zeros out any old location and making a note that someone has to fill in the correct location later. But the compiler can't generate any code at all unless it knows whether THIS$HERE$THING is a BYTE or a WORD.

To help the compiler, any module that uses THIS$HERE$THING without declaring it must at least tell the compiler what sort of a thing it is. It does this by saying that THIS$HERE$THING is a WORD that is declared external to this module. In PL/M-86 this is written:

DECLARE THIS$HERE$THING WORD EXTERNAL;

Although this looks like a declaration, it is not; it merely specifies the type of THIS$HERE$THING but does not reserve any memory for it. The compiler can now generate the right kind of code for the assignment statement, but it still doesn't know what memory location to put in the code.

In the module where THIS$HERE$THING is really declared, it would be nice to tell the compiler that some other module is going to use THIS$HERE$THING. Then the compiler could make a note of the location of THIS$HERE$THING so that later someone can fill that location into the code generated by the other module. Thus we write the declaration as

DECLARE THIS$HERE$THING WORD PUBLIC;

to make it clear to the compiler that this declaration is public information, available for use by other modules.

After all the modules have been compiled, someone still has to go around reading all the notes left by the compiler. These notes are attached to the code generated for each module, and they specify either (1) where the location of THIS$HERE$THING has to be written into the code or (2) what the location of THIS$HERE$THING is. The location of THIS$HERE$THING can then be written into the appropriate places in the code. This process is referred to as *linking* the code of the various modules together. A person or a program that does this linking is called a *linker*. Don't panic; you won't have to be a linker. When you receive your PL/M-86 compiler, you'll also find a linker program in the same package.

The following example illustrates the use of modules. The first module is the main program and uses SUCCESSOR and COUNT.

```
M1:
    DO;                                          /* first module */
        DECLARE COUNT BYTE PUBLIC;               /* here's a declaration */
        SUCCESSOR:
        PROCEDURE (X) BYTE PUBLIC;               /* here's another */
            DECLARE X BYTE;
            RETURN X+1;
        END SUCCESSOR;
    END M1;
M2:
    DO;                                          /* second module */
        DECLARE ARG BYTE;                        /* this is a declaration */
        DECLARE COUNT BYTE EXTERNAL;             /* this is not */
        SUCCESSOR:
        PROCEDURE (X) BYTE EXTERNAL;             /* nor is this */
            DECLARE X BYTE;
        END SUCCESSOR;
        ARG = 3;
        COUNT = SUCCESSOR(ARG);
    END M2;
```

Tying It All Together

Let's finish up by returning to our traffic light example. The example was introduced in Fig. 1.3 to show a typical microprocessor application. By the time we were into Chap. 4, we knew enough to be able to design an 8086 system that would control the traffic light. This was shown in Fig. 4.16. Now we can write a program that can be used in that system.

The traffic light is situated on a main highway at the intersection with a small cross street. The light is to behave as follows. It will normally be green for the highway and red for the cross street. After the number of cars lined up in the cross street exceeds 5, the light will become red on the highway and blinking yellow on the cross street. This will continue until there are no more cars left in the cross street.

The system shown in Fig. 4.16 has the traffic light connected as a memory-mapped output port at memory location 1000 (hexadecimal). Let us assume that the individual bulbs in the light are wired up so they correspond to the bits in location 1000 as follows:

(leftmost bit)   7   Red bulb on main highway
                   6   Yellow bulb on main highway
                   5   Green bulb on main highway
                   4   Left-turn bulb on main highway
                   3   Red bulb on cross street
                   2   Yellow bulb on cross street
                   1   Green bulb on cross street
(rightmost bit)   0   Left-turn bulb on cross street

The system also has an input port (not shown in Fig. 4.16), which tells the processor how many cars are waiting in the cross street. This port receives its information from sensors (along with some counting circuitry) buried in the roadway. Let us assume that this input is connected as port 50.

The following PL/M-86 program will cause the traffic light to behave the way we specified:

```
TRAFFIC$LIGHT:
    DO;
            DECLARE LIGHTS BYTE AT (1000H);      /* memory-mapped output */
            DECLARE CAR$COUNT LITERALLY  'INPUT(50)';      /* input */
            DECLARE MAIN$RED LITERALLY '80H';    /* names for individual bulbs */
            DECLARE MAIN$YELLOW LITERALLY '40H';
            DECLARE MAIN$GREEN LITERALLY '20H';
            DECLARE MAIN$LEFT$TURN LITERALLY '10H';
            DECLARE CROSS$RED LITERALLY '08H';
            DECLARE CROSS$YELLOW LITERALLY '04H';
            DECLARE CROSS$GREEN LITERALLY '02H';
            DECLARE CROSS$LEFT$TURN LITERALLY '01H';

    DELAY:
            PROCEDURE (X);                       /* causes an X second delay */
                DECLARE X BYTE;
                        .
                        .
                        .
            END DELAY;

    START:
            LIGHTS = MAIN$GREEN +CROSS$RED;  /* normal setting */
            IF CAR$COUNT>5 THEN              /* too many cars waiting */
              DO;                            /* let them go through */
                LIGHTS = MAIN$YELLOW +CROSS$RED;  /* stop highway */
                CALL DELAY(3);
                DO WHILE CAR$COUNT>0;  /* start cross street */
```

```
        LIGHTS = MAIN$RED
        CALL DELAY(1);
        LIGHTS = MAIN$RED +CROSS$YELLOW;
        CALL DELAY (1);
      END;
   END;
   GO TO START;              /* and repeat the cycle */
END;                         /* of program */
```

Let's add a degree of complexity to the system. This time we'll make all the traffic lights in the town become blinking red (in all directions) whenever a fire alarm is sounded. Assume we have two signals that are sent from the firehouse to every traffic light. One of these signals indicates the alarm has been sounded; the other indicates the all clear situation.

We'll connect the alarm signal to the INTR pin on our processor and incorporate some circuitry to convey the corresponding interrupt type (say it's 10) to the processor at the appropriate time. The all clear signal we'll connect as input port 51, so that all 1's (true) are read from this port when the emergency is over and all 0's (false) otherwise. And we'll include the following procedure declaration in our program:

```
FIRE$ALARM:
     PROCEDURE INTERRUPT 10;
          DECLARE SAVED$LIGHTS BYTE;
          DECLARE ALL$CLEAR LITERALLY 'INPUT(51)';
          SAVED$LIGHTS = LIGHTS;        /* we need to restore these later */

          DO WHILE NOT ALL$CLEAR;       /* blinking red */
               LIGHTS = 0;
               CALL DELAY (1);
               LIGHTS = MAIN$RED +CROSS$RED;
               CALL DELAY (1);
          END;
          LIGHTS = SAVED$LIGHTS;        /* restore old settings */
     END FIRE$ALARM;
```

We'll stop the design here. But you might want to try modifying the program to do more elaborate things, such as controlling the northbound lights independently of the southbound lights, controlling the left turn arrow, varying the delays to accommodate for peak hours, and anything else you can think of.

In Conclusion

This chapter was not meant to be a compendium of all the features and rules in PL/M-86 (the *Intel PL/M-86 Programming Manual* does that very well). Instead, it attempted to present most of the features of the language in a form that was easy to digest and conveyed enough information so that you could write meaningful programs. We didn't cover many of the fine details (like "thou shalt not declare interrupt procedures except on the outermost level of the program"), which, although important, really get in the way when you're trying to learn the language. We also didn't present some of the dispensable features (like type

ADDRESS for compatibility with an earlier version of PL/M) so that attention could be focused on the more useful features.

Finally, if you've been keeping track of all the facilities provided by the 8086 and comparing them to the things you can write in PL/M-86, you've probably discovered that there's no way to generate the string instructions, the shift or rotate instructions, or the LOCK prefix. These facilities, although not a part of the PL/M-86 language, are available by calling built-in procedures (procedures that the compiler knows about and you didn't have to write). A description of the built-in procedures can be found in the *Intel PL/M-86 Programming Manual* and will not be presented here.

8

8086

High-Level-Language

Programming (Pascal)

Who Needs High-Level Languages?

Programs for the 8086 can be written either at the level of the problem to be solved (high level) or at the level of the processor on which the problem is to be solved (low level). The low-level approach is necessary when programs don't fit into the amount of memory that's been allocated for them. But there are times when concentrating on the problem is more advantageous than concentrating on the processor. It's at those times that high-level languages and compilers prove indispensable.

Virtues often attributed to high-level language programs are high reliability, portability, ease of maintenance, and being self-documenting. High reliability is another way of saying that the program has a good chance of doing what's expected of it. Portability means the program can be moved from one processor to another. Ease of maintenance refers to the fact that future changes can be made with little difficulty. And self-documenting means that its easy to read and understand.

To illustrate these points, let's write a program that finds the smallest number divisible by three that is greater than 100. The answer, of course, is 102; but let's see how the 8086 can be used to figure it out.

One way to solve the problem would be to start with zero and keep adding three until the result exceeds 100. More specifically, start with X being zero and, while X is less than or equal to 100, add three to X.

A high-level programming language would let you write down the program directly from the verbal description of the solution. In the programming language called Pascal, this would look like:

```
X := 0;
while X< = 100 do X := X + 3;
```

207

Note that the above program could be written without giving any thought to the instruction set of the 8086. The program would be fed into a compiler, which generates the 8086 instructions for us.

Now let's try to write an assembly-language (low-level) program to find the result. We need to convert the description of the solution into a sequence of steps corresponding to 8086 instructions.

1. Reserve a byte in memory for X.

2. Move a zero into that byte for X.

3. Add three to X.

4. Compare the value in X to 100.

5. If the comparison indicates X does not exceed 100, go back to step 3.

6. We've got the result, so halt.

From these steps, we can write the program in ASM-86, an assembly language for the 8086.

```
1.   X          DB      ?
2.              MOV     X,0
3.   REPEAT     ADD     X,3
4.              CMP     X,100
5.              JNA     REPEAT
6.              HLT
```

Now that you've seen the different levels of programming of the 8086, it's up to you to make a choice. If you still believe in low-level programming exclusively, the remainder of this chapter would be of little interest to you. However, if you believe you may have some use for high-level languages, read on.

The most popular high-level languages are Pascal, COBOL, BASIC, and FORTRAN. COBOL is a popular language in commercial data-processing applications. FORTRAN is used frequently in applications involving numerical computations. BASIC is a favorite language, especially among microcomputer hobbyists, because of its simplicity and its interactive nature; BASIC programs are often executed directly without first being compiled into machine-language instructions.

Pascal is a language that was originally intended to be used for teaching purposes. It has been gaining in popularity recently for uses other than teaching and may supplant PL/M-86 as the language of choice for programming the 8086. Pascal is discussed in detail in this chapter.

Structure of Pascal Programs

Let's not waste time introducing our first Pascal program.

```
1. program Adder;
2.    const
```

```
3.     Scale = 2;
4.   var
5.     Sum: Integer;
6.     Next: Integer
7.   begin {add inputs divided by scale factor until total exceeds 100}
8.   Sum := 0;
9.   while Sum< = 100 do
10.     begin
11.     Read(Next);
12.     Sum := Sum + (Next div Scale);
13.     end;
14.   Write(Sum)
15.   end.
```

Without knowing a thing about Pascal, we can read and almost understand the program above. Line 1 seems to be telling us that the name of the program is Adder. Line 2 must mean that we are going to define some **const**ants and, in particular, line 3 defines the constant called Scale to have the value of 2. Line 4 looks like we're about to declare some **var**iables and lines 5 and 6 tell us that these variables are named Sum and Next and can take on integer values. Line 7 seems to be **begin**ning something which line 15 must be **end**ing. The period on line 15 has a strong overtone of finality which looks like the end of the program. The English on line 7 is telling us what it is that this program hopes to accomplish. So far, none of these lines have generated any instructions. Line 8 looks like the first instruction—moving zero into Sum. Lines 9 through 13 seem to be related; they are grouped together and start off with **begin** and finish with **end**. They seem to be repeatedly reading in values, **div**iding them by 2, and adding the result to Sum until Sum exceeds 100. This is just what the comment on line 7 promised we would do. Finally, line 14 looks like it's writing out the final value of Sum.

From this example, let's try to generalize about the structure of a Pascal program. It starts off with a heading that introduces the program name, and it ends with a period. The remainder of the program seems to be divided between a description of the items (primarily data) used by the program (such as Sum:Integer) and the actions performed by the program on this data [such as Sum := Sum + (Next **div** Scale)]. The data description occurs in sections of the program that are preceded with words like **const** (definition of constants) and **var** (declaration of variables). The actions performed by the program are described by a sequence of statements bounded by the words **begin** and **end** (although more **begin-end** pairs may appear within these statements). Semicolons are used profusely; they separate adjacent statements, terminate each data description, and pop up in other assorted places as well. The structure of a Pascal program is shown below:

program name;
    label   {we'll learn about labels later}
        label-declaration, label-declaration, ... , label-declaration;

    const
        constant-definition;
        constant-definition;

```
                    .
                    .
                    .
          constant-definition;

type                              {we'll also learn about types later}
          type-definition;
          type-definition;
                    .
                    .
                    .
          type-definition;

var
          variable-declaration;
          variable-declaration;
                    .
                    .
                    .
          variable declaration;

          procedure-or-function-declaration;    {be patient, ...}
          procedure-or-function-declaration;    {... we'll learn about these too}
                    .
                    .
                    .
          procedure-or-function-declaration;

begin
          statement;
          statement;
                    .
                    .
                    .
          statement
end.
```

The programs presented here all display a consistent indentation pattern. Such indentation is not part of the program structure. It is purely optional as far as a Pascal compiler is concerned but is highly recommended to make the programs easier for us to read and understand. As an extreme example of this point, consider the following unindented version of the preceding program. It would present no additional difficulty to any Pascal compiler (in fact, it would compile faster) but would be much less comprehensible to us.

```
program Adder;const Scale = 2;var Sum:Integer;Next:Integer;begin
{add inputs divides by scale factor until total exceeds 100} Sum: = 0;
while Sum< = 100 do begin Read(Next);Sum: = Sum + (Next div Scale);end;Write(Sum)end.
```

Tokens

Before examining the kinds of definitions, declarations, and statements from which Pascal programs are built, we must become familiar with the building blocks of these three bigger building blocks. The smaller building blocks consist of such things as *identifiers, reserved words, delimiters, constants,* and *comments.* They are sometimes called *tokens.*

Identifiers   Identifiers are names that you, the programmer, are free to make up. An example of an identifier in the sample program already discussed is Sum. An identifier is a sequence of letters (upper or lower case) and numbers (digits) starting with a letter. Examples of identifiers are the following:

> X
> GAMMA
> Jack5

No distinction is made between upper or lower case letters in identifiers so the last identifier above is indistinguishable from the identifier written as JACK5. For the most part, identifiers in this chapter will be written like English proper nouns (first letter in upper case, remaining letters in lower case) except where interspersing upper and lower case letters helps to clarify the intended meaning of the identifier. For example, the identifier Pagenine might look like a mean-ingless word whereas PageNine conveys its meaning clearly.

Reserved Words   Reserved words look like identifiers, but they have special meaning in the language, and you may not use them as identifier names. In our sample program, we saw such reserved words as **begin, end, var,** and **while.** Thus, it would be perfectly acceptable for us to make up an identifier name like Ending as in

var Ending: Integer;

but it would be improper for us to write

var End: Integer:

because **end** is a reserved word.

To distinguish reserved words from identifiers, reserved words will be writ-ten in boldface characters throughout this chapter (don't look for the shift-to-boldface key when typing your program—you probably won't find it and it's not necessary). A complete list of Pascal reserved words is given in Table 8.1.

Table 8.1 Reserved Words in Pascal

and	do	if	or	then
array	else	in	packed	to
begin	end	label	procedure	type
case	file	mod	program	until
const	for	nil	record	var
div	function	not	repeat	while
downto	goto	of	set	with

Delimiters   Delimiters are the nonalphanumeric character sequences appearing in Pascal programs. In our sample program, we saw such delimiters as $<=$ and ;. Each delimiter has a special meaning in the language, and we will become exposed to most of them in this chapter. A complete list of delimiters in Pascal is given in Table 8.2.

Table 8.2 Delimiters in Pascal

+	<	{	.	<>
−	>	}	,	<=
*	[	(	:	>=
/	]	)	;	:=
=		'	^	..

Constants   Constants are the fixed values appearing in Pascal programs. In our sample program, we saw such constants as 0, 2, and 100. These are *integer constants*; Pascal also allows for *real constants, character constants*, and *Boolean constants*. And, if that's not enough, we'll see later (in the section on enumerated types) how Pascal lets us create other types of constants that we might desire.

An integer constant can be any nonfractional value within some reasonably large range. Pascal compilers that generate code for the 8086 usually use -32767 to $+32767$ as that range.

A real constant is a number containing either a decimal point or an E (or both). The E indicates multiplication by a power of 10. For example, 1E6 means 1 times 10 to the sixth power ($1*10^6$) or one million. Examples of real constants are 15.6, 138., -3.14, 7E3, and $1.32E-7$.

A character constant is a single character enclosed within apostrophes. An apostrophe itself may be the character within a character constant by writing it as two consecutive apostrophes. Examples of character constants are 'a', ';', and ''''. The last example is the character constant consisting of the apostrophe character. Character constants are not numbers and cannot be used in place of integer or real constants in the program. But that's no problem, since we probably have no interest in writing such things as Sum := Sum + 'a' anyhow. What we do want to be able to do is treat character constants as characters—assign them to variables (Ch: = 'f'), compare them to other characters (**while** Ch<'G' **do** ...), and make decisions based on which character we have (**if** Ch = 'q' **then** ...). All of these things *are* allowed in Pascal.

Pascal also provides for something called *string constants*, but they are limited in how they can be used. We won't discuss string constants until we are actually ready to use them.

There are only two Boolean (or logical) constants—True and False. But that's all we need because, logically speaking, a thing either "is" or it "isn't." Like character constants, Boolean constants cannot be used in place of numbers so we can't write nonsense like Sum := True + 1. What we can do is assign

Boolean constants to variables (Raining : = True) that we can later use to base decisions on (**while** Raining **do** ...).

Note that we always capitalize Boolean but not real or integer or character. That's because Boolean is named for a person, George Boole. Boole developed an algebra of logic (called Boolean algebra) over the two element field True and False.

Comments   Comments are sequences of characters enclosed within the delimiters { and }. They have no meaning to the compiler but should be used generously in your program to keep reminding you of what you are doing. Although comments like

I := 0;   {I becomes zero}

would be absurd, comments like

I := 0;   {initialize array index prior to first iteration}

go a long way to making a program more readable.

Expressions

One more building block, namely expressions, must be introduced before we can build definitions, declarations, and statements. The expression itself is built up from some of the tokens just described.

Loosely speaking, an expression is a sequence of operands and operators that can be combined to produce a value. So now we must introduce both operands and operators and indicate how they are combined to produce the value of an expression.

If you have read and understood the section in Chap. 6 on expressions in assembly-language programming, you might find the following analogy interesting. In assembly-language programming, the instruction mnemonics (not the expressions) correspond to the items that get executed (instructions) when the program is run. In high-level languages, there are no instruction mnemonics; the expressions represent sequences of instructions that get executed when the program is run. Assembly-language expressions are evaluated at the time the program is being assembled; high-level language expressions are evaluated when the program is run.

Operands   An operand is something that has a value. The simplest kind of operand is a constant. Thus, 15, 2.7E5, 'z', and False are all operands. Another kind of operand is a variable representing a value. Frequently, this is simply an identifier, such as Sum in the sample program. Unlike a constant, the value represented by a variable is not known until you execute the program and will usually take on different values at different times during the execution.

Another operand is an expression itself, perhaps enclosed in parentheses, and used in some bigger expression such as in 3*(Sum + 2). The purpose of the parentheses is to force the order in which the operators are applied. If we make generous use of parentheses to make the ordering explicit, we won't have to memorize a bunch of "silly" rules about which operators get evaluated first.

Operators   An operator takes the value of one or more operands and produces a new value. There are four kinds of operators in Pascal—*arithmetic operators, relational operators, logical operators,* and *set operators.*

Arithmetic operators are nothing more than the familiar addition operator (+), subtraction operator (−), multiplication operator (*), and division operator) (/). But these operators cannot be used on just any operands. For example, we cannot (nor would we ever want to) write things like True + '$'. Arithmetic operators can be applied to numeric (integer or real) operands only; they cannot be applied to operands of any other *type* such as Boolean operands or character operands.

From the preceding paragraph, it appears as though types are an important concept, so let's introduce that concept now. A *type* is a collection of distinct values that a variable may assume. Every constant has a particular value and so belongs to some type. When we discussed constants, we saw that they fell into at least four different types—integer, real, character, and Boolean. Every variable, when it is declared, must have a type specified for it. In our sample program, we saw such declarations as Sum:Integer. And, finally, the results produced by each operator will be of some specified type. So, for each operator, there must be a rule that tells us the type of the result produced.

Now let's consider the rule for the addition and subtraction operators. The rule is simple. It states that (1) each operand must be either an integer or a real and (2) if both operands are integers, the result will be an integer, otherwise the result will be a real. For example,

an integer operand added to an integer operand gives an integer result,
a real operand added to a real operand gives a real result,
and an integer operand added to a real operand gives a real result.

Furthermore, you cannot add such things as Booleans to characters (nor may you add apples to oranges).

Such restrictions might appear to make the language harder to learn by giving us more rules to memorize. On the contrary, they make the language easier because we only have to remember one general rule—"you can only add what makes sense"—rather than having to memorize a bunch of rules like "if you add a character to a Boolean you get something altogether different." And besides, you probably didn't mean to add such things anyhow, so the compiler can help prevent you from making certain kinds of errors. But if you are persistent and really want to add such things, Pascal provides a function (it's called Ord but we'll learn about it later) that lets us convert many things into integers.

The rule for multiplication is the same as for addition and subtraction. But what about division? If it also used the same rule, dividing 9 (an integer) by 4 (another integer) would give an integer and we couldn't get an answer of 2.25 (a real). So the division operator (/) always gives a real result, even if both operands are integers. Now there are times when we are working with integers because reals have no meaning in our application, and we would like to remain with integers no matter what arithmetic operations we perform (someday I'd like to meet the average family with its 2.1 children). For this, Pascal provides us with another division operator, **div**, that takes two integer operands and produces an integer quotient by simply discarding any fractional part of the result. Thus, 19 **div** 7 is 2 and -19 **div** 7 is -2.

An operator related to **div** is **mod**. Both take two integer operands and produce an integer result. If both operands are positive, the result produced by **mod** is the remainder that results after dividing the two integers. Thus, 19 **mod** 7 is 5. But **mod** is not really a remainder operator. What it's actually doing in this example is subtracting (adding if the first operand were negative) enough 7s from 19 until the result is in the range of 0 to 6 (that's $7-1$). An example illustrating the use of **mod** would be to find the relative position within a century for any given year. For example, 1776 **mod** 100 is 76, 1215 **mod** 100 is 15, and -67 (that's 67 B.C.) **mod** 100 is 33 (33 years since the start of the first century B.C.).

The relational operators are equal ($=$), not-equal ($<>$), less-than ($<$), greater-than ($>$), less-than-or-equal ($<=$), and greater-than-or-equal ($>=$). In case you're puzzled how we get not-equal from $<>$, consider not-equal as the combination of less-than-or-greater-than. Now $<>$ makes sense (of course, $\neq$ would have made more sense, but it doesn't exist on standard keyboards).

The two operands of a relational operator must both be of the same type and the result is of type Boolean. For example, 6>5 yields True; 1.5=2.1 yields False; 'A'<>'a' yields True; and 7='7' is an invalid comparison (they're of different types).

Relational operators point out the interesting fact that the collection of values that make up a type is ordered. It's not surprising that the collection of integer values is ordered (we assumed this when we wrote the expression 6>5 above). We might not even be surprised to learn that the collection of character values is ordered so that the expression 'b'>'a' yields True. (For 8086 Pascal at least, the ordering of character constants is the same as the ordering of their associated ASCII codes.) But it is surprising to learn that the constants of a type like Boolean are ordered. In particular, Pascal considers that False<True yields the result True.

The logical operators are the usual **and**, **or**, and **not**. The operands of these operators must be of type Boolean and the result will also be a Boolean. For example,

True **and** True is True	True **or** True is True	
True **and** False is False	True **or** False is True	**not** True is False
False **and** True is False	False **or** True is True	**not** False is True
False **and** False is False	False **or** False is False	

Some words are in order for those of you who have read and understood the chapter on PL/M. Besides **and**, **or**, and **not**, PL/M has another logical operator called exclusive-or (**xor**). This operator returns a result of True if one or the other but not both of its operands are True, and returns a result of False otherwise. But this is exactly what the not-equal (<>) operator does in Pascal so we have no need for an exclusive-or operator. PL/M contains an exclusive-or operator distinct from the not-equal operator because, unlike Pascal, the logical operators in PL/M do not take Boolean operands; instead they operate on the equivalent of integer operands and perform bit-by-bit logical operations on corresponding bits in the two operands. So the logical operators of PL/M are not equivalent to the logical operators of Pascal even though the operators have the same names (**and**, **or**, and **not**).

We'll have to postpone a discussion of set operators until after we learn about sets.

Definitions, Declarations, and Statements

Now that we've met the trees (tokens and expressions in our case), let's step back and take a look at the forest (program). A Pascal program consists of a description of the data (and other items) used in the program followed by a description of the actions performed by the program on these items. The first category can be further subdivided into *definitions* of concepts and *declarations* of objects. The actions performed by the program are described by *statements*.

A definition introduces a name that can be used in place of some concept of the language. In the sample program, we defined the name Scale to have the same meaning as the constant 2. A declaration introduces an object of a particular type, associates a name with that object, and indicates any restrictions on how we intend to use the object. In response to the declaration, a compiler would allocate memory for the object if necessary. For example:

var
     Cost: 0..99; {a particular subrange of integers}

This declaration introduces an integer variable, gives it the name Cost, and says that we intend to keep our cost below 100.

A statement describes actions to be performed by the processor and causes the compiler to generate code that performs these actions. The actual code generated is influenced by the definitions and declarations. For example:

Cost := Cost + 3

This statement instructs the compiler to generate code that increases the value of Cost by 3. Because of the preceding declaration, the compiler has enough information to generate some instructions that inform us (when our program is executing) if we make an error and Cost gets above 99. Furthermore, the declaration has told the compiler that it should increase Cost by generating instructions that perform integer arithmetic rather than floating-point (real) arithmetic.

Statements

Some of the statements in Pascal are *assignment statements, selective statements, repetitive statements*, and *compound statements*. Each of these statements will be described in this section. Two other classes of statements, *procedure-invocation statements*, and **with** *statements* will be described in later sections—procedure-invocation statements in the section describing procedures and **with** statements in the section describing records.

Semicolons are used to separate adjacent statements. For example, three consecutive statements would be written as

```
A := 5; B := 0; C := 7
```

Of course the above example could have been written on three lines instead of one. In either case, there is no need for a semicolon after the 7. Inserting a semicolon there would not be wrong; rather it would mean that we actually have four statements instead of three, where the fourth statement contains no tokens and performs no actions (the empty statement). Let's see how these three statements would look in a program:

```
program Semicolons;
... {data description section}
begin
A := 5;
B := 0;
C := 7
end.
```

Again, notice that there is no need for a semicolon after the 7. But if later we decide to add a statement following C := 7, we must remember to go back and put in the semicolon. There's a good chance we'll forget, so let's simply avoid the problem and always follow every statement with a semicolon. The program examples in the remainder of this chapter will contain such semicolons.

Assignment Statements   The simplest kind of statement is the assignment statement. It causes the value of an expression to be assigned to a variable. The format of an assignment statement is as follows:

```
variable := expression
```

Some examples of assignment statements are shown below:

```
Length := 5; Width := 2*Length
```

Some other high-level languages, notably FORTRAN and PL/M, use " = " instead of the more cryptic ": = " to separate the variable from the expression in an assignment statement. Pascal uses the ": = " symbol so that we can easily recognize when we are making an assignment and when we are applying the equal-to relational operator. For example, statements of the form

Match := I = J

are much easier for us to understand than

Match = I = J {invalid in Pascal, valid in PL/M}

The meaning of the first statement (and the intended meaning of the second statement) is to assign the Boolean value of True to Match if the value of I is equal to the value of J, and otherwise assign False to Match.

Just as Pascal keeps us from adding apples to oranges, it also prohibits us from assigning apples to oranges. In other words, both the value being assigned and the variable it is assigned to must be of the same type. Thus, if Count is declared to be an integer, we can write

Count := 117

but we cannot write

Count := 6.5

One exception: we can assign integer values to real variables. So if Weight was declared to be a real, we can write:

Weight := 117

The following program is an example that uses assignment statements:

```
program Factorial;
  var
    Fact1: Integer;
    Fact2: Integer;
    Fact3: Integer;
    Fact4: Integer;
  begin {compute 1!, 2!, 3!, and 4!}
  Fact1 := 1;
  Fact2 := 2*Fact 1;
  Fact3 := 3*Fact2;
  Fact4 := 4*Fact 3;
  {you'll probably want to do something with the factorial results here}
  end.
```

Selective Statements   There aren't very many interesting programs we could write with just assignment statements. Once we can make decisions and select which assignment statements we want the processor to perform, programming starts to become fun. The two selective statements—the *if statement* and the *case statement*—gives us this capability.

The **if** statement has the form:

if expression **then** statement

An example of an **if** statement is

if Speed>55 **then** Fine := 25

The **if** statement tells what to do if the expression is true. A natural question to ask is, "If not, then what?" The answer is nothing, unless we're told what **else** to do as in the following **if** statement:

if Height<6 **then** Clearance : = 6 – Height **else** Clearance : = 0

So another form of the **if** statement is

if expression **then** statement **else** statement

In either form, the expression must return a Boolean result; the selection will be based on that result.

Note that there is no semicolon after the statement that is sandwiched between **then** and **else**. To include such a semicolon, as in

if Height<6 **then** Clearance : = 6 – Height; **else** Clearance : = 0

would be an error because a semicolon separates adjacent statements and "**else** Clearance : = 0" is not a statement (it is a part of the **if** statement). So, although we can be careless everywhere else and end all statements with semicolons, within an **if** statement we must be careful and not end the sandwiched statement with a semicolon.

The following program illustrates the use of the **if** statement in computing income taxes:

```
program Tax;
  var
     Exemptions,Age: Integer;
     Salary,Tax: Real;
  begin
  Read(Salary); Read(Age);
  Exemptions := 1;
  if Age>65 then Exemptions := Exemptions + 1;
  Salary := Salary – 750.00*Exemptions;
  if Salary<1000.00 then Tax := .14*Salary
  else Tax := 140.00 + .20*(Salary – 1000.00);
  Write(Tax);
  end.
```

Now here's an example of when not to use an **if** statement. Although the statement

if Temperature<32.0 **then** Freezing : = True **else** Freezing : = False

is perfectly valid, it could be stated simply as

Freezing : = Temperature<32.0

The **if** statement has the ability to select one or the other of two statements to be executed depending on the truth or falsity of an expression. The **case** statement is a more general selective statement. It selects one out of a collection of statements based on the value (not necessarily a Boolean value) of an expression. It has the form:

case expression **of** value:statement; value:statement; ... ; value:statement **end**

An example of a **case** statement is

```
case DayOfChristmas of
     1: PartridgeInAPearTree := PartridgeInAPearTree + 1;        {first day}
     2: TurtleDoves := TurtleDoves + 2;                          {second day}
     3: FrenchHens := FrenchHens + 3;                            {third day}
     4: CallingBirds := CallingBirds + 4;                        {fourth day}
     5. GoldenRings := GoldenRings + 5;                          {fifth day}
     6: GeeseALaying := GeeseALaying + 6;                        {sixth day}
     7: SwansASwimming := SwansASwimming + 7;                    {seventh day}
     8: MaidsAMilking := MaidsAMilking + 8;                      {eighth day}
     9: DrummersDrumming := DrummersDrumming + 9;                {ninth day}
    10: PipersPiping := PipersPiping + 10;                       {tenth day}
    11: LadiesDancing := LadiesDancing + 11;                     {eleventh day}
    12: LordsALeaping := LordsALeaping + 12                      {twelfth day}
end
```

If, in the above example, the value of DayOfChristmas is 7, the only statement that is executed is:

SwansASwimming := SwansASwimming + 7

The above **case** statement is equivalent to the following collection of **if** statements:

```
if DayOfChristmas = 1 then
     PartridgeInAPearTree := PartridgeInAPearTree + 1
else if DayOfChristmas = 2 then
     TurtleDoves := TurtleDoves + 2
else if DayOfChristmas = 3 then
     FrenchHens := FrenchHens + 3
else if DayOfChristmas = 4 then
     CallingBirds := CallingBirds + 4
else if DayOfChristmas = 5 then
     GoldenRings := GoldenRings + 5
else if DayOfChristmas = 6 then
     GeeseALaying := GeeseALaying + 6
else if DayOfChristmas = 7 then
     SwansASwimming := SwansASwimming + 7
else if DayOfChristmas = 8 then
     MaidsAMilking := MaidsAMilking + 8
else if DayOfChristmas = 9 then
     DrummersDrumming := DrummersDrumming + 9
else if DayOfChristmas = 10 then
     PipersPiping := PipersPiping + 10
else if DayOfChristmas = 11 then
     LadiesDancing := LadiesDancing + 11
else if DayOfChristmas = 12 then
     LordsALeaping := LordsALeaping + 12
```

The **case** statement was not really necessary; we can always use a bunch of **if** statements as just illustrated. However, when the **case** statement is appropriate, it makes the program simpler.

A less seasonal example of a **case** statement would be

```
case Year of
    1981: Days := 365;
    1982: Days := 365;
    1983: Days := 365;
    1984: Days := 366;
    end
```

This **case** statement could be abbreviated to

```
case Year of
    1981,1982,1983: Days := 365;
    1984: Days := 366;
    end
```

Compound Statements   The **if** statement just described permits us to specify only one statement after the word **then** and only one statement after the word **else**. But there are times that we might want to execute several statements if a condition is true and possibly several other statements otherwise. A compound statement is a collection of statements wrapped together to form a single statement; it can be used following **then** or following **else** or any other place that a single statement can be used. The form of a compound statement is

```
begin statement; statement; ... ; statement end
```

Now a more complicated **if** statement would look like this:

```
if Minutes> =60 then
    begin
    Hours := Hours + 1;
    Minutes := Minutes – 60;
    end
```

Let's now consider the following **if** statements

```
if Speed>55 then
    if MeanJudge then Fine := 100
    else Fine := 25
```

Here we have two **if**s and one **else**. The **else** is said to be *dangling* because it could go with either **if**. It's obvious from the way we wrote it that we meant for the **else** to go with **if** MeanJudge and not with **if** Speed>55. If we meant for it to be otherwise, we probably would have written

```
if Speed>55 then
    if MeanJudge then Fine := 100
else Fine := 25
```

But Pascal doesn't care how we indent our lines; to a Pascal compiler both forms are interpreted the same way. And the way Pascal interprets a dangling **else** is to associate it with the most-recent **if** that can accept it (**if** MeanJudge in our

case). If we wanted the **else** to go the other way, we would have to "undangle"
it as in

if Speed>55 **then**
        begin if MeanJudge **then** Fine := 100; **end**
else Fine := 25

The compound statement makes the enclosed **if** into a completed statement so
it can no longer accept an **else**. The above **else** is no longer dangling, since there
is only one **if** that can accept it.

   Repetitive Statements   So far, we have seen how to write a program
that executes statements in sequence, one after another. We also want the ability
to execute one or more statements repeatedly. Pascal provides the ability to repeat
for a given number of times (*for statement*), for as long as a given condition is
sastisfied (*while statement*), or until a given condition is satisfied (*repeat-until
statement*). Repetitions can also be accomplished using the more elementary *goto
statement*.
   The **goto** statement has the form:

goto label

The label is an unsigned integer. The following example illustrates the use of the
goto statement:

1492: America := True;

        .
        .
        .

    goto 1492

A few words about **goto**s and labels are in order here. A label is a name, not a
number (it only looks like a number). We can't substitute **goto** 1490+2 in the
above example. It certainly would have been nicer if labels looked like identifiers
(**goto** Start, for example) instead. But **goto**s were purposely made ugly to dis-
courage us from using them. It's often hard to follow the flow in a program heavily
laced with **goto**s. Fortunately, most of the things we might want to do with **goto**s,
we can do with the higher-level repetitive statements instead. And the latter are
much easier to read. This point will become clearer as we learn about these other
repetitive statements.
   The **for** statement has the form:

    for variable := expression **to** expression **do** statement

An example of a **for** statement is

    for I:=1 **to** 7 **do** Factorial := I*Factorial

The effect of the above example is to assign the values 1, 2, 3, 4, 5, 6, 7 to I,
and after each assignment execute the statement

    Factorial := I*Factorial

This is roughly equivalent to

```
    I := 1;
10:
    IF I< = 7 then
            begin
            Factorial := I*Factorial;
            I := I+1;
            goto 10;
            end
```

If we initialized Factorial to 1 prior to executing the above **for** statement, 7! would be the final value of Factorial. Note how much easier it is to read (and comprehend) the **for** statement than the equivalent statements involving a **goto**. (There is a subtle distinction between these two forms. In the second version, I gets assigned a value of 8 the last time through the loop, whereas in the **for** statement I never gets assigned any value other than 1 through 7.)

We can use the **for** statement to assign values in decreasing, rather than increasing, order. For example:

for I: = 7 **downto** 1 **do** ...

would assign the values 7, 6, 5, 4, 3, 2, 1 to I in that order.

The following program illustrates how the **for** statement is used to compute the number of leap years in the 21st century.

```
program Leaps;
  var
      Years: 2000..2099;
      LeapYears: 0..100;
  begin
  LeapYears := 0;
  for Years: = 2000 to 2099 do
    if (Years mod 4) = 0 then LeapYears := LeapYears + 1;
  Write(LeapYears);
  end.
```

The **while** statement has the form:

while expression **do** statement

An example is the following:

while Debt>0 **do** Debt := Debt + Interest − Payment

The effect of the above example is to repeatedly execute the statement as long as the value of Debt is greater than 0. This is equivalent to:

```
20:
    if Debt>0 then
            begin
            Debt := Debt + Interest − Payment;
            goto 20;
            end
```

The **repeat-until** statement is just the opposite of the **while** statement. The **while** statement is repeated as long as a condition is true; the **repeat-until** statement is repeated as long as a condition is false. The **while** statement tests its condition prior to performing its other actions; the **repeat-until** statement tests its condition after performing the other actions. The form of the **repeat-until** statement is:

repeat statement; statement; ... ; statement **until** expression

An example of a **repeat-until** statement is

```
repeat
      Minutes := Minutes + 1;
      if Minutes = 60 then begin Hours := Hours + 1; Minutes := 0; end;
      until Hours = 5
```

Note that even though there is more than one statement in the sequence of repeated statements above (there's an assignment statement and an **if** statement), we did not need to use a compound statement. All of the other repetitive statements (except the **goto**) could only repeat a single statement (or a single compound statement); the **repeat-until** statement can repeat an entire sequence of statements. There's no esoteric reason that Pascal permits this here and not elsewhere; it's simply an accidental side-effect of writing the terminating condition after rather than before the repeated statements (the repeated statements are bracketed by the words **repeat** and **until** so there is no need to bracket them with **begin** and **end**).

Definitions and Declarations

Now that we've learned almost all we need to know about statements, it's time to learn about the descriptive sections (the definitions and declarations) of the program. There can be up to five descriptive sections. These sections are:
—label declarations
—constant definitions
—type definitions
—variable declarations
—procedure and function declarations
Not all five sections need be present, but those that are present must appear in the above order; unlike some other high-level languages, Pascal is very strict on this ordering.

Label Declarations   Every label used in the program (remember the **goto** statement) must be introduced in a label declaration. An example of a program containing a label declaration is

```
program Labeled;
      label 1;
      var I: Integer;
      begin
```

.
.
.

if I = 0 **then goto** 1;

.
.
.

1:**end;**

A label declaration can introduce more than one label as follows:

label 10,20,30;

Note that adjacent labels in the declaration are separated by commas and the last label is followed by a semicolon.

Variable Declarations   All variables used in our program must be declared. Such declarations inform the compiler of the type associated with each variable. With this knowledge, the compiler can determine what kind of code to generate (for example, integer add or floating-point add). Furthermore, the compiler can prevent you from making certain kinds of errors (such as assigning apples to oranges) that it knows you didn't want to make.

Certain high-level languages (such as FORTRAN and BASIC) do not require that variables be declared. You just go ahead and use them and, by doing so, you are telling the compiler that they exist. Furthermore, the first letter of a variable's name could be used to indicate the type of the variable (for example, all variables starting with I are integers). Such a language might seem to be easier to use because it does not require us to write as much. But what happens when we make a spelling error and write an assignment statement like

Carrect := Correct + 1

The Pascal compiler would know that we never declared Carrect and so it could tell us that we have an error in the above statement. But a language that doesn't require declarations would just think that Carrect is another variable and make an assignment to it. Then we'd have a hard time trying to find out why our program didn't perform correctly. So we can be thankful that Pascal requires us to declare our variables.

An example of some variable declarations is the following:

var

I,J,K: Integer;	{declaring three integer variables}
Speed,Acceleration: Real;	{declaring two real variables}
Ch: Char;	{declaring a character variable}
Found: Boolean;	{declaring a Boolean variable}
Weight: Real;	{declaring another real variable}

Let's make some observations from the above example. For one thing, note that several variables of the same type can be declared together (such as was done with I, J, and K) so that the type (Integer in this case) need be written only once. Note, also, the use of semicolons; they must appear after each declaration of a variable (or variables) of a particular type.

Procedure and Function Declarations   We'll introduce procedures and functions shortly so let's defer a discussion of their declarations until then.

Constant Definitions   As a convenience, Pascal lets us define a name for a constant. For example:

const
        Pi = 3.141592653579893;

Then we can use Pi later on in the program as a shorthand for 3.141592653579893. A more important use for constant definitions is to define a name for a constant whose value we might want to change next week (or next month, or next year). Rather than use that constant throughout the program, we give the constant a name like

const
        BufferSize = 32;

and use BufferSize throughout the program. Now we need only make the change in one place. And, even if we never intend to change its value, a named constant enhances the readability of our program so that someone else won't have to decipher mystical statements like

if Day>280 **then** ...

when we really meant

if Day>GestationPeriod **then** ...

Type Definitions   Just as the constant definition lets us give a name to a constant, a type definition lets us give a name to a new type. For example, we could define

type
        Years = Integer;
        Dollars = Integer;

and then declare some variables having these types as in

var
        X: Years;
        Y: Dollars;

It is true that we could have declared both X and Y to be of type Integer and it would not affect the behavior of our program. By declaring them to be of type Years and Dollars instead, we are conveying some additional information to other readers of our program about the intended usage of the variables X and Y. Some other high-level languages might even tell us that we made a mistake if we tried adding a variable of type Years to a variable of type Dollars, but Pascal doesn't go that far (since they were both derived from integers, Pascal considers this as adding red apples to green apples—a lesser sin than adding apples to oranges).

In the next section, we'll learn much more about other kinds of types that Pascal lets us define.

Types

There's been a lot said about types already in this chapter. They're obviously pretty important. In this section, we'll review the types we've already met, become introduced to some more types, and even learn how to create our own types.

As we've already learned, a type specifies a collection of distinct values that a variable of that type may take on. For example, a variable of type Boolean can have one of the two Boolean values—True and False. A type can either be a *simple* type (such as an integer, a real, a character, or a Boolean), a *structured* type, which is a collection of simple types, or a *pointer* type whose values identify (point to) variables that become created when the program is executing.

Simple Types

We've already been exposed to the standard simple types—namely Integer, Real, Boolean, and Char. These types are actually predefined for us; in other words, they are known to the Pascal compiler without our having to include type definitions for them in our program. Now we'll learn how to create types of our own choosing (enumerated types) as well as how to restrict the values in a type (subrange types).

Enumerated Types   The standard simple types have not been defined for any particular application; they are general enough to be used in a wide variety of cases. But if we are writing a program for a particular application, might there not be some specialized types that we would find quite useful? For example, if we are writing a program to control all the traffic lights in town, a type that specifies the three traffic-light settings would be nice to have. Pascal lets us create such a type by enumerating a collection of identifiers that are the values of that type. For example

(Green,Yellow,Red)

is the type we want. Besides creating a new type, we have just created three new constants, namely Green, Yellow, and Red. We could define variables of this new type by writing

Light1,Light2,Light3: (Green,Yellow,Red)

or we could define a name for the new type and use that name when declaring variables.

type
    Setting = (Green,Yellow,Red);
var
    Light1,Light2,Light3: Setting;

The order in which we enumerate the identifiers is important. The ordering in the preceding example implies that Green is less than Yellow, which in turn is less than Red. We can take advantage of these relations as in the following:

```
if Light1<Light2 then ... {traffic controlled by Light1 has right-of-way}
for Light1:=Green to Red do ... {step through one full cycle}
```

Pascal even provides us with some functions that rely on this ordering. In particular, Succ(Yellow) gives the value that is the successor to Yellow (Red in this case), Pred(Yellow) gives the predecessor to Yellow (that's Green), and Ord(Yellow) gives the enumerated order (starting from 0) of Yellow (1 in this case).

How about an example? Here's a program that counts the weekdays in this decade. It uses two enumerated types, Day and Month.

```
program Calendar;
type
        Date = 1..31;
        Day = (Mon,Tue,Wed,Thu,Fri,Sat,Sun);
        Month = (Jan,Feb,Mar,Apr,May,Jun,Jul,Aug,Sep,Oct,Nov,Dec);
        Year = 1980..1989;

var
        ThisDate,MaxDate: Date;
        ThisDay: Day;
        ThisMonth: Month;
        ThisYear: Year;
        WeekDays: Integer;
begin
{start at first day of decade}
ThisDay := Tue; ThisYear := 1980; ThisMonth := Jan; ThisDate := 1;
WeekDays := 1; {starting day is a weekday}

repeat {go through entire decade}

    {determine number of days in month}
    case ThisMonth of {see if we've exhausted this month yet}
        Sep,                            {Thirty days hath September,}
        Apr,Jun,Nov:                    {April, June, and November;}
            MaxDate := 30;
        Jan,Mar,May,Jul,Aug,Oct,Dec:
            MaxDate := 31;              {All the rest have thirty-one,}
        Feb:                            {Excepting February alone:}
            if (ThisYear mod 4)<>0 then
                MaxDate := 28           {Which hath but twenty-eight in fine,}
            else MaxDate := 29;         {Till leap year gives it twenty nine.}
    end;
    {increment date}
    if ThisDate<>MaxDate then ThisDate := ThisDate+1
    else {go on to next month}
            begin
            if ThisMonth<>Dec then ThisMonth := Succ(ThisMonth)
            else begin ThisMonth := Jan; ThisYear := ThisYear+1; end;
            ThisDate := 1;
            end;
```

```
{increment day}
if ThisDay<Sun then ThisDay := Succ(ThisDay) else ThisDay := Mon;

{count weekdays}
if ThisDay<Sat then {it's a weekday}
      WeekDays := WeekDays+1;
```

until (ThisMonth = Dec) **and** (ThisDate = 31) **and** (ThisYear = 1989);

Write(WeekDays); {here's the answer}
end.

Subrange Types   A type whose values are a subset of the values of some other type is

0..9

Since 0 and 9 are both integers, the above type consists of the integer values in the range from 0 to 9. This is called a *subrange* of type Integer. We can declare subrange variables by writing

var
      X: 0..9;

or equivalently with

type
      Digit = 0..9;
var
      X: Digit;

Subranges are not distinct types; X above is still considered to be an integer even though the values it may take on are more restricted than the integer values. This means we may add X to any·other integer variable without being accused of mixing types. We must be careful when assigning to a subrange variable. The compiler will not prevent us from writing X := Y where Y is declared by Y:Integer. But when our program is running, it might happen that the value of Y is greater than 9 (or less than 0). In general, such an error cannot be detected when our program is being compiled. At best, the compiler might generate code that will test for this condition when the program is executing and will print out an error message if it occurs.

Since subranges are not new types, why do we need them? They just place more restrictions on us and appear to make it harder for us to write programs. In truth, they make it harder for us to write *incorrect* programs. If we know that a variable should only take on a particular range of values, we can assert this fact by declaring the variable to be a subrange. Then, if our program has an error in it and the variable gets out of range, there is the possibility that we will be alerted. At the very least, by using a subrange we have documented some important piece of information about how our program should behave after the last bug has been removed.

Subrange types are not restricted to being integers. We can, for example, declare the variable Ch to be of type character but restrict its values to lower-case letters only. Such a declaration would be

var
    Ch: 'a'..'z';

Structured Types

The structured types are such things as arrays, records, sets, and files. Each of these types will now be examined in detail.

Arrays   Variables of simple types have only one value at any one time. But frequently certain values are related, and programs can be simplified by grouping related values together. For example, consider a program that reads in the age (to the nearest year) of 10 people and then determines how many of them are over 40. The following is the hard way to solve the problem:

```
program Over40TheHardWay;
    var
            Age1,Age2,Age3,Age4,Age5,Age6,Age7,Age8,Age9,Age10: 0..150;
            Over40: 0..10;
    begin
    ... {read in the ages}
    Over40 := 0; {initialize the count}
    if Age1>40 then Over40 := Over40 + 1;
    if Age2>40 then Over40 := Over40 + 1;
    if Age3>40 then Over40 := Over40 + 1;
    if Age4>40 then Over40 := Over40 + 1;
    if Age5>40 then Over40 := Over40 + 1;
    if Age6>40 then Over40 := Over40 + 1;
    if Age7>40 then Over40 := Over40 + 1;
    if Age8>40 then Over40 := Over40 + 1;
    if Age9>40 then Over40 := Over40 + 1;
    if Age10>40 then Over40 := Over40 + 1;
    ... {do something with the result}
    end.
```

Obviously the variables Age1, Age2, ..., Age10 are related to each other in the sense that all of them are ages. Pascal allows such related variables to be grouped together as one variable with 10 integer values. Such a variable, Age, would be declared by:

Age: **array**[1..10] **of** 0..150

where **array**[1..10] **of** 0..150 is a type. The subrange 1..10 is called the *index* of the array. The individual components (called *elements*) in the array Age are of type 0..150 and can be referred to as Age[1], Age[2], ..., Age[10]. Now the previous program can be rewritten as follows:

```
program Over40TheEasyWay:
var
    Age: array[1..10] of 0..150;
    Over40: 0..10;
    I: 1..10;
begin
... {read in the ages}
Over40 := 0; {initialize the count}
for I:= 1 to 10 do if Age[I]>40 then Over40 := Over40+1;
... {do something with result}
end.
```

The elements and index of an array may be other than (subranges of) integers as shown below:

```
var
    LotsOfInts: array['a'..'z'] of Integer;
    LotsOfReals: array[0..5] of Real;
    LotsOfCharacters: array[-50..50] of Char;
    LotsOfBooleans: array[Char] of Boolean;
```

The following is an example of an array indexed by a subrange of characters:

```
program CountLetters;
var
    Ch: Char;
    Count: array['a'..'z'] of 0..100;
begin
for Ch:= 'a' to 'z' do Count[Ch] := 0; {clear the count}
repeat
    Read(Ch): {read in the next letter}
    Count[Ch] := Count[Ch]+1; {increment the count for that letter}
    until Count[Ch]=100; {stop when we get 100 of any one letter}
... {do something with result}
end.
```

The following is an example of an array indexed by a type rather than a subrange of a type:

```
Count: array[Char] of 0..100
```

In this case, we would get an array that has an element coresponding to every value of type Char (the previous array had elements corresponding to the lowercase letters only).

Now there are some restrictions on what types we can use for the index of an array. For one thing, it must be a simple type (a structured type won't do). For another, we can't use a real type such as

```
RealIndex: array[Real] of ... {no good}
```

because there is no way we could ever count the number of values of type real and the array would have to have an infinite number of elements (that's more than the number of memory locations in most processors).

Finally, we can have arrays like

MultiIndex: **array**[1..10,1..100] **of** ...

This is called a two-dimensional array (arrays of even higher dimensions are also possible) and has an array element for every pair of possible values of each index. In this case, there are 10*100 different elements and they are accessed by such names as MultiIndex[5,30].

All of the above declarations of array variables defined their own array types. Alternatively, they could have equally well used a previously defined array type as in

type
  MyArray = **array**[1..10] **of** 0..150;
var
  Age: MyArray;

This same comment applies to all other types as well so I won't bore you by repeating this over and over again.

Records   A *record* (called a *structure* in PL/M) is another method of grouping related variables together. An example of a record is

RelatedThings:
  record
  ExactThing: Integer;
  ApproximateThing: Real;
  end {of record}

and the individual components (called *fields*) in the record can be referred to as RelatedThings.ExactThing and RelatedThings.ApproximateThing. There are several obvious differences between records and arrays:

1. The components of an array are called elements; the components of a record are called fields.
2. The elements of an array are all of the same type, while the fields of a record may be of differing types.
3. An element in an array is referred to by its index (which may be a variable whose value is not known when the program is being compiled). A field in a record is referred to by its name (which is always known at compile time).

When we access a component of a record, we have to indicate both the name of a record variable and the name of a field. For example, to increment the integer field of the above record, we would write

RelatedThings.ExactThing := RelatedThings.ExactThing + 1

If we frequently access the fields of a particular record variable, we can simplify matters by using a **with** statement as follows:

```
with RelatedThings do
      begin {no need to mention RelatedThings on the lines below}
      ExactThing := ExactThing + 1;
      ApproximateThing := ApproximateThing + 1;
      end
```

The fields of a record need not be simple types. An example of a record field being an array is as follows:

```
type
   Gender = (Male,Female);
   Person =
      record
      Name: array[1..15] of Char;
      Age: 0..150;
      Sex: Gender;
      end;
var
   John: Person;
```

The individual fields in this record can be referred to as John.Name[1], John. Name[2], ..., John.Name[15], John.Age, and John.Sex.

It's time for us to look at an example involving records. Consider a company that keeps all its payroll information in a computer file. Every payday the company runs its payroll program, which reads this file and prints the paychecks. But now it's raise time, and the company wants to give everybody a 12% cost-of-living raise. So it executes the following program:

```
program Raises:
   var
      PayCheck:
         array[1..100] of
            record
            Name: array[1..15] of Char;
            Salary: Real;
            end
      I: 1..100;
      begin
      ... {read in the payroll file}
      for I:=1 to 100 do {increase everyone's salary}
         PayCheck[I].Salary := 1.12 * PayCheck[I].Salary;
      ... {write out the updated file}
      end.
```

All the variables of a particular record type need not have the same structure. For example, consider the record

```
type
   Gender = (Male,Female);
   Person =
      record
```

```
Name: array[1..15] of Char;
Age: 0..150;
case Sex:Gender of
   Male: (Bearded: Boolean);
   Female: (ChildBirths: 0..69);      {see Guinness Book of World Records}
end;
var
   John,Jane: Person;
```

This definition of person has all the fields of the previous definition of person (including a Sex field), but it has one additional field that was not in the previous definition. This added field differs, depending on the value of the Sex field. If the value of the Sex field is Male, the added field is a Boolean variable called Bearded; if Sex is Female, the added field is an integer called ChildBirths. For example, suppose we made the assignment

```
John.Sex := Male;     {this is not surprising}
```

Now we can make reference to the component John.Bearded but the component John.ChildBirths would be meaningless. Similarly, if Jane.Sex were assigned the value Female, we could refer to Jane.ChildBirths but not to Jane.Bearded. (The preceding example was meant to illustrate variant records only; any inferences to sexist stereotypes is purely unintentional).

Sets and Set Operators   A set is a collection of distinct values, all of the same type. To illustrate this, let's consider the type

```
type
   Fruit = (Apple,Orange);
```

There are only two values of type Fruit, namely Apple and Orange. But there are four possible sets of Fruit values—namely the set consisting of both Apple and Orange, the set consisting of only Apple, the set consisting of only Orange, and the set consisting of no values. These four sets are designated by [Apple,Orange], [Apple], [Orange], and [ ] respectively (there is no difference between the set designated by [Apple,Orange] and the set designated by [Orange,Apple]). Each of these four sets is a value of some new type (they're certainly not Fruit values) and that type is called *set of Fruit*. A set-of-Fruit type can be defined by

```
type
   FruitBowl = set of Fruit;
```

and some FruitBowl variables can be declared by

```
var
   MyBowl,YourBowl : FruitBowl;
```

In this example, Fruit is the *base type* of the type FruitBowl. Of course the above variable declarations could have been written without ever defining the type Fruit,

type
   FruitBowl = **set of** (Apple,Orange);
var
   MyBowl,YourBowl: FruitBowl;

or without ever defining the type FruitBowl,

type
   Fruit = (Apple,Orange);
var
   MyBowl,YourBowl: **set of** Fruit;

or without defining any types at all.

var
     MyBowl,YourBowl: **set of** (Apple,Orange);

As a more interesting example (sets of a base type containing only two values are not very interesting), let's look at sets of characters. An example of a set of characters is ['a','e','i','o','u']; this set consists of the five vowels. There are obviously a very large number (2^{128}) of different sets of characters and each of these sets is a value of the type set-of-character. Another example of a set of characters is the set of nine digits and is written as ['1','2','3','4','5','6', '7','8','9']. But this can be written in a simpler form, namely ['1'..'9'].

We can declare a variable of type set-of-character by writing

Vowels: **set of** Char;

and then we can write statements like

Vowels := ['a','e','i','o','u'];

Now that we have been introduced to sets, what can we do with them? Sets can be used to simplify the task of making certain kinds of decisions. For example, instead of testing the value of a character variable with

if (Ch = 'a') **or** (Ch = 'e') **or** (Ch = 'i') **or** (Ch = 'o') **or** (Ch = 'u') **then** ...

we could write

if Ch **in** Vowels **then** ...

We have just seen our first set operator, namely **in**, which appeared in the expression Ch **in** Vowels. The expression consists of two operands and an operator. The second operand is of type set (set-of-characters in this case) and the first operand is in the base type (character in this case) of the set. The **in** operator returns the Boolean value True if the element of the base type is in the particular set, otherwise it returns the Boolean value False.

Some other set operators that also return a Boolean result are set-equality (=), set-inequality (<>), subset (<=), and superset (>=). The operands of these operators are both set operands having the same base type. For example:

['a'..'z']=['1'..'9'] yields False
        (set of letters and set of numbers are different)

['a','e','i','o','u']<=['a'..'z'] yields True
        (set of vowels is contained in the set of letters)

['q']>=[ ] yields True (every set contains the empty set)

['1'..'9']<>[1..9] is invalid
        (operands do not have same base type)

A word about the subset ("<=") and superset (">=") operators is in order. We have already met these symbols in connection with relational operators, except there we called them less-than-or-equal and greater-than-or-equal. We just happen to be redefining for set operations some (but not all) of the symbols that were previously defined for relational operations. The symbols "<" and ">" are not defined for set operations.

The remaining set operators are set-union (+), set-difference (−), and set-intersection (*). Each of these operators takes two set operands and produces a set result. The base type of the two operands must be the same and the result will have that base type as well. The effect of these three set operators is illustrated in the following lines of code:

```
Letters := ['a'..'z'];
Vowels := ['a','e','i','o','u'];
Digits := ['0'..'9'];
Consonants := Letters − Vowels;            {difference of two sets}
AlphaNumerics := Letters + Digits;         {union of two sets}
ExtendedVowels := Vowels + ['y'];          {another union}
Shared := Consonants * ExtendedVowels;     {intersection of two sets}
```

After executing the above lines of code, Consonants would consist of all the lower-case letters with the exception of the five lower-case vowels, AlphaNumerics would consist of all the lower-case letters together with the digits, ExtendedVowels would consist of the five vowels along with the "sometimes-vowel" 'y', and Shared would consist of the only character that is both in ExtendedVowels and Consonants—namely 'y'.

Before leaving the topic of sets, let's contrast them with arrays. The components of both are called elements and, in both cases, the elements must all be of the same type. But that's where the similarity ends. The value of an array is completely specified by specifying a value (in the underlying type) for each position in the array; the value of a set is completely specified by specifying whether or not each value in the underlying type is contained in the set. From this, we can deduce the following differences between sets and arrays:

1. All arrays of the same type (such as **array**[1..10] **of** Integer) have the same number of elements (10 in this case); each set of the same type (such as **set of** Fruit) can have a different number of elements (0, 1, or 2 in this case).

2. Several elements in an array can have the same value; each element in a set is unique.
3. An individual element in an array can be accessed (by specifying its index). The individual elements in a set are never accessed.

Files   A file is an ordered sequence of elements, all of the same type. But this is not very different from an array. There are, however, two fundamental differences between files and arrays:

1. An array contains a specified number of elements; a file does not.
2. Any element in an array can be accessed at any time (by simply specifying its index); the elements in a file must be accessed sequentially (we can't access the tenth element until after we've accessed the preceding nine elements).

Arrays are usually (but need not be) kept in the addressable memory of the processor during the entire execution of the program. Files, on the other hand, are usually kept on some external memory device such as magnetic tape or disk. This distinction is not inherent in the Pascal language (Pascal doesn't care where its variables are stored as long as the execution of the program comes up with the correct answers). However, it is just this distinction that explains why files were defined the way they were. Specifically, a magnetic tape can be accessed only sequentially and you can always put another element onto the tape (the end of the tape is usually pretty far away). Disks, of course, can be accessed randomly, but Pascal programs do not take advantage of this fact when accessing files that are stored on disks.

File variables are declared just like any other variable. The following is a declaration of two files:

```
Infile,Outfile: file of Integer;
```

The individual elements in a file are accessed by writing statements like

```
Read(Infile,I,J,K); Write(Outfile,I + J + K)
```

The statements on the above line will read the next three elements from the file Infile; store their values in the variables I, J, and K; and write the sum of the values into the next element in the file Outfile. Whenever Read or Write do not specify a file name, a default system file (possibly an interactive console) is used. The default file for Read is named Input and the one for Write is named Output. This is exactly how Read and Write were used in our sample program.

Now if we are always reading or writing into the "next" element of a file, we need some means of starting from the beginning of the file. This is accomplished by writing

```
Reset(Infile); Rewrite(Outfile)
```

Rewrite gets us to the beginning of a file that we are going to Write to; Reset gets us to the beginning of a file that we are going to Read from. ResetForWrite and ResetForRead would have been more descriptive (but, alas, more cumbersome) names. If the files are actually stored on magnetic tape, both Reset and Rewrite will cause the corresponding tape drive to be rewound (Infile and Outfile would be on two different tape drives).

Why do we have to specify, when we start to use a file, whether we will be reading from or writing to that file? Answer: Because reading from a file doesn't change the length of the file whereas writing to it does. When we Rewrite a file, we start with an empty file (if the file previously exists, we are going to overwrite it) and append elements to it with each succeeding Write that we execute. When we Reset a file, we start at the beginning of an existing file whose elements will be accessed with each succeeding Read that we execute. The end of a file being written to is always immediately after the last element we wrote. The end of a file being read is usually not after the last element we read; it could be further out in the file but we can always get to it if we do enough Reads. So, when we start to use a file, we must commit ourselves to either reading from or writing to that file; we cannot do both.

We need some way of knowing when we've read the last element in a file. This can be tested for as follows:

if Eof(Infile) **then** ...

where Eof is an abbreviation for end-of-file.

An example is certainly in order at this time. Let's consider a program that reads in an unspecified (but probably very large) number of telephone numbers and then prints out the numbers with all the numbers in the local area preceding all the remaining numbers. This list might then be used by a telephone canvasser who first wants to survey the local people and, if time permits, survey some of the others. Since the numbers written out will not be in the same order as the numbers read in, we will need to temporarily store the numbers during the execution of the program. But we can't use an array to store them in, since we don't know how many numbers there will be and, therefore, we don't know how big an array to declare. In this case, a file will do just fine.

```
program Telephone;
    var
        Number:      {this is phone number to be read or written}
            record
            Prefix: 000..999;
            Suffix: 0000..9999;
            end;
        Nearby,Faraway: file of Number;
    begin

    {prepare to write to files}
    Rewrite(Nearby); Rewrite(Faraway);

    Read(Number); {get the first phone number}
    while Number.Prefix<>0 do {zero indicates end of phone numbers}
```

```
begin
if Number.Prefix = 775 then {it's a local number}
   Write(Nearby,Number)
else {it's not a local number}
   Write(Faraway,Number);
Read(Number); {get the next phone number}
end;
```

```
{we have finished writing so prepare to read from beginning of files}
Reset(Nearby); Reset(Faraway);
```

```
{read back the local numbers and print them out}
while not Eof(Nearby) do
   begin Read(Nearby,Number); Write(Number); end;
```

```
{read back the remaining numbers and print them out}
while not Eof(Faraway) do
   begin Read(Faraway,Number); Write(Number); end;
```

```
end.
```

Certain files might exist before our program starts to execute (they supply input data to our program) and others will exist after our program completes its execution (they contain the results generated by our program). These files constitute an external environment for our program. We've already been using two such files without even realizing it—namely Input and Output. These files are the system files that Read and Write use when no explicit files are mentioned. Depending on what computer system you are executing your program on, Input might be a card reader, a paper-tape reader, the console keyboard, or some other input device. Similarly, Output might be a printer, a card or paper-tape punch, a console screen, or some other output device.

The rules of the Pascal language state that the external environment is mentioned on the first line (called the *header*) of the program. So a program that reads from the file Input and writes to the file Output would start off with

```
program MyProg(Input,Output);
```

However, many compilers have chosen to use a different method of specifying the environment. In particular, the popular 8086 Pascal compilers want us to specify the external name of the file whenever we start to use the file. An external name of a file is the name by which that file is known to the operating system that controls the execution of our program. Thus, the Rewrite and Reset lines in the above example would be changed to

```
Rewrite(Nearby,'name1'); Rewrite(Faraway,'name2');
Reset(Nearby,'name1'); Reset(Faraway,'name2');
```

where name1 and name2 would be the external names of our two files.

Pointer Types

All of the variables we have met up to now are declared before we ever execute our program. If we need five integers, we declare five integer variables when we write the program. Pascal provides no means for letting the program decide (when it is executing) that it needs to declare a sixth integer. In other words, we can't write a program such as

if X>Y **then var** Z: Integer; {a declaration made when program is executing}

Before we learn about a way that does let us create variables when the program is executing, let's see why we would want to do such a thing. Suppose we wanted to write a program that simulates the traffic flow at some intersection. The number of cars in the intersection will vary as the program executes; new cars will be entering the intersection and, with luck, those cars in the intersection will eventually leave it. Each car is a variable in our program and would probably be represented by a record. We could contain the cars in an array of records and declare the size of the array to be at least as big as the maximum numbers of cars that we ever expect to be in the intersection at any one time. We might need other such variables in our program (perhaps to represent the people in the intersection) and we would have to declare maximum size (worse case) arrays for these as well. Even though the maximum number of people and the maximum number of cars might never be in the intersection at the same time, we have been forced to allocate enough memory for such an event. We have probably declared an excessive amount of memory, and it might even be more memory than is actually available to our program. If we weren't forced to declare our variables in advance, but could create them when our program was executing instead, we might not need as much memory to perform our simulation.

When we declare a variable, we give it a name by which we can refer to it throughout our program; if we create a variable when the program is running, we will need some alternate means of referring to it. We can do this by storing the identity of each created variable in some other variable called a *pointer variable*. The pointer variable is then said to "point" to the created variable. The values taken on by pointer variables are identities of other variables, but such values do not fall into the realm of any type we have met so far. So we must introduce a new type; if the created variables are integers, the variables that point to them are type pointer-to-integer.

Besides taking on values that are identities of other variables, a pointer variable can also take on the value of **nil**. A pointer variable having such a value does not point to anything. Thus, **nil** is a good value to use for initializing pointer variables.

A pointer variable can be declared by writing

var
    Nextint: ^Integer; {read this as "pointer to integer"}

This declares Nextint to be a variable whose value is the identity of some other variable (that will be created when the program is running) and the value of that created variable will be an integer. We can now create the integer variable with the next statement

New(Nextint)

and we can refer to the created variable by writing Nextint˄ as in the following:

Nextint˄ := 5; X := Nextint˄

Everything looks fine—we've seen how to create variables without having to declare them, and we learned how to refer to these created variables. But we haven't solved the problem of dealing with that traffic simulation. If we have to declare a pointer variable for every variable that we are going to create, we are no better off than before. But there is a way for us to declare only one pointer variable that points to the last created variable and have each created variable point to the variable that was created just before it. Consider the following type definition for our created variables:

```
type Car =
  record
  Speed: Real
  ... ; {other fields relating to the particular car}
  PreviousCar: ˄Car;
  end;
```

Our pointer variable would be declared with

```
var
  LastCar: ˄Car;
```

We would initialize LastCar by writing the statement

LastCar := **nil**

and each time we wanted to create a new car we would execute the following statements:

```
TempCar := LastCar; {TempCar is a temporary variable, also of type ˄Car}
New(LastCar); {create a new car and store its identity in LastCar}
LastCar˄.PreviousCar := TempCar; {last car created now points to car created before it}
```

Now suppose we wanted to do something to every car we created, such as double its speed. We could do this with the following **while** statement:

```
TempCar := LastCar; {start with last car created}
while TempCar<>nil do
  begin
  TempCar˄.Speed := 2 * TempCar˄.Speed; {double the speed}
  TempCar := TempCar˄.PreviousCar; {go to the next car}
  end;
```

Procedures and Functions

A very important concept in programming is the subroutine or procedure. It provides the ability to execute a section of code at several different places in the program without having to repeat the code at each of these places. Consider, for example, the problem of making change for a dollar.

```
program MakingChange;
  const
     LastCoin = 8;
  var
     Coins: array[1..LastCoin] of 1..50;{this is the result}
     Change: 0..99; {number to be converted}
     I:1..LastCoin; {index into Coins array}
  begin
  Change := 100 – ...; {write the cost here}
  I := 1; {initialize the index}
  while Change> = 50 do {half dollars}
     begin
     Coins[I] := 50;
     I := I+1;
     Change := Change – 50;
     end;
  while Change> = 25 do {quarters}
     begin
     Coins[I] := 25;
     I := I+1;
     Change := Change – 25;
     end;
  while Change> = 10 do {dimes}
     begin
     Coins[I] := 10;
     I := I+1;
     Change := Change – 10;
     end;
  while Change> = 5 do {nickels}
     begin
     Coins[I] := 5;
     I := I+1;
     Change := Change – 5;
     end;
  while Change> = 1 do {pennies}
     begin
     Coins[I] := 1;
     I := I+1;
     Change := Change – 1;
     end;
  while I< = LastCoin do {zero out rest of coins}
     begin
     Coins[I] := 0;
     I := I+1;
     end;
  end.
```

Note that the sequence of code

```
     Coins[I] := X;
     I := I+1;
     Change := Change – X;
```

for different values of X occurs in several places. It sure would simplify the program if we could write this code only once and then call upon it from different places in the program. Pascal lets us do just that by declaring the code to be a procedure as follows:

```
program MakingChangewithProcedures;
  const
    LastCoin = 8;
  var
    Coins: array[1..LastCoin] of 1..50; {this is the result}
    Change: 0..99; {number to be converted}
    I:1..LastCoin; {index into Coins array}
  procedure NextCoin(X:1..50); {this is a procedure declaration}
    begin
    Coins[I] := X; {X is specified when procedure is called upon}
    I := I+1;
    Change := Change-X;
    end; {of NextCoin}

begin
Change := 100-...; {write the cost here}
I := 1; {initialize the index}
while Change> =50 do NextCoin(50); {half dollars}
while Change> =25 do NextCoin(25); {quarters}
while Change> =10 do NextCoin(10); {dimes}
while Change> =5 do NextCoin(5); {nickels}
while Change> =1 do NextCoin(1); {pennies}
while I< =LastCoin do NextCoin(0); {zero out rest of coins}
end.
```

This example has illustrated the fact that a procedure is a section of code that is declared rather than executed. It appears along with the other declarations and definitions. It has the same structure as the program itself (it can contain definitions, declarations, and statements) except it starts off with a *procedure heading* instead of a program heading. It can be called into execution (invoked) from other parts of the program simply by mentioning its name; this is referred to as a *procedure-invocation statement*.

We have already been using two procedures without even realizing it—namely Read and Write. These two procedures are actually predeclared for us (much like the predefined types such as Integer); in others words, they are known to the Pascal compiler without our having to include procedure declarations for them in our program.

Passing Information   In many applications, we need to send input information to a procedure and receive output information (results) back. The simplest method of sending information to a procedure is by placing the information in a particular variable (or variables) before calling the procedure. The variable I in the MakingChange program was such a variable. The same variable is used every time the procedure is called and the procedure knows to look in that variable for its information. The procedure can return results in such variables as well. Such variables are known as *global variables*. An example of transferring information through a global variable is the following:

Procedure Declaration	*Procedure Invocation*
procedure UpCount;	UpCount;
begin	
Count := Count + 1;	
end;	

In this example, Count is a global variable used both for sending information to the procedure and for receiving information from the procedure.

Another method of sending information to a procedure is by specifying the information every time the procedure is called. Information passed in this manner is called a *parameter*. An example of a parameter is the 50 in

NextCoin(50)

Within the body of the procedure, there is a variable corresponding to each parameter; the names of these variables are designated in the procedure heading as, for example, X in

procedure NextCoin(X:1..50);

An example using parameters is shown below:

Procedure Declaration	*Procedure Invocation*
procedure CheckSize(I,J:Integer);	**var** Max,Min: Integer;
begin	.
if I<J **then** Count := Count + 1;	.
end;	CheckSize(Max,Min);

In this example, the values (not the locations) of Max and Min are passed to CheckSize and become the initial values of I and J (I and J are called *value parameters*). CheckSize does not know where Max and Min are located and therefore cannot change their values.

If a parameter indicates the location of a value instead of the value itself, the procedure could either fetch the value from that location or place a result in that location or both. Such a parameter is called a *variable parameter* (the procedure can vary its value). Variable parameters are so denoted by preceding their names with the word **var** in the procedure heading. The following example illustrates the use of variable parameters.

Procedure Declaration	*Procedure Invocation*
procedure Switch(**var** I,J:Integer);	**var** First,Last: Integer;
var	.
Temp: Integer;	.
	.
begin	
Temp := I;	Switch(First,Last);

```
I := J;
J := Temp;
end;
```

Of course, we could denote every parameter as being a variable parameter and then we wouldn't have to think about whether it will be used to supply information to the procedure or receive results from the procedure. But this has several drawbacks. For one thing, the compiler would have to generate a greater number of instructions (in the object code) for fetching parameter values. For another, we wouldn't be able to pass constants as parameters. And, most important, we would be overriding the protection Pascal is offering us to ensure that certain values that *should* not be altered by a given procedure are *indeed* not altered.

A function is very similar to a procedure except it offers one more way that a result can be returned. In particular, the name of the function is its result. A function is not called into execution with a procedure-invocation statement; instead it is called upon by using its name as an operand in an expression. Let's look at the following example:

Function Declaration
```
function PhoneBill(Units:0..1000): Real;
   begin
   PhoneBill := 5.00 + .05*Units;
   end;
```

Function Invocation
```
Expenses := PhoneBill(78) + ElectricBill(113) + ...;
```

Functions are distinguished from procedures in two ways. First, each function must contain at least one assignment statement that assigns a value to its own name. Second, a fuction specifies the type (Real in the example above) of the result to be returned.

Thus, we have seen three ways ot sending information to procedures and functions and three ways of receiving information back. These ways are summarized below:

Sending to Procedure/Function	*Receiving from Procedure/Function*
global variables	global variables
value parameters	variable parameters
variable parameters	function name

Recursion   It is sometimes desirable to have a procedure (or function) call itself. In some sense, this is like looking at the reflection of a mirror in a mirror. Pascal doesn't object to recursive procedures, providing that the procedures will eventually stop calling and start returning. As ?n example, let's write a program that uses a recursive function to calculate factorials. One way to calculate 7! (pronounced "seven factorial") would be to calculate 6! and multiply the result by 7. So the factorial function, when asked for the factorial of X, could use the factorial function (which means calling itself) to calculate the factorial of X – 1 and then multiply that result by X. But if we're not careful, this may never end. So to make sure the sequence of function calls terminates, the factorial function will return the result 1 (without calling any other functions) when asked for the factorial of 1. The Pascal program that calculates 7! is shown here:

```
program Fact7;
var X:Integer;
function Factorial(I:1..7): Integer;
   begin
   if I = 1 then Factorial := 1
   else Factorial := I*Factorial(I – 1);
   end;
X := Factorial(7); write (X);
end.
```

One reason we're mentioning recursive procedures and functions here is because some languages (notably FORTRAN) do not permit recursion.

Block Structure and Scope

So far we have seen how to introduce items (constants, labels, types, variables, procedures, and functions) in one part of a program and use them somewhere else in the program. But we've never said just where in the program we can refer to these items once they're introduced. The portions of a program in which the name of an item is recognized is called the *scope* of the item.

Before we can talk about scope, we must introduce the concept of a block. A *block* is a unit of the program that consists of a descriptive part (declarations and definitions) and an action part (statements). We have seen three places where blocks occur in Pascal—namely in procedure declarations, in function declarations, and in the outermost level of the program itself. Some of the the declarations in the descriptive part of a given block could be procedure or function declarations, so we can have blocks within blocks. Such inner blocks are said to be *nested* within the outer blocks.

Now we can define the scope of an item. The scope is specified by the following equation:

```
scope  =  block in which item is introduced
       +  all nested blocks
       -  those nested blocks that introduce another item with the same name
```

One restriction on the scope of an item is that the item must be introduced before it is used (this makes the compiler's life much simpler) with the exception of pointer types (the compiler has agreed to work overtime for us here). Let's clarify and motivate these scope rules with some examples.

Example 1: Scope includes block in which item is introduced.

```
var X: Integer;
begin
X := X+1; {of course this is within the scope of X}
end;
```

Example 2: Scope includes nested blocks as well.

```
var X: Integer;
procedure P;
  var Y: Integer;
  begin
  X := Y+1; {this is also within the scope of X}
  end;
begin
...
end;
```

Example 3: Scope does not include nested blocks in which name is reintroduced.

```
var X: Integer;
procedure P;
  var X: array(1..10) of Integer;
  begin
  X := X+1; {error since this is outside the scope of integer X}
  X[3] := X[2]+1; {however this is within the scope of array X}
  end;
begin
X := X+1; {and this is within the scope of integer X}
end;
```

Example 4: Scope does not include outer block.

```
var Y: Integer;
procedure P;
  var X: Integer;
  begin
  ...
  end;
begin
X := X+1; {error since this is outside the scope of X}
end;
```

Example 5: Items must be introduced before being used.

```
TYPE
      A = array[1..10] of B; {error since B not yet introduced}
      B = array[1..5] of Integer; {sorry, too late}
```

(It should be noted that some 8086 Pascal compilers, notably Intel's, do allow you to use an item before it is introduced.)

Example 6: Labels present no additional problems.

```
label 1;
procedure X;
   begin
   goto 1; {ok since the label has already been introduced}
   end;
begin
1: ... {and here's where the label is}
end;
```

Example 7: What about two (or more) procedures that call each other?

```
procedure A(C:Char); Forward; {introduces A and C without declaring A}
procedure B(I:Integer);
      begin
      A('x'); {ok since A has been introduced though not declared}
      end;
procedure A; {here's the declaration for A but without reintroducing C}
      begin
      B(5); {ok since B has been declared}
      end;
```

Note that we used something new above, namely Forward. This allows us to introduce a procedure and its parameters, but defer the declaration of the procedure until later. By doing so, we can have procedures that call each other and yet be able to introduce each procedure before it is called.

Example 8: Pointer types can be used before being introduced.

```
type
   Car =
      record
      Number: 0001..9999;
      Owner: ^Person; {ok even though we haven't introduced Person yet}
      end;
   Person =
      record
      Age: 0..150;
      Vehicle: ^Car; {ok even if we hadn't introduced Car yet}
      end;
begin
...
end;
```

In the last example, it would be impossible to introduce both Car and Person before either one is referenced, since each one has a component that points to the other. This explains why pointer types are exceptions to the "introduce before using" rule.

Now what effect does a **with** statement have on scope? A **with** statement does not allow us to refer to any items (record components in particular) that we could not have referred to otherwise; it just makes it a little easier to refer to them. It might, however, reduce the scope of certain items as shown in the following example:

```
var
  A:
    record
    B:Char;
    end;
procedure P;
  var B: Boolean;
  begin
  with A do
    begin
    B := True; {no good, we can no longer reference Boolean B}
    B := 'x'; {but we can reference character B in record A directly}
    end;
  end;
```

Input and Output

No discussion of a programming language would be complete without a description of how to get data into the program and how to get answers out. In our early example, we saw how to get data in with Read(Next) and how to get results out with Write(Sum). Later, when we met files, we learned that all reads and writes are really to files, and the default files Input and Output are used if no other file is specified. And when we studied procedures we realized that Read and Write were actually procedures that are predeclared for us.

There's a strange thing about the Read and Write procedures; they can take on as many (or as few) parameters as we feel like passing to them. For example, we can read the next integer from a file of integers with Read(IntFile,I), or we can read the next five integers with Read(IntFile,I,J,K,L,M). No procedure or function that we declare ourselves can do that.

Although we can define a file that contains objects of almost any type (no, we can't define a file of files), probably the most universally used files are files of characters. We could declare a file of characters by writing

MyChars: File of Char;

Even more useful than a file of characters would be a file of lines of text. (Imagine what would happen if we wanted to write all the characters in this book to a printer and they all came out on one line). Such files are called *text files* and are declared by

MyText: Text;

Both of the above files, MyChars and MyText, contain characters. But the characters in MyText are grouped together to form lines, whereas those in MyChars are not. When MyText is sent to a printer, the line structure is made visible to us. But the file still has lines even when it resides on some nonvisual media such as a disk; in this case, the lines are conceptually defined to be sequences of characters separated by end-of-line markers.

We now need some means of generating an end-of-line marker when we write to a text file and some means of recognizing an end-of-line marker when we read from a text file. Pascal provides two procedures, Readln and Writeln, for this purpose. The parameters to these procedures are the same as the parameters to Read and Write. And these procedures perform the same actions as Read and Write but, in addition, perform the following actions: Writeln will write out an end-of-line marker after it writes out those characters requested of it; Readln, after reading in those characters requested of it, will read and discard characters until it reads in an end-of-line marker. And Pascal provides the function Eoln (end of line) which allows us to determine if we've just read in the last character preceding an end-of-line marker.

What we need now is an example that illustrates the line structure of text files. What better example is there than copying one text file to another while preserving the line structure?

```
program CopyLines;
var
    Ch:Char; {variable in which to store characters being transferred}
    SourceFile,DestFile: Text; {declaring the two files}
begin
Reset(SourceFile,'file1'); {external name of source file is file1}
Rewrite(DestFile,'file2'); {external name of destination file is file2}
while not Eof(SourceFile) do {transfer all characters in the source file}
    begin
    while not Eoln(SourceFile) do {transfer all characters on next line}
        begin
        Read(SourceFile,Ch); {read in next character from source file ...}
        Write(DestFile,Ch); {... and write it to destination file}
        end;
    Readln(SourceFile); {read past the end-of-line marker}
    Writeln(DestFile); {write out an end-of-line marker}
    end;
end.
```

We've been using text files throughout this chapter without even being aware that we were doing so. The default files Input and Output are text files so we were using a text file in our sample program when we wrote Read(Next). But Next was declared to be an integer and now we are reading it from a file containing characters and end-of-line markers. This points out another property of text files. Namely, Read and Write to textfiles can transfer more than just characters; they can transfer numeric objects (integers or reals) and the numeric values are automatically translated to or from a sequence of characters representing the values. For example, if the next four characters in the text file Input were '5', '9', '8', and ' '; the call to Read(Next) would read in the first three, translate them to the integer value 598, and assign this value to the integer variable Next.

We can also write (but not read) a string of characters to a text file as in

```
Write('hello')
```

True, this is no different from

```
Write('h','e','l','l','o')
```

but it is much easier to write. Note the use of a string constant—namely 'hello'. Back when we learned about constants, we were told that such things existed but had limited use. Here's one place we can use them.

As a final example, the following program will ask us if we want it (the program) to stop. It will continue to do so until we respond by typing a line starting with the character 'y' (presumably the rest of the line contains the characters 'e' and 's' but the program doesn't bother testing for them).

```
program Looping;
var
    Ch: Char;
begin
repeat
    Writeln('do you want to stop the program?'); Readln(Ch);
    until Ch = 'y';
end.
```

Aside about Standard Pascal

For years the Pascal "bible" has been the *Pascal User Manual and Report* by Jensen and Wirth (Springer-Verlag, 1975). Recently there has been activity to "standardize" the Pascal language. That work is still in progress, but draft proposals have been published by the International Standards Organization (DP7185 Specification for the Computer Programming Language Pascal, ISO/TC 97/SC 5 N, January 1981).

This aside is mentioned at this time because the next topic, separate compilations, is not described in either the Jensen-Wirth report or the ISO draft proposal. As a result, different Pascal compilers for the 8086 have chosen to recognize different forms of separate compilation facilities. Two such forms are described here. The first introduces separate compilations in a manner that does not deviate from the proposed standard, instead it adds the facility by specifying certain details that the proposed standard expressly designated as being implementation-dependent. The second form, which is recognized by Intel's Pascal compiler, does deviate from the proposed standard.

Separate Compilations

So far, all the programs we have written have been self-contained. It is also possible to write a program that has some "missing" procedures or functions. These missing routines might appear in some other Pascal programs. This collection of programs would be compiled separately but must be tied together (bound) before they could be executed. This permits a program to be subdivided among several programmers. It also permits a single programmer to partition his program into small, easily comprehended sections.

Two different methods of performing separate compilations are described below. The choice of which method you will use is *not* up to you; it's determined by whichever compiler is available to you.

First Method   The following example illustrates one method of performing separate compilations

```
program Slave;
var
   Count: Integer;
function Successor(X:Integer): Integer;
   begin
   Successor := X + 1;
   end;
begin
end.


program Master;
var
   Count: Integer;
function Successor(X:Integer): Integer;
   Extern;
begin
Count := 3;
Count := Successor(Count);
end.
```

The program Slave doesn't do anything (there are no statements between the outermost **begin** and **end**), but it does contain the declaration for the function Successor. The program Master is responsible for doing all the work, and it calls upon Successor for assistance in carrying this out. There is no declaration for Successor in Master; there is only a heading for the function and an indication that the declaration is outside the program Master (Extern).

Note that items that are declared or defined in Master (Count in particular) also appear in Slave. This is necessary so that the compiler can get itself into the same state (frame of mind) when compiling the body (in Slave) that it was in when it expected to find the body in Master and found an Extern instead.

At this time it would be worthwhile to contrast the form

procedure X; Forward;   {see section on Block Structure and Scope}

with

procedure Y; Extern;

Both are instances of missing bodies. But Forward says that the body will eventually appear in this program, whereas Extern says that the body is somewhere outside this program.

Second Method   The following example illustrates an alternate method for performing separate compilations. This is the form recognized by Intel's Pascal compiler.

```
module Slave;

   public Slave;
   function Successor(X:Integer): Integer;

   private Slave;
   function Successor(X:Integer): Integer;
      begin
      Successor := X + 1;
      end;


module Master;

   public Slave;
   function Successor(X:Integer): Integer;

   program Master;
   var
      Count: Integer;
      begin
      Count := 3;
      Count := Successor(Count);
      end.
```

Now instead of talking about programs, we are talking about modules. The module Slave doesn't do anything on its own (it has no statements that aren't buried inside procedure or function declarations), but it does contain the declaration for the function Successor. The module Master is responsible for doing all the work, and it calls upon Successor for assistance in carrying this out. There is no declaration for Successor in Master; there is only a heading for the function and an indication that the declaration is outside the module Master (**public**).

A module contains either a main program (such as Master above) or a nonmain program (such as Slave above). The name of the module must be the same as the name of the main or nonmain program it contains. A main program takes the form of a program as already described; it consists of a program heading (**program** ...;), followed by a description of items used in the program (definitions and declarations), followed by actions performed by the program on these items (statements), followed by a period. A nonmain program consists of a private heading (**private** ...;), followed by a description of items used in the (nonmain) program, followed by a period. Note that a nonmain program does not contain an action part.

In addition to a main or nonmain program, a module also contains an interface specification. This is the section that begins with the word **public**. The interface specification tells which items in the current module are available to other modules, and which items in other modules are available to the current module.

The nonmain program Slave contains no actions (nonmain programs never do), but it does contain the declaration for the function Successor. The interface section of the module Slave indicates that the function Successor declared in this module is available to other modules. The main program Master contains actions (main programs are responsible for doing all the work) and calls upon Successor for assistance. The interface section of the module Master indicates that the function Successor declared in the module Slave is available to the current module.

Combining the Separate Compilations   The two programs (modules) in either method above are compiled separately and can be compiled in either order. Let's look at the compilation process in a little more detail. When the compiler encounters the call to Successor in program Master, it generates a call instruction. But the address of Successor is not known at that time, so the compiler cannot complete the address field of this instruction. Instead it generates a dummy address field (a field containing any old address) and makes a note that the correct address must be filled in later. This note remains attached to the object code of program Master. When the compiler encounters the body of Successor in program Slave, it picks an address for Successor and can make a note of the address so that later this address can be inserted into the object code of Master. After both programs have been compiled, all notes are read and the address of Successor is written into the appropriate place in the object code of program Master. This latter process is referred to as *binding* or *linking*.

Note that even though the body of Successor is missing in Master, its heading (with all its parameter information) is still present. To understand why, consider what happens when the compiler encounters the call for Successor (in Master). It must generate code that somehow passes the parameters to Successor. This code depends on the types of the parameters and on whether the parameters are value parameters or variable parameters. And this is exactly the information that is contained in the heading of Successor. However, the compiler does not need to know anything else about Successor at this time, so its entire body could indeed be outside of Master. In fact, the body could be changed at some later date, and the code that the compiler generates to call Successor would be unaffected.

Up to now we have been assuming that the program containing a missing routine and the program containing the body of that routine were both written in Pascal. In reality, either of them could be written in some "foreign" language instead. This permits us to write a Pascal program that calls on routines that are written in some other high-level language or even in assembly language. Such a facility is essential when we want to do things that are outside the realm of Pascal (like reading the contents of a particular location in memory).

Tying It All Together

Let's finish up by returning to our traffic light example. The example was introduced in Fig. 1.3 to show a typical microprocessor application. By the time we were into Chap. 4, we knew enough to be able to design an 8086 system that would control the traffic light (Fig. 4.16). Now we can write a Pascal program for the system.

The traffic light is situated on a main highway at the intersection with a small cross street. The light is to behave as follows. It will normally be green for the highway and red for the cross street. After the number of cars lined up in the cross street exceeds 5, the light will become red on the highway and blinking yellow on the cross street. This will continue until there are no more cars left in the cross street.

The system shown in Fig. 4.16 has the traffic light connected as a memory-mapped output port at memory location 1000 hexadecimal. Let us assume that the individual bulbs in the light are wired up so they correspond to the bits in the memory location as follows:

(leftmost bit)	7	Red bulb on main highway
	6	Yellow bulb on main highway
	5	Green bulb on main highway
	4	Left-turn bulb on main highway
	3	Red bulb on cross street
	2	Yellow bulb on cross street
	1	Green bulb on cross street
(rightmost bit)	0	Left-turn bulb on cross street

The system also has an input port (not shown in Fig. 4.16) that tells the processor how many cars are waiting in the cross street. This port receives its information from sensors (along with some counting circuitry) buried in the roadway. Let us assume that this input is connected as port 50 (decimal).

The Pascal program below will cause the traffic light to behave the way we specified. Three external assembly-language routines are used in this program. One causes a delay for a given number of seconds. This could have been written in Pascal by using a **for**-statement that, after some experimentation, produces the right amount of delay. But such a routine would be highly dependent on both the 8086 timing characteristics (we could not use this program with some other microprocessor in the future) and on the particular compiler we are using (a different compiler or a different version of the same compiler might generate slightly different code causing the timing of the **for**-statement to change). So the delay routine is a very good candidate for assembly-language programming. The remaining assembly-language routines are used for reading or writing to specific memory addresses or Input/Output ports. Such actions cannot be accomplished directly in Pascal and must be done in assembly language.

```
program TrafficLight;

const {names for individual bulbs}
   MainRed = 128;
   MainYellow = 64;
   MainGreen = 32;
   MainLeftTurn = 16;
   CrossRed = 8;
   CrossYellow = 4
   CrossGreen = 2;
   CrossLeftTurn = 1;

type
   Byte = 0..255; {an eight-bit quantity}
   MemoryAddress = record {an address in 8086 memory space}
      SegmentLo,SegmentHi: Byte;
      OffsetLo,OffsetHi: Byte;
      end;
   IOAddress = record {an 8086 IO port number}
      OffsetLo,OffsetHi: Byte;
      end;
var
   Lights: MemoryAddress; {memory-mapped output}
   CarCount: IOAddress; {input port}

{external assembly-language routines}
procedure Delay(X:Byte); Extern; {causes an X second delay}
procedure MemoryWrite(Addr:MemoryAddress; X:Byte); Extern;
function IORead(Addr:IOAddress): Byte; Extern;

begin
Lights.SegmentHi := 0; Lights.SegmentLo := 0; {memory address of ...}
Lights.OffsetHi := 16; Lights.OffsetLo := 0; {...Lights is 1000H}
CarCount = 50; {port number of CarCount}

repeat
   MemoryWrite(Lights,MainGreen + CrossRed); {normal setting}
   if IORead(CarCount)>5 then {too many cars waiting}
   begin {let them through}
      MemoryWrite(Lights,MainYellow + CrossRed); {stop highway}
      Delay(3);
      while IORead(CarCount)>0 do {start cross street}
         begin
         MemoryWrite(Lights,MainRed);
         Delay(1);
         MemoryWrite(Lights,MainRed + CrossYellow);
         Delay(1);
         end
      end
   until False; {should loop forever}

end.
```

Now we have the beginnings of a traffic-light control program. You might want to try modifying it to do more elaborate things, such as controlling the northbound lights independently of the southbound lights, controlling the left-turn arrow, varying the delays to accommodate for peak hours, and anything else you can think of.

Summary

This chapter was not meant to be a compendium of all the features and rules in Pascal (Jensen and Wirth's *Pascal User Manual and Report* published by Springer-Verlag does that very well). Instead, it attempted to present most of the features of the language in a form that was easy to digest, and convey enough information so that you could write meaningful programs. We didn't cover many of the fine details (like "thou shalt not jump into a repetitive statement"), which, although important, really get in the way when you're trying to learn the language. We also didn't present some of the dispensable features (like packing of structured types) so that attention could be focused on the more necessary features.

9

References

The earliest document describing the 8086 was an Intel internal publication (1) describing the 8086 architectural specification, which went through several revisions during 1976 and 1977 until it arrived in its final form (2). The first published article, which in effect announced the processor to the world, appeared in a trade magazine in February of 1978 (3). The first technical article appeared in June of that year and was published in the IEEE *Computer* magazine (4). The next month marked the first shipments of 8086's to customers and the publication of the first official 8086 manual (5). This was followed by other Intel publications, which describe the 8086 assembly language (6), the PL/M-86 language (7), and Intel's version of Pascal (8). Finally, the 8088 was announced (9) and described in Intel literature (10). Most recently, a description of the architectural evolution that traces the features of the 8086 back to the earliest microprocessors has been published (11).

1. S.P. Morse, "Intel 8086 Instruction Set," Intel internal documentation, August 13, 1976 (Revision 0), October 22, 1976 (Revision 1), February 18, 1977 (Revision 2).
2. S.P. Morse, W.B. Pohlman, B.W. Ravenel, "Intel 8086 Architectural Specification," Intel internal documentation, January 12, 1978.
3. B.J. Katz, S.P. Morse, W.B. Pohlman, B.W. Ravenel, "8086 Microcomputer Bridges the Gaps between 8- and 16-bit Designs," *Electronics,* February 16, 1978.
4. S.P. Morse, W.B. Pohlman, B.W. Ravenel, "The Intel 8086 Microprocessor: A 16-bit Evolution of the 8080," *Computer,* June 1978.
5. *MCS-86 User's Manual,* Intel Corp., July 1978.
6. *MCS-86 Assembly Language Reference Manual,* Intel Corp., 1978.
7. *PL/M-86 Programming Manual,* Intel Corp, 1978
8. Pascal-86 User's Guide, Intel Corp., 1981.

9. J. Bartlett and R. Retter, "CPU Brings 16-Bit Performance to 8-Bit Systems," *Electronic Design*, March 15, 1979.
10. *The 8086 Family User's Manual*, Intel Corp., October 1979.
11. S.P. Morse, B.W. Ravenel, S. Mazor, W.B. Pohlman, "Intel Microprocessors—8008 to 8086," *Computer*, October 1980; also *Computer Structures: Principles and Examples*. McGraw-Hill, 1982.

Appendix A

Instruction Set Summary

Reprinted by Permission INTEL Corp.

DATA TRANSFER

MOV = Move:

	7 6 5 4 3 2 1 0	7 6 5 4 3 2 1 0	7 6 5 4 3 2 1 0	7 6 5 4 3 2 1 0
Register/memory to/from register	1 0 0 0 1 0 d w	mod reg r/m		
Immediate to register/memory	1 1 0 0 0 1 1 w	mod 0 0 0 r/m	data	data if w 1
Immediate to register	1 0 1 1 w reg	data	data if w 1	
Memory to accumulator	1 0 1 0 0 0 0 w	addr-low	addr-high	
Accumulator to memory	1 0 1 0 0 0 1 w	addr-low	addr-high	
Register/memory to segment register	1 0 0 0 1 1 1 0	mod 0 reg r/m		
Segment register to register/memory	1 0 0 0 1 1 0 0	mod 0 reg r/m		

PUSH = Push:

Register/memory	1 1 1 1 1 1 1 1	mod 1 1 0 r/m
Register	0 1 0 1 0 reg	
Segment register	0 0 0 reg 1 1 0	

POP = Pop:

Register/memory	1 0 0 0 1 1 1 1	mod 0 0 0 r/m
Register	0 1 0 1 1 reg	
Segment register	0 0 0 reg 1 1 1	

XCHG = Exchange:

Register/memory with register	1 0 0 0 0 1 1 w	mod reg r/m
Register with accumulator	1 0 0 1 0 reg	

IN = Input from:

Fixed port	1 1 1 0 0 1 0 w	port
Variable port	1 1 1 0 1 1 0 w	

OUT = Output to:

Fixed port	1 1 1 0 0 1 1 w	port
Variable port	1 1 1 0 1 1 1 w	
XLAT = Translate byte to AL	1 1 0 1 0 1 1 1	
LEA = Load EA to register	1 0 0 0 1 1 0 1	mod reg r/m
LDS = Load pointer to DS	1 1 0 0 0 1 0 1	mod reg r/m
LES = Load pointer to ES	1 1 0 0 0 1 0 0	mod reg r/m
LAHF = Load AH with flags	1 0 0 1 1 1 1 1	
SAHF = Store AH into flags	1 0 0 1 1 1 1 0	
PUSHF = Push flags	1 0 0 1 1 1 0 0	
POPF = Pop flags	1 0 0 1 1 1 0 1	

ARITHMETIC

ADD = Add:

Reg./memory with register to either	0 0 0 0 0 0 d w	mod reg r/m		
Immediate to register/memory	1 0 0 0 0 0 s w	mod 0 0 0 r/m	data	data if s:w=01
Immediate to accumulator	0 0 0 0 0 1 0 w	data	data if w=1	

ADC = Add with carry:

Reg./memory with register to either	0 0 0 1 0 0 d w	mod reg r/m		
Immediate to register/memory	1 0 0 0 0 0 s w	mod 0 1 0 r/m	data	data if s:w=01
Immediate to accumulator	0 0 0 1 0 1 0 w	data	data if w=1	

INC = Increment:

Register/memory	1 1 1 1 1 1 1 w	mod 0 0 0 r/m
Register	0 1 0 0 0 reg	
AAA=ASCII adjust for add	0 0 1 1 0 1 1 1	
DAA=Decimal adjust for add	0 0 1 0 0 1 1 1	

SUB = Subtract:

Reg./memory and register to either	0 0 1 0 1 0 d w	mod reg r/m		
Immediate from register/memory	1 0 0 0 0 0 s w	mod 1 0 1 r/m	data	data if s:w=01
Immediate from accumulator	0 0 1 0 1 1 0 w	data	data if w=1	

SBB = Subtract with borrow

Reg./memory and register to either	0 0 0 1 1 0 d w	mod reg r/m		
Immediate from register/memory	1 0 0 0 0 0 s w	mod 0 1 1 r/m	data	data if s:w=01
Immediate from accumulator	0 0 0 1 1 1 0 w	data	data if w=1	

DEC = Decrement:

7 6 5 4 3 2 1 0   7 6 5 4 3 2 1 0   7 6 5 4 3 2 1 0   7 6 5 4 3 2 1 0

Register/memory	1 1 1 1 1 1 1 w	mod 0 0 1 r/m
Register	0 1 0 0 1 reg	
NEG=Change sign	1 1 1 1 0 1 1 w	mod 0 1 1 r/m

CMP = Compare:

Register/memory and register	0 0 1 1 1 0 d w	mod reg r/m		
Immediate with register/memory	1 0 0 0 0 0 s w	mod 1 1 1 r/m	data	data if s:w=01
Immediate with accumulator	0 0 1 1 1 1 0 w	data	data if w 1	
AAS=ASCII adjust for subtract	0 0 1 1 1 1 1 1			
DAS=Decimal adjust for subtract	0 0 1 0 1 1 1 1			
MUL=Multiply (unsigned)	1 1 1 1 0 1 1 w	mod 1 0 0 r/m		
IMUL=Integer multiply (signed)	1 1 1 1 0 1 1 w	mod 1 0 1 r/m		
AAM=ASCII adjust for multiply	1 1 0 1 0 1 0 0	0 0 0 0 1 0 1 0		
DIV=Divide (unsigned)	1 1 1 1 0 1 1 w	mod 1 1 0 r/m		
IDIV=Integer divide (signed)	1 1 1 1 0 1 1 w	mod 1 1 1 r/m		
AAD=ASCII adjust for divide	1 1 0 1 0 1 0 1	0 0 0 0 1 0 1 0		
CBW=Convert byte to word	1 0 0 1 1 0 0 0			
CWD=Convert word to double word	1 0 0 1 1 0 0 1			

LOGIC

NOT=Invert	1 1 1 1 0 1 1 w	mod 0 1 0 r/m
SHL/SAL=Shift logical/arithmetic left	1 1 0 1 0 0 v w	mod 1 0 0 r/m
SHR=Shift logical right	1 1 0 1 0 0 v w	mod 1 0 1 r/m
SAR=Shift arithmetic right	1 1 0 1 0 0 v w	mod 1 1 1 r/m
ROL=Rotate left	1 1 0 1 0 0 v w	mod 0 0 0 r/m
ROR=Rotate right	1 1 0 1 0 0 v w	mod 0 0 1 r/m
RCL=Rotate through carry flag left	1 1 0 1 0 0 v w	mod 0 1 0 r/m
RCR=Rotate through carry right	1 1 0 1 0 0 v w	mod 0 1 1 r/m

AND = And:

Reg./memory and register to either	0 0 1 0 0 0 d w	mod reg r/m		
Immediate to register/memory	1 0 0 0 0 0 0 w	mod 1 0 0 r/m	data	data if w=1
Immediate to accumulator	0 0 1 0 0 1 0 w	data	data if w=1	

TEST = And function to flags, no result:

Register/memory and register	1 0 0 0 0 1 0 w	mod reg r/m		
Immediate data and register/memory	1 1 1 1 0 1 1 w	mod 0 0 0 r/m	data	data if w=1
Immediate data and accumulator	1 0 1 0 1 0 0 w	data	data if w=1	

OR = Or:

Reg./memory and register to either	0 0 0 0 1 0 d w	mod reg r/m		
Immediate to register/memory	1 0 0 0 0 0 0 w	mod 0 0 1 r/m	data	data if w=1
Immediate to accumulator	0 0 0 0 1 1 0 w	data	data if w=1	

XOR = Exclusive or:

Reg./memory and register to either	0 0 1 1 0 0 d w	mod reg r/m		
Immediate to register/memory	1 0 0 0 0 0 0 w	mod 1 1 0 r/m	data	data if w=1
Immediate to accumulator	0 0 1 1 0 1 0 w	data	data if w=1	

STRING MANIPULATION

REP=Repeat	1 1 1 1 0 0 1 z
MOVS=Move byte/word	1 0 1 0 0 1 0 w
CMPS=Compare byte/word	1 0 1 0 0 1 1 w
SCAS=Scan byte/word	1 0 1 0 1 1 1 w
LODS=Load byte/wd to AL/AX	1 0 1 0 1 1 0 w
STDS=Stor byte/wd from AL/A	1 0 1 0 1 0 1 w

CONTROL TRANSFER

CALL = Call:

	7 6 5 4 3 2 1 0	7 6 5 4 3 2 1 0	7 6 5 4 3 2 1 0
Direct within segment	1 1 1 0 1 0 0 0	disp-low	disp-high
Indirect within segment	1 1 1 1 1 1 1 1	mod 0 1 0 r/m	
Direct intersegment	1 0 0 1 1 0 1 0	offset-low	offset-high
		seg-low	seg-high
Indirect intersegment	1 1 1 1 1 1 1 1	mod 0 1 1 r/m	

JMP = Unconditional Jump:

Direct within segment	1 1 1 0 1 0 0 1	disp-low	disp-high
Direct within segment-short	1 1 1 0 1 0 1 1	disp	
Indirect within segment	1 1 1 1 1 1 1 1	mod 1 0 0 r/m	
Direct intersegment	1 1 1 0 1 0 1 0	offset-low	offset-high
		seg-low	seg-high
Indirect intersegment	1 1 1 1 1 1 1 1	mod 1 0 1 r/m	

RET = Return from CALL:

Within segment	1 1 0 0 0 0 1 1		
Within seg. adding immed to SP	1 1 0 0 0 0 1 0	' data-low	data-high
Intersegment	1 1 0 0 1 0 1 1		
Intersegment. adding immediate to SP	1 1 0 0 1 0 1 0	data-low	data-high
JE/JZ=Jump on equal/zero	0 1 1 1 0 1 0 0	disp	
JL/JNGE=Jump on less/not greater or equal	0 1 1 1 1 1 0 0	disp	
JLE/JNG=Jump on less or equal/not greater	0 1 1 1 1 1 1 0	disp	
JB/JNAE=Jump on below/not above or equal	0 1 1 1 0 0 1 0	disp	
JBE/JNA=Jump on below or equal/not above	0 1 1 1 0 1 1 0	disp	
JP/JPE=Jump on parity/parity even	0 1 1 1 1 0 1 0	disp	
JO=Jump on overflow	0 1 1 1 0 0 0 0	disp	
JS=Jump on sign	0 1 1 1 1 0 0 0	disp	
JNE/JNZ=Jump on not equal/not zero	0 1 1 1 0 1 0 1	disp	
JNL/JGE=Jump on not less/greater or equal	0 1 1 1 1 1 0 1	disp	
JNLE/JG=Jump on not less or equal/greater	0 1 1 1 1 1 1 1	disp	

	7 6 5 4 3 2 1 0	7 6 5 4 3 2 1 0
JNB/JAE=Jump on not below/above or equal	0 1 1 1 0 0 1 1	disp
JNBE/JA=Jump on not below or equal/above	0 1 1 1 0 1 1 1	disp
JNP/JPO=Jump on not par/par odd	0 1 1 1 1 0 1 1	disp
JNO=Jump on not overflow	0 1 1 1 0 0 0 1	disp
JNS=Jump on not sign	0 1 1 1 1 0 0 1	disp
LOOP=Loop CX times	1 1 1 0 0 0 1 0	disp
LOOPZ/LOOPE=Loop while zero/equal	1 1 1 0 0 0 0 1	disp
LOOPNZ/LOOPNE=Loop while not zero/equal	1 1 1 0 0 0 0 0	disp
JCXZ=Jump on CX zero	1 1 1 0 0 0 1 1	disp

INT = Interrupt

Type specified	1 1 0 0 1 1 0 1	type
Type 3	1 1 0 0 1 1 0 0	
INTO=Interrupt on overflow	1 1 0 0 1 1 1 0	
IRET=Interrupt return	1 1 0 0 1 1 1 1	

PROCESSOR CONTROL

CLC=Clear carry	1 1 1 1 1 0 0 0	
CMC=Complement carry	1 1 1 1 0 1 0 1	
STC=Set carry	1 1 1 1 1 0 0 1	
CLD=Clear direction	1 1 1 1 1 1 0 0	
STD=Set direction	1 1 1 1 1 1 0 1	
CLI=Clear interrupt	1 1 1 1 1 0 1 0	
STI=Set interrupt	1 1 1 1 1 0 1 1	
HLT=Halt	1 1 1 1 0 1 0 0	
WAIT=Wait	1 0 0 1 1 0 1 1	
ESC=Escape (to external device)	1 1 0 1 1 x x x	mod x x x r/m
LOCK=Bus lock prefix	1 1 1 1 0 0 0 0	

Footnotes:

AL = 8-bit accumulator
AX = 16-bit accumulator
CX = Count register
DS = Data segment
ES = Extra segment
Above/below refers to unsigned value.
Greater = more positive;
Less = less positive (more negative) signed values
if d = 1 then "to" reg; if d = 0 then "from" reg
if w = 1 then word instruction; if w = 0 then byte instruction

if mod = 11 then r/m is treated as a REG field
if mod = 00 then DISP = 0*, disp-low and disp-high are absent
if mod = 01 then DISP = disp-low sign-extended to 16-bits, disp-high is absent
if mod = 10 then DISP = disp-high: disp-low

if r/m = 000 then EA = (BX) + (SI) + DISP
if r/m = 001 then EA = (BX) + (DI) + DISP
if r/m = 010 then EA = (BP) + (SI) + DISP
if r/m = 011 then EA = (BP) + (DI) + DISP
if r/m = 100 then EA = (SI) + DISP
if r/m = 101 then EA = (DI) + DISP
if r/m = 110 then EA = (BP) + DISP*
if r/m = 111 then EA = (BX) + DISP
DISP follows 2nd byte of instruction (before data if required)

*except if mod = 00 and r/m = 110 then EA = disp-high: disp-low.

if s:w = 01 then 16 bits of immediate data form the operand.
if s:w = 11 then an immediate data byte is sign extended to
     form the 16-bit operand.
if v = 0 then "count" = 1; if v = 1 then "count" in (CL)
x = don't care
z is used for string primitives for comparison with ZF FLAG.

SEGMENT OVERRIDE PREFIX

    0 0 1 reg 1 1 0

REG is assigned according to the following table:

16-Bit (w = 1)	8-Bit (w = 0)	Segment
000 AX	000 AL	00 ES
001 CX	001 CL	01 CS
010 DX	010 DL	10 SS
011 BX	011 BL	11 DS
100 SP	100 AH	
101 BP	101 CH	
110 SI	110 DH	
111 DI	111 BH	

Instructions which reference the flag register file as a 16-bit object use the symbol FLAGS to represent the file:

FLAGS = X:X:X:X:(OF):(DF):(IF):(TF):(SF):(ZF):X:(AF):X:(PF):X:(CF)

Appendix B

Opcode Space

Most 8086 instructions contain their opcode entirely in the first byte of the instruction. However, there are some instructions that spill the opcode over into certain bits of the following byte. The portion of the opcode that is contained in the first byte is called the *primary opcode,* and the portion that spills over (if any) is called the *secondary opcode.* This appendix shows how the 8086 instructions are laid out in a matrix called the *opcode space.*

The matrix entries correspond to the instruction opcodes. Each entry contains the mnemonic of the instruction having that opcode as well as the settings of any fields that distinguish the opcode from other opcodes that have the same instruction mnemonic. For example, the primary opcodes AC and AD both correspond to the LODS (load string) mnemonic. The primary opcode space entry for AD (intersection of row A and column D) contains LODS w, indicating that this instruction loads a word (**w** field is 1). The entry for AC is simply LODS, indicating this is a byte load (**w** field is 0).

Each entry in the matrix specifies not only the instruction but also any arguments used by the instruction. The following notation is used for specifying the arguments:

1. **r/m** means one of the arguments is specified by a **mod** and **r/m** field.
2. **reg** means one of the arguments is specified by a **reg** field.
3. **imm** means one of the arguments is specified as immediate data.
4. **mem** means the memory address of one of the arguments is specified directly.
5. if a register name is given explicitly, that register is one of the arguments.
6. if there are two arguments, the destination argument appears first.

As an example, consider the instruction whose opcode is 29. The entry in the primary opcode space at the intersection of row 2 and column 9 tells us that the instruction is SUB (subtract). The **w** field is set indicating that it is a word

1. Primary Opcode Space

	0	1	2	3	4	5	6	7	8	9	A	B	C	D	E	F
0	ADD r/m,reg	ADD w r/m,reg	ADD d reg,r/m	ADD d w reg,r/m	ADD AL,imm	ADD w AX,imm	PUSH ES	POP ES	OR r/m,reg	OR w r/m,reg	OR d reg,r/m	OR d w reg,r/m	OR AL,imm	OR w AX,imm	PUSH CS	
1	ADC r/m,reg	ADC w r/m,reg	ADC d reg,r/m	ADC d w reg,r/m	ADC AL,imm	ADC w AX,imm	PUSH SS	POP SS	SBB r/m,reg	SBB w r/m,reg	SBB d reg,r/m	SBB d w reg,r/m	SBB AL,imm	SBB w AX,imm	PUSH DS	POP DS
2	AND r/m,reg	AND w r/m,reg	AND d reg,r/m	AND d w reg,r/m	AND AL,imm	AND w AX,imm	SEGMENT ES	DAA	SUB r/m,reg	SUB w r/m,reg	SUB d reg,r/m	SUB d w reg,r/m	SUB AL,imm	SUB w AX,imm	SEGMENT CS	DAS
3	XOR r/m,reg	XOR w r/m,reg	XOR d reg,r/m	XOR d w reg,r/m	XOR AL,imm	XOR w AX,imm	SEGMENT SS	AAA	CMP r/m,reg	CMP w r/m,reg	CMP d reg,r/m	CMP d w reg,r/m	CMP AL,imm	CMP w AX,imm	SEGMENT DS	AAS
4	INC AX	INC CX	INC DX	INC BX	INC SP	INC BP	INC SI	INC DI	DEC AX	DEC CX	DEC DX	DEC BX	DEC SP	DEC BP	DEC SI	DEC DI
5	PUSH AX	PUSH CX	PUSH DX	PUSH BX	PUSH SP	PUSH BP	PUSH SI	PUSH DI	POP AX	POP CX	POP DX	POP BX	POP SP	POP BP	POP SI	POP DI
6																
7	JO	JNO	JB/JNAE	JNB/JAE	JE/JZ	JNE/JNZ	JBE/JNA	JNBE/JA	JS	JNS	JP/JPE	JNP/JPO	JL/JNGE	JNL/JGE	JLE/JNG	JNLE/JG
8	...	... w	...	... s w	TEST r/m,reg	TEST w r/m,reg	XCHG r/m,reg	XCHG w r/m,reg	MOV r/m,reg	MOV w r/m,reg	MOV reg,r/m	MOV w reg,r/m	MOV r/m,seg	LEA reg,r/m	MOV seg,:/m	POP r/m
9	XCHG AX,AX	XCHG CX,AX	XCHG DX,AX	XCHG BX,AX	XCHG SP,AX	XCHG BP,AX	XCHG SI,AX	XCHG DI,AX	CBW	CWD	CALL inter	WAIT	PUSHF	POPF	SAHF	LAHF
A	MOV AL,mem	MOV AX,mem	MOV mem,AL	MOV mem,AX	MOVS	MOVS w	CMPS	CMPS w	TEST AL,imm	TEST w AX,imm	STOS	STOS w	LODS	LODS w	SCAS	SCAS w
B	MOV AL,imm	MOV CL,imm	MOV DL,imm	MOV BL,imm	MOV AH,imm	MOV CH,imm	MOV DH,imm	MOV BH,imm	MOV AX,imm	MOV CX,imm	MOV DX,imm	MOV BX,imm	MOV SP,imm	MOV BP,imm	MOV SI,imm	MOV DI,imm
C			RET intra •	RET intra	LES reg,r/m	LDS reg,r/m	MOV r/m,imm	MOV w r/m,imm			RET inter •	RET inter	INT type 3	INT	INTO	IRET
D	...	... w	... v	... v w	AAM	AAD		XLAT	ESC 0	ESC 1	ESC 2	ESC 3	ESC 4	ESC 5	ESC 6	ESC 7
E	LOOPNZ/LOOPNE	LOOPZ/LOOPE	LOOP	JCXZ	IN AL,port	IN w AX,port	OUT port,AL	OUT w port,AX	CALL intra	JMP intra	JMP inter	JMP short	IN AL,var	IN w AX,var	OUT var,AL	OUT w var,AX
F	LOCK		REP/REPNE/REPNZ	REPE/REPZ	HLT	CMC	...	... w	CLC	STC	CLI	STI	CLD	STD	...	... w

*** means see Secondary Opcode Space

subtraction. Furthermore, the destination operand is specified by the **r/m** (and **mod**) field, and the source operand is specified by the **reg** field. Thus the instruction will subtract the contents of the word operand specified by the reg field from the contents of the word operand specified by the **mod** and **r/m** fields and place the result back into the operand specified by the **mod** and **r/m** fields.

To illustrate the use of a secondary opcode, consider the instruction whose primary opcode is F7. The primary opcode space contains *** at the intersection of row F and column 7, indicating the existence of a secondary opcode. This primary opcode space also contains a **w,** indicating that whatever the instruction does, it does it on words. The secondary opcode space entry for F7 is found by looking at the row labeled F7. There are seven different instructions that all have the primary opcode F7. Suppose that our instruction contained a 3 in the opcode portion of its second byte. The secondary opcode space entry for row F7 and column 3 is NEG **r/m**. So the instruction will negate the word specified by the **mod** and **r/m** fields.

2. Secondary Opcode Space (opcode in second byte)

	0	1	2	3	4	5	6	7
80-81	ADD r/m,imm	OR r/m,imm	ADC r/m,imm	SBB r/m,imm	AND. r/m,imm	SUB r/m,imm	XOR r/m,imm	CMP r/m,imm
83	ADD r/m,imm		ADC r/m,imm	SBB r/m,imm		SUB r/m,imm		CMP r/m,imm
8F	POP r/m							
D0-D3	ROL r/m	ROR r/m	RCL r/m	RCR r/m	SHL/SAL r/m	SHR r/m		RAR r/m
F6-F7	TEST r/m,imm		NOT r/m	NEG r/m	MUL r/m	IMUL r/m	DIV r/m	IDIV r/m
FE	INC r/m	DEC r/m	CALL intra	CALL inter	JMP intra	JMP inter	PUSH r/m	
FF	INC w r/m	DEC w r/m						

Appendix C

ASCII Codes

1. Non Printable ASCII Characters

hex	abrev	intent		hex	abrev	intent
00	NUL	null or time fill		10	DLE	data line escape
01	SOH	start of heading		11	DC1	device control 1 (X-ON)
02	STX	start of text		12	DC2	device control 2 (TAPE)
03	ETX	end of text		13	DC3	device control 3 (X-OFF)
04	EOT	end of transmission		14	DC4	device control 4 (TAPE)
05	ENQ	enquiry		15	NAK	negative acknowledge
06	ACK	acknowledge		16	SYN	synchronous idle
07	BEL	bell		17	ETB	end of transmission blocks
08	BS	backspace		18	CAN	cancel
09	HT	horizontal tabulation		19	EM	end of medium
0A	LF	line feed		1A	SUB	substitute
0B	VT	vertical tabulation		1B	ESC	escape
0C	FF	form feed		1C	FS	file separator
0D	CR	carriage return		1D	GS	group separator
0E	SO	shift out		1E	RS	record separator
0F	SI	shift in		1F	US	unit separator
				7F	DEL	delete

2. Printable ASCII characters

hex	char	hex	char	hex	char	hex	char	hex	char	hex	char
20		30	0	40	@	50	P	60	`	70	p
21	!	31	1	41	A	51	Q	61	a	71	q
22	"	32	2	42	B	52	R	62	b	72	r
23	#	33	3	43	C	53	S	63	c	73	s
24	$	34	4	44	D	54	T	64	d	74	t
25	%	35	5	45	E	55	U	65	e	75	u
26	&	36	6	46	F	56	V	66	f	76	v
27	'	37	7	47	G	57	W	67	g	77	w
28	(	38	8	48	H	58	X	68	h	78	x
29	)	39	9	49	I	59	Y	69	i	79	y
2A	*	3A	:	4A	J	5A	Z	6A	j	7A	z
2B	+	3B	;	4B	K	5B	[	6B	k	7B	{
2C	,	3C	<	4C	L	5C	\	6C	l	7C	¦
2D	–	3D	=	4D	M	5D	]	6D	m	7D	}
2E	.	3E	>	4E	N	5E	^	6E	n	7E	~
2F	/	3F	?	4F	O	5F	_	6F	o	7E	

Index